THAT THE WORLD MAY KNOW

Howard G. Hageman
in collaboration with
Ruth Douglas See

Illustrated by Hans Zander

THE COVENANT LIFE CURRICULUM

Published by the CLC Press
Richmond, Virginia

THE COVENANT LIFE CURRICULUM
the authorized curriculum
of the following denominations

ASSOCIATE REFORMED PRESBYTERIAN CHURCH

CUMBERLAND PRESBYTERIAN CHURCH

MORAVIAN CHURCH IN AMERICA

PRESBYTERIAN CHURCH IN THE UNITED STATES

REFORMED CHURCH IN AMERICA

affiliate denomination:
THE EVANGELICAL COVENANT CHURCH OF AMERICA

Unless otherwise noted, Scripture quotations are from the *Revised Standard Version of the Bible*, copyrighted 1946 and 1952 by the Division of Christian Education of the National Council of Churches, and used by permission.

© Marshall C. Dendy 1965
Printed in the United States of America
Second Printing 1967
4815-WB-2316

Contents

1. Why History? 5
   Christianity and History; God's New People

   ### PART I. THE CHURCH AGAINST THE WORLD

2. After the Apostles 13
   The Martyrs; The Apologists
3. Our Debt to the Heretics 21
   *The Gnostics; Marcion and the Old Testament;
   Speaking in Tongues*
4. The Age of Creed-Making 29
   *Arius; Athanasius Against the World;
   Consolidating the Faith*

   ### PART II. THE CHURCH IN A BREAKING WORLD

5. The City of God 39
   *Can the Church Survive?; Introducing Augustine;
   A Theology of History*
6. The Monastic Movement 47
   *Overcoming Individualism; The Monastic Organizer;
   Evaluating Monasticism*
7. The Monks March 55
   *To Scotland; To Holland; Mission Produces Mission;
   Missionary Strength and Weakness*
8. The Two Swords 64
   *The First Pope; The Greatness of Gregory;
   The First Emperor*
9. The Cross and the Crescent 73
   The Eastern Church; The Church Behind the Curtain

   ### PART III. THE CHURCH SEEKS TO CONTROL THE WORLD

10. The Dark Ages 83
    Filling the Vacuum; Light in the Darkness
11. Men of Light 91
    The Cathari; The Waldenses; Dominic; Francis of Assisi
12. The Age of the Builders 99
    *The Intellectual Challenge; Thomas Aquinas;
    From Climax to Decline*
13. Dark Night and Morning Stars 107
    *The Babylonian Captivity; The Council of Constance;
    John Hus; Brethren of the Common Life*

PART IV. THE CHURCH REFORMS ITSELF

14. Here I Stand 117
    The Unhappy Monk; Tetzel's Challenge;
    The Breach Widens; The Later Luther
15. The Radical Reformation 125
    Anabaptist Leaders; The Radical Radicals; Menno Simons;
    The Anabaptist Contribution
16. That Frenchman 133
    The Visitor Who Stayed; Calvin's Contribution
17. They Went to School in Geneva 142
    The Scottish Reformation; John Knox; After Knox;
    The Dutch Reformation; William the Silent;
    The Development of the Dutch Church

PART V. THE WORLD CHALLENGES THE CHURCH

18. Thrust and Counterthrust 153
    The Counter-Reformation; The Council of Trent;
    Protestant Scholasticism; The Thirty Years' War
19. Puritan and Pietist 161
    The Puritans; The Pietists
20. The World Is My Parish 169
    The Inner Awakening; The Outer Awakening;
    The Broadening Movement

PART VI. THE CHURCH FACES NEW WORLDS

21. The New World of America 181
    Massachusetts Bay; New Netherland; The Dissenters
22. The Great Awakening 190
    They Prepared the Way; Whitefield's Mission to America;
    Baptists and Methodists; The Liberals
23. On the Frontiers 199
    Geographical Frontiers; Missionary Frontiers;
    Social Frontiers
24. Our Own Time 208
    Discouraging Signs; Hopeful Signs
25. Conclusion: Good Friday and Easter 216
    Can We Still Believe in Progress?; Death and
    Resurrection; Good Friday and Easter

Notes 221

I
Why History?

History is bunk! It was Henry Ford who said it. And if you are like many people, you couldn't agree with him more! At least you would say that history is a bore—all those dates to memorize, all those strange people doing absurd things. Who cares about Napoleon at Waterloo or Caesar at the Rubicon? What difference does it make anyway? This is the twentieth century!

In fact, did you ever stop to think that this is the real reason why some persons find the Bible boring? It's not just the strange language (they could read a modern translation) or the difficult names. These things are simply convenient excuses. The big reason why the Bible bores them is the simple fact that an enormous amount of the Bible is history. Take all the history out of the Bible and there really wouldn't be very much left—a book of poems, some proverbs, a few letters would be about all. Whether it be the long history of the people of Israel, the shorter history of the young Christian church, or the single history of a man named Jesus, there's no getting away from it. Most of the Bible is history.

When you stop to think about it, that's an odd thing. (And if you've never stopped to think about it, now is a good time to try.) After all, the Bible is a religious book. We should expect a religious book to be just that—a book containing religious truths, moral advice, ethical prescriptions. We should expect a religious book to tell us how to be religious.

But we open the Bible and what do we find? History and more history! If it isn't some Israelitish king attacking the Amalekites, it's some eager missionary preaching in Colossae or Thessalonica. Even the names twist our tongues. You open the Bible for some sound religious advice and you read about Tirhakah, king of Ethiopia. You open the Bible for moral guidance and you read about some woman named Lydia. It's all very confusing. If the Bible is a religious book, why should it have so much history? If it's a history book, why should it claim to be religious?

That is actually a very important question. Suppose we think about it. All of the world's other great religions really have no history. Yes, there was someone who expounded them—Buddha, Confucius, Mohammed. Of course, each had a personal history. But that really doesn't matter too much. For these religions are all religions of abstract ideas, religions of general teachings and propositions. It would make no real difference to Buddhism, for example, if Buddha had been Indian or Puerto Rican. The religious ideas of Confucius would be the same whether Confucius were Chinese or Brazilian. What matters is not the history, but the teachings, the ideas.

Because that is the way all the other great religions of the world work, we naturally assume that that is the way Christianity works, too. In fact, we often try to make it work that way, try to reduce the Christian gospel to some neat and concise formula like the Golden Rule or the thirteenth chapter of First Corinthians. "There it is," we say; "that's Christianity in a nutshell."

But Christianity doesn't work that way. We have to face the stubborn fact that Christianity has a history. There's the Bible with page after page to prove it. All those Israelitish kings and those strange people in the Mediterranean churches belong there. They cannot be washed out as if they didn't matter. They matter enormously. For alone among the world's religions the Christian gospel is not ideas but history. Our faith is not a set of propositions, but a story.

This, then, is where we must begin. No Christian can ever get away from history. Even the Apostles' Creed—that statement of Christian propositions, if you like—has a historical pivot. Right there in the middle of the Creed, like a fossil in a rock, is Pontius Pilate, a little Roman politician of whom no one would ever have heard otherwise. What is he doing in the Apostles' Creed? He is there to remind us that we can never dissolve the Christian gospel into a set of ideas with no roots in history. Our gospel is located in a series of events which happened in a particular place and at a particular time—"under Pontius Pilate."

CHRISTIANITY AND HISTORY

Why should there be this close relation between Christianity and history? Here are three reasons to think about.

1. All of the other great religions have assumed that God (or the gods) is in heaven while men are on earth. While occasional messengers may come from heaven to earth, they are two separate and distinct realms, having little to do with each other.

The Bible is different because of its insistence from the very first words of Genesis on that God is not confined to heaven or a mere spectator of the earthly show, but that he is a real and active participant in history. The God of the Bible is not only interested but involved in events on earth. When a Greek or a Chinese fell downstairs, he probably said "Ouch" (or something less polite). But when a Hebrew fell downstairs, he probably said, "I wonder why God pushed me." In other words, the God of the Bible is no static idea beyond the clouds, but an active, dynamic participant in the things that happen, involving himself in them to make his influence felt, his will done.

As soon as we have said that, we have involved ourselves in history. After all, history is simply the record of events. If we believe that God is involved in the things that happen, then we have said that he is involved in history. We must record the things that happen and study them carefully because it is in them that we see God at work.

Because of our training, we tend to look for evidence of God in created things—the arrangement of the stars, the construction of the human eye. That kind of approach seldom interested the Hebrew. He looked for evidence of God in the things that happened, in the battles that were fought, the kings that were deposed, the nations that rose and fell on the scene of history. In his tradition the best place to look for God today would be in the headlines of the newspaper!

Nor did the Hebrew of Bible times shrink from the full logic of his belief. Though he may have had only a limited acquaintance with world affairs, the nations that he did know, the Egyptians, the Assyrians, the Babylonians, were all part of the story in which God involved himself. What happened to them was part of the pattern of his purpose.

Perhaps now we can begin to understand why history was so very important to the biblical point of view. It was the theater in which God acted. If you wanted to know God, you had to know history. For it was in the things that happened that God was at work.

2. But now we must narrow this down a bit. After all, all history, even that part of it which the Hebrew could know, is a pretty big theater. The picture gained from it would be a bewildering one because of the size of it. While the Bible never denies that God is to be found in all events, in all history, it claims that he can be best seen and known in a particular and specialized history, that of the people of Israel.

The Bible claims that it was in this history that God chose to do his closest and most specialized work. It is silly to waste time by arguing why God chose this particular history; it is like asking why grass is green and not blue. The better approach is to examine the claim and see what it means. What it means, put simply, is that the history of Israel is also the history of God, the record of his mighty acts. From the day that Abraham was summoned to leave his home and go into a land of which he had never heard to the very end of the Old Testament story, the history of the people of Israel cannot be understood in the same way as the history of the people of Persia or the people of India. The history of the people of Israel must be interpreted in the light of God's purposes, his activity, his will.

To be sure, the people of Israel, like every other nation, had their own purposes, aims, and activities. But the fascinating thing about their history is the very way in which God used their stubborn determination toward their own purposes to achieve his purpose, the way God worked through their history to accomplish his will and reveal his purpose.

As a result, it would not be too much to say that all that the Old Testament knows about God, it knows from what he has done in history, specifically in the history of his people Israel. For example, the Old Testament declares that he is a God of grace, delivering those who do not deserve deliverance. How does it know that? Not because one fair day God wrote in the sky "I am a God of grace" nor even because he whispered the statement in someone's ear. The Old Testament can say it because in the history of Israel it happened time and again. Yes, it happened superbly on that day by the shore of the Red Sea when a horde of slaves found themselves trapped between the angry waters in front of them and the marching tread of Pharaoh's army behind them. There was no hope—and yet they were delivered.

If history is important to the understanding of God, the history of Israel is absolutely essential. Apart from that history, what could be said of the nature and character of the God whom we worship? He would be what a college student once called him, an oblong-shaped blur. But because in the history of Israel he acted again and again, we can know and say, a God of grace, a God of judgment, a God of mercy.

We must know the history recorded in the Bible, therefore, not for its own sake. For its own sake it is of no greater value than the history of any other nation. A person could know the history of Israel back to front and still miss its real point. We must know the history of Israel because in that history the character of God is disclosed to us. It is in what he has done that God has made himself known. And he has done it in the history of this people whose story is recorded in the Bible.

3. Now we must push our question about history a step further. Did God cease to act in history when the Bible came to an end? When Paul reached the city of Rome (it is about at this point in history that the New Testament record breaks off), was that the end of God's activity in our human story? Does it make any sense to say that God began to act in history with Abraham and ended with Paul? Can we draw the conclusion that since A.D. 65 he has been doing nothing?

Of course that would be ridiculous. While we know that he acted decisively, even finally, in history in the person of Jesus Christ, we also believe that he has not stopped nor will he stop until he has brought all history under the control of Christ. Once involved in the human story, God will not leave it until he has made it over completely to his pattern.

But in what history does God work today? While certainly we must believe that he works in all history, is there a particular people in whose story he continues to make himself and his purposes known as once he did in the people of Israel? If so, what people is it? Is it, as many people appear to think, the United States of America? If God still has chosen people through whose history he particularly works, who would your candidate for the position be?

GOD'S NEW PEOPLE

The answer is the Christian church. This is God's new people. We do not often enough think of the church in this way. At first, it may even seem a strange way to think of it. If we were asked to name the founder of the Christian church, we should of course reply, Jesus Christ. In a deep sense, we should be right. But in another sense, we should be wrong. For the founder of the church was Abraham.

In other words, the New Testament contends that the real successor to the people of Israel is the people of the church. They are the new people through whom God works. Just as in the time of the Old Testament he made himself known in the history of Israel, so in the history of the church he continues his work and accomplishes his purposes. It is through the people of the church that God is at work to complete his will for the world.

The one real book of history in the New Testament is the Acts of the Apostles. It tells the story of the Christian church from its baptism by the Holy Spirit on the day of Pentecost until Paul reaches Rome some thirty years later. There New Testament history ends.

Yet in one sense we can say that the acts of the apostles still continue. For if the church is the new Israel, the people whose history God uses for his purposes, then all that has happened in the story of that people since the gospel was brought to Rome until now is still part of what was begun at Pentecost. The bringing of the gospel to Western Europe, the development of monasteries and cathedrals, the Protestant Reformation, the religious revival of the Wesleys—these are all part of the story. For these are all part of the history of that people through whom God still works in his world.

If you agree, then you cannot deny that it is important that we know the story of the church, just as we must know the story of Israel. Once again, that knowledge is never for its own sake. We can be wonderfully versed in the facts of church history and still miss the point completely. But we must know that history because it is in and through that history that we trace the pattern of God's continuing activity, a pattern now made fully and finally clear in Jesus Christ.

History is bunk! If you do not believe in God, that may be true. But to those who believe in the God of the Bible, that can never be true. For that God is not detached from the human scene. And while he has the whole human scene under his direction and control, there has always been and will always be some particular part of that scene in which we can trace him more clearly. In our time that part of the human scene is the history of the Christian church.

We shall be looking at that history not to become experts in dates and events, able to tell who was pope in Rome when Columbus discovered America or what was John Wesley's mother's maiden name. But we shall be looking at the history of the church to discover from it what we can of the way God works in his world, the pattern of his purpose.

So let the curtain go up! The drama will contain rogues and villains, saints and martyrs, deeds of heroism, acts of cowardice. But even while the story unfolds, this is the question to keep in mind: Is there pattern and purpose in this series of events?

A modern historian has said that there is no pattern in history. Hegel, the great German philosopher, once remarked that the only thing we can learn from history is that nobody ever learns anything from history.

What do we Christians learn from the history of the people of which we are a part, the history of the church?

PART I
THE CHURCH AGAINST THE WORLD

•

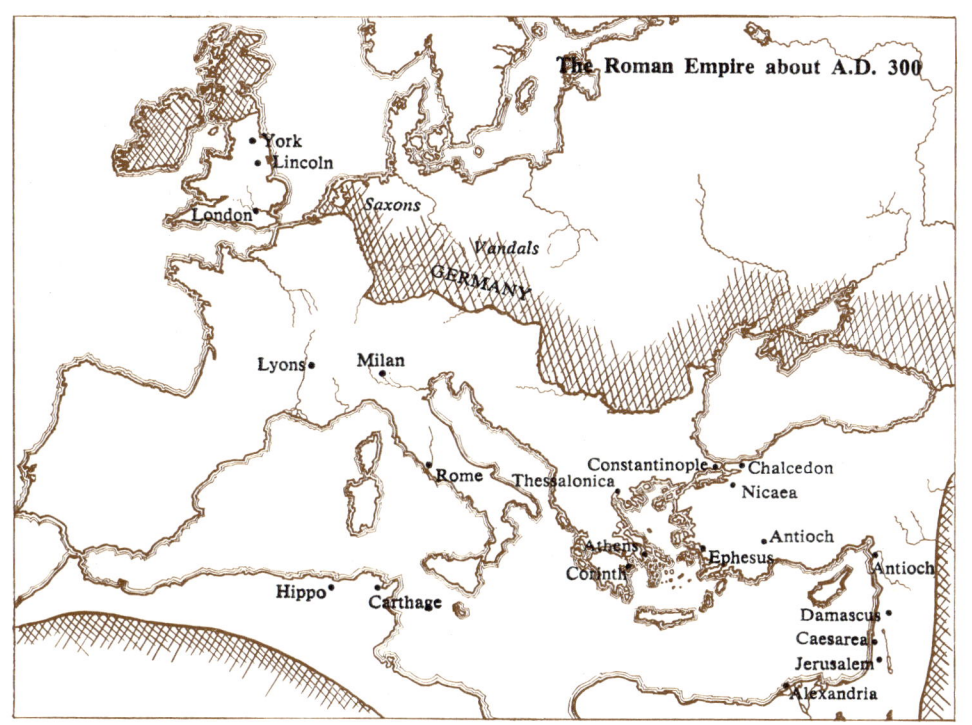

•

AS this broken bread, once scattered upon the mountains, has been gathered together and been made one, so may thy Church be gathered together from the ends of the earth into thy Kingdom. For thine is the glory and the power through Jesus Christ for ever. . . . Amen.[1]
—*The Didache*, about A.D. 100

MAY God the Father, and the Eternal High Priest Jesus Christ, build us up in faith and truth and love, and grant to us our portion among the saints with all those who believe on our Lord Jesus Christ. We pray for all saints, for kings and rulers, for the enemies of the Cross of Christ, and for ourselves we pray that our fruit may abound and that we may be made perfect in Christ Jesus our Lord. Amen.[2]
—Bishop Polycarp, martyred A.D. 155

MERCIFUL Lord, the Comforter and Teacher of Thy faithful people, increase in Thy Church the desires which Thou hast given, and confirm the hearts of those who hope in Thee by enabling them to understand the depth of Thy promises, that all Thine adopted sons may even now behold, with the eyes of faith, and patiently wait for, the light which as yet Thou dost not openly manifest; through Jesus Christ our Lord. Amen.[3]
—Ambrose of Milan, A.D. 340–397

2

After the Apostles

Scholars will probably go on debating the question as long as time lasts. But let's assume that we are not far from the truth if we say that all the books in the New Testament were written before the year A.D. 150. Perhaps you will recall from your history book that it was in the year 313 that the Emperor Constantine recognized that Christianity was a legitimate religion. Now suppose that you were asked to tell what you know of the main events in the story of the Christian church between those two dates. What would you reply?

The one answer that almost everyone could give would be "persecution." In fact, many of us have a very vivid picture of Christians being thrown to the lions, used as human torches, or subjected to varieties of cruel tortures by the Roman Empire. And there can be no doubt that the answer is a correct one. The big thing in the history of the church for those two centuries was persecution. Had we been Christians living in that time we should always have had this fact in our minds.

Yet we really ought to know something more about the fact of persecution than that. We ought to know, for example, that persecution was not a daily occurrence all during this period but rather occurred in sporadic outbursts. In fact they were such definite events that we can number them. From the time of Nero in A.D. 64 to the last persecution under the Emperor Diocletian in 303 there were ten. This is not to say that there were not continual local harassments and annoyances. There probably were. But organized persecution of Christians on an empire-wide basis was sometimes separated by many years. Between Diocletian's persecution and the last one before it, for example, more than forty years elapsed. In other words, Christians were not forced to spend all their time hiding from the police. Though they always had to live in terrifying uncertainty of the next blow, they had long periods of time in which to extend their numbers and, more importantly, to think about themselves and their mission in the world.

A study of each of the ten persecutions would reveal somewhat different reasons for the outburst of imperial violence. But underlying all of them were certain basic factors which we must understand. Even though the persecutions were sometimes separated by long periods of time, why did they occur at all? Why did the Roman Empire seek to stamp out Christianity? This question becomes more fascinating when we recall that the empire had a great record for religious tolerance. Within its bounds the wildest assortment of religions could be found—all left to go their own way unmolested except for Christianity.

To answer our question we shall pass by all of the local reasons and occasional excuses. They had their part to play doubtless, but it was at best a very minor one. To answer our question we shall ask another. How would you feel toward a group of people in your community who refused to salute the flag and remained seated at any public gathering when "The Star-Spangled Banner" was sung?

Let us suppose that having noticed these rather public actions, you had become interested and done some further investigating. Your research had shown that for the most part this group was made up of people who lived on the wrong side of town. When you tried to attend one of the meetings which they held in their houses, you were not admitted. Neighbors had told you, however, that the goings-on were pretty dreadful, including eating a body and drinking its blood!

Sometimes you had heard one of them preaching in the park. He had spoken about being a citizen of another kingdom in which the President of the United States had no authority. In fact the preacher had said that he and his companions owed their primary obedience to this leader and not to the President. You were not surprised to hear this, however, since you had noticed that many had refused to serve in the army or in any branch of military service.

You had also noticed that many never appeared at any public celebration. They avoided the Halloween parade and were never seen at the Fourth of July celebration. They did not even attend football games or go to the movies ... If you knew a group of people like this in your community, what would you think of them?

Well, you might think of them exactly as the Roman authorities thought of them. When they did not think of the Christians as a harmless, though unpleasant group of antisocial people, they thought of them as dangerous revolutionaries whose ideas and practices threatened the stability of the empire. When that empire was in no particular trouble, Christians were tolerated, though disliked. But when the empire had heavy going, as it did many times during the two centuries in question, the Christians were the first to be blamed and punished.

Nor were the Roman authorities acting unreasonably. Leaving to one side all of the unwarranted gossip about them and their own uncooperative and antisocial attitude, Christians did for the most part come from the lower class: ex-slaves and little dispossessed people, the very element among which revolution always starts. They did talk quite openly about their loyalty to another kingdom and another King whenever any conflict arose between Him and the emperor. No matter which way you looked at it, Christians were like a fifth column whenever the empire was in danger. If they ever had their way, there would no longer be an empire.

THE MARTYRS

With this temper on the part of the government, it is not surprising that many of the great names during these first centuries after the apostles are the names of martyrs, of men and women who witnessed to their loyalty to Jesus Christ even at the cost of their lives. Indeed, it would be difficult to name a Christian leader during these two centuries who was not finally a martyr. They acquitted themselves well, these little insignificant people, when the test came.

Take, for example, one of the earliest cases of which we have a record. About the year 120 the leader of the congregation in Antioch was arrested and taken to Rome for trial. He occupied himself on his journey by writing letters to several other congregations. While most of his letters are concerned with matters of church organization and doctrine, Ignatius gives us an occasional glimpse of his own attitude toward what he knows is to be his future. That attitude is almost enthusiastic. He cannot wait to get to Rome and to make his witness there by his death.

Or perhaps you have heard the story of the martyrdom of Polycarp,

Suffer as a Christian

The First Epistle of Peter is, as J. B. Phillips calls it, a "letter to young churches." It was clearly written to instruct and encourage new Christians in a time of persecution. Look, for example, at these words:

And now, dear friends of mine, I beg you not to be unduly alarmed at the fiery ordeals which come to test your faith, as though this were some abnormal experience. You should be glad, because it means that you are called to share Christ's sufferings. One day, when He shows Himself in full splendour to men, you will be filled with the most tremendous joy. If you are reproached for being Christ's followers, that is a great privilege, for you can be sure that God's Spirit of glory, unseen by you, is resting upon you. But take care that none of your number suffers as a murderer, or a thief, a rogue or a spy! If he suffers as a Christian he has nothing to be ashamed of and may glorify God in Christ's name."[1] (1 Peter 4:12–19)

leader of the congregation in Smyrna. He was probably the last survivor of those who had actually known and talked with some of Jesus' friends. When he was brought before the authorities in 155, moved by his great age, they tried to persuade him to change his mind about his loyalty to Christ. But the old man was insulted by the suggestion that after so many years he should deny his Lord. It was almost with joy that he went from his trial to his death.

Ignatius and Polycarp are only two examples from an almost endless list. How can we account for them? Only by remembering what the word *martyr* really means. These people were not fanatics in love with death. They loved life as much as you do. But they deeply believed that the future belonged to Jesus Christ. Because that was the deepest message of their hearts, they had to preach it, even to the last and most difficult thing any man can do. By dying they witnessed to their unshakable belief in the very thing that they had been saying during their lives.

We have come upon a partial answer to a question which may have been forming in your mind. How is it that in the face of such opposition a faith which required the sacrifice not only of normal social life and contacts but, at any given moment, could require the sacrifice of life itself not only survived but actually grew? What compelled an ever increasing number of people in the Roman Empire to abandon a normal kind of life for one as demanding as the Christian way of life in these days undoubtedly was?

The real answer, of course, lies in the nature of that faith itself. What better demonstration of the nature of that faith could there have been than this almost endless line of witnesses? You could dismiss the first Christian martyrs as a bunch of deluded crackpots. But when martyrdom went on year after year, even the most comfortable Roman citizen had to stop and ask questions. Certainly there was nothing in his religion (if indeed he had one) which could command that kind of devotion. Since the Roman citizen of these centuries lived in a time of great anxiety and uncertainty, the continuing evidence that these Christians must have found something stable and real often caused him to visit their meetings, to ask questions, to take their preachers seriously. The sermons preached by the martyrs were probably the most effective in the history of the church.

THE APOLOGISTS

The church in these centuries after the apostles had other forms of propaganda as well. Though the martyrs were the most dramatic exhibit the Christians had to offer, we must not forget the work of another group called *apologists*. It's a poor word in our vocabulary, suggesting people who make excuses. So let's call them what they were, propagandists, people who tried to interpret the Christian faith to their neighbors in the Roman Empire.

Interpreting the faith was more of a job than you may at first realize. It is a fairly simple job for you and me since the Christian vocabulary is pretty much a part of the culture in which we live. But in the time of which we are speaking, not only the Christian vocabulary but the whole Christian story was obviously and undeniably Jewish. The story centered in Palestine; it presupposed a knowledge of what we call the Old Testament—yet the people they wanted to persuade didn't speak a single word of Hebrew and thought of Palestine, if they thought of it at all, as a rather messy little place off there somewhere. Their intellectual and religious heroes were the great masters of Greek philosophy.

We can list the names of some of these propagandists. Some wrote in Greek, others in Latin, depending upon that part of the empire in which they lived. The most famous of them were Justin the Martyr, Lactantius, Tertullian, Origen, and Clement of Alexandria. Theirs are no romantic stories of heroic exploits, though as Justin's name indicates, many of them also paid with their lives for their faith. Theirs is simply the story of hard intellectual endeavor to make the Christian faith attractive and meaningful to the world around them. And that is never glamorous.

We can do justice to their work only by reading it, but we can summarize the aims of these early Christian propagandists by saying that they had both a negative and a positive intention. Negatively they did not hesitate to point out all the weaknesses in the traditional Roman religion, the foibles of the gods, the foolishness and even the immorality which were attributed to them in the popular mythologies. They did not hesitate to take on the great Greek philosophers either, pointing out the inconsistencies and deficiencies in the systems of men like Plato, Zeno, and Epicurus.

". . . what the soul is in a body"

How could the Christians state their case in a suspicious and often hostile world? One famous attempt to do so is the anonymous "Epistle to Diognetus," written about A.D. 200. Diognetus, apparently, was a man of influence who had expressed interest in the Christian faith. This excerpt suggests the writer's case for Christianity.

This kind of writing required men of large education. The apologists were that. They had studied the philosophies of the men they attacked. In the case of at least one, Justin the Martyr, there had been personal experience of some of these philosophies and personal disillusionment over their failure fully to satisfy human need. The fact that as early as the middle of the second century the Christian church was able to command the services of educated men like these is clear proof that it was not only those from the other side of town who were Christians. Christianity had obviously begun to claim men from intellectual circles as well.

This effort to meet the mind that was trained in Greek philosophy inevitably had two results in the way in which the apologists presented the Christian gospel. For one thing, while they had to point out the ways in which the great philosophers failed to answer some of the deepest human questions, they could not make an all-out attack on those philosophers. They needed them as a bridge to the men whom they wished to reach with the Christian message. It became their task, therefore, to show how the philosophers had really been preparing the way for Christ. Clement of Alexandria, for example, went so far as to claim that the story of Greek philosophy was just as much a preparation for the gospel in the pagan world as the Old Testament was in the Jewish.

Some of the apologists, men like Tatian and Tertullian, were deeply distrustful of this line of approach. Far better, in their opinion, to concede nothing to the pagan world, to condemn it all as worthless, than to try to find points of connection between that world and the Christian gospel. In their opinion there were no points of connection. Jesus Christ and his gospel had nothing to do with the world of pagan philosophy except to replace it. But theirs was definitely a minority opinion. The great majority of the apologists sought ways in which the best of pagan philosophy could be incorporated in the Christian message. Christianity, the answer to the deepest longings of the best philosophers of ancient Greece and Rome—that was the line along which they worked.

> For Christians are not distinguished from the rest of mankind either in locality or in speech or in customs. For they dwell not somewhere in cities of their own, neither do they use some different language, nor practise an extraordinary kind of life. . . . They dwell in their own countries, but only as sojourners; they bear their share in all things as citizens, and they endure all hardships as strangers. Every foreign country is a fatherland to them, and every fatherland is foreign. . . . Their existence is on earth, but their citizenship is in heaven. They obey the established laws, and they surpass the laws in their own lives. . . . Doing good they are punished

(While it is not history, it is interesting to observe that the difference in opinion among the apologists is still a real one in the mission of the church to the world today. When we ask the best way to present the gospel to the Hindu or the Moslem, we still find the same two answers. There are those who believe it is best presented as something totally new and different, while there are those who argue that it is best presented as the answer to the unfulfilled aspirations of the highest in Hinduism or Islam.)

The second result of the apologists' presentation of Christianity was that it was presented as a philosophy, as a way of life. Not only are all the specifically Hebrew features of the story eliminated, but the center of reference has been changed. In the letters of Paul that center is in the cross and resurrection of Jesus Christ. In the writings of the apologists it is in the way of life which Jesus Christ makes possible. Not that either the cross or the resurrection are denied; they are there as part of the story. But they are much in the background. The foreground is entirely concerned with the kind of person that the gospel produces.

Of course, we must remember that writings like these were produced to attract the dissatisfied pagan. Once attracted, he would doubtless receive solid theological instruction as part of his training before baptism. Still it is interesting to observe the way in which these apologists stressed the visible results of the Christian faith. They emphasized the moral transformation that Christianity produced. To win converts these propagandists accentuated the way in which Christianity made a man not only contented individually but sensitive and responsible socially. "If you doubt that Christianity is the best philosophy of life," they said, "simply look at the lives of those in the Christian community compared with the lives of those in your pagan society."

It says much for the life of the Christian community in those days and of the ordinary people who made it up that it could stand this test. One wonders whether our lives as Christians could meet the same test or whether a modern propagandist might not be running a great risk if he tried such an argument. But the life of that community must have

---

as evil-doers; being punished they rejoice, as if they were thereby quickened by life . . .

In a word, what the soul is in a body, this the Christians are in the world. . . . The soul is enclosed in the body, and yet itself holdeth the body together; so Christians are kept in the world as in a prison-house, and yet they themselves hold the world together. . . . So great is the office for which God hath appointed them, and which it is not lawful for them to decline.[2]

been able to deliver the goods. For almost two hundred years the apologists continued to make just such an appeal and it must have had results.

These propagandists for the Christian cause have often been accused of giving away too much. In seeking to make Christianity presentable to the ancient world, it is said, they made it too much a philosophy, too little a theology. But again we point out that theological instruction was not their business. Their job was to interest the pagan world and that meant meeting the pagan world in terms which it could understand. If Lactantius or Origen were alive today, they would probably be taking graduate courses in nuclear physics or radio astronomy so that they could present the Christian faith to the modern pagan! It was their faith, after all, that no area of human life or thought could be alien to Jesus Christ and his gospel.

What accounted for the growth of the Christian movement in these years after the apostles? There was the steadfast devotion of the martyrs; the intellectual integrity of the apologists. Above all there was the loyal, quiet living of thousands of ordinary Christians who, as someone has said, "out-thought," "out-lived," and "out-died" the pagans around them. The greatest reason for the growth of the church was to be found in the fact that when the world watched it, strange and unattractive as many of its ways seemed, the world could come to only one conclusion: "Behold, how these Christians love one another!"

3

Our Debt to the Heretics

Even in these centuries when through the witness of the martyrs and the propaganda of the apologists the Christian gospel was making its way in the empire, there began to develop within its own ranks movements which forced it to ask questions about itself. For within the fellowship of the Christian church there were those who disagreed as to the nature and meaning of the gospel which was being proclaimed to the world.

They have come down in history as the first of a long line of people known as *heretics*. The word has acquired so many overtones in our ears that we should do well to remind ourselves that basically it means nothing more than *those who have made a choice*. To be sure, it was decided that they made the wrong choice—and with that decision there is no disagreement. But in their own way by forcing the church to make up its mind they unwittingly performed a service. For if they had not insisted upon their points, the truth might have remained concealed or undefined.

There is another interesting fact about these heretics of eighteen hundred years ago. Though the positions they held were ruled out of bounds by the decision of the church at the time, these viewpoints had a strange way of recurring in the later history of the church. Heresy dies hard, it would seem. If we have eyes to see, it does not take much vision to discover many of these ideas from long centuries ago still lurking even in our modern Protestantism.

THE GNOSTICS

The greatest internal rival of the Christian faith in these centuries was a movement called Gnosticism. It would be more accurate to call Gnosticism *movements* since it had many leaders and many expressions in the early Christian world. Derived from the Greek word meaning knowledge, Gnosticism, however it was expressed, always based its claim on some hidden wisdom, some secret knowledge which it professed to offer to its believers. Actually, it was older than Christianity, and when Christianity came on the scene, it simply tried to incorporate the Christian witness into its own system.

It is clear from the New Testament that some form of Gnosticism was already threatening the integrity of the Christian faith in the time of the apostles. There are passages in the writings of John, especially those which attack people who say that Jesus Christ did not come in the flesh, which are clearly aimed at the Gnostic creed.

For that creed, though it might find scores of expressions and variations at the hands of different Gnostic thinkers, always centered in this: The real world, the good world, was the world of spirit. The world of material things was bad and the source of all wickedness. From such a premise it followed that human beings were evil only because they had physical bodies. The human spirit, if only it could be liberated from the prison of the flesh, was good.

Yet even more important conclusions followed from the Gnostic premise. A good God must have made the world of spirit. But the material world, being evil and the source of all contamination, must be the work of an evil spirit, a wicked god. It is obvious, therefore, that when Jesus came into this world, he could not have had a human body. That would have made him subject to the power of evil. Jesus was pure spirit, being sent by the good God. He only *seemed* to have a body. It was this aspect of Gnosticism to which John was objecting.

Before we dismiss the Gnostic interpretation of religion as a weird one and wonder who could ever believe such stuff, we ought to remember two things about it. In the first place it won such acceptance in the ancient world because it said some of the things which the best thinkers of the ancient world had themselves said. The great philosopher Plato, for example, had spoken of the body as the tomb of the soul. Physical existence seemed to many of the best ancient thinkers not only a drag on the life of the spirit but a positive hindrance to it. The Gnostics were merely stretching out into a system some of the most widely held insights of ancient thinkers.

Even more significant is the way in which the Gnostic ideology has lingered right on into the modern Protestant world. Before you dismiss

Beware of False Teachers!

These short passages were written from three corners of the Roman Empire in the early centuries of the Christian church. Here are warnings against false teachers from the pens of three famous early church Fathers, Ignatius of Antioch (born c. A.D. 35), Irenaeus of Lyons (c. A.D. 130–c. 200), Clement of Alexandria (c. A.D. 150–c. 215). The heresies about which each writes are described in this chapter of the study book. Why were these false teachings very dangerous?

the Gnostics as a bunch of crackpots, have a look at the variety of ways in which some Protestants condemn the physical world if not as the work of the devil, as something pretty close to it. What is our modern idea of the destruction of the body and the immortality of the soul? What are many of our puritanical ideas about the wickedness of sex?

Our tendency toward Gnosticism goes even deeper than that when you think about it. Have you ever heard a good Christian say that the business of the church is saving souls and that it should stick to that business and keep its nose out of such matters as racial equality, political freedom, economic justice, the use of nuclear weapons? Have you perhaps thought that way yourself sometimes? Well, to what extent must we say, then, that Gnosticism is still alive in present-day Christianity?

However we may answer that one, it is clear that in Gnosticism the church faced an internal enemy of no mean strength. And it is important to see why in the opinion of Christian leaders and thinkers of that day Gnosticism was an enemy with whom no compromise could be made. The basic assumptions of Christianity and Gnosticism simply could not be reconciled. Gnosticism was completely the wrong choice.

Christian leaders rejected Gnosticism not simply because the Scriptures knew nothing of the Gnostic division of the world into a material world and a spiritual world or man into a body and a soul. It was basically because the scriptural witness clearly affirmed that the entire world, physical and spiritual, was God's creation. There were not two creators, a good one and a bad one. "In the beginning God created the heavens and the earth" (Gen. 1:1).

These Christian leaders did not deny that there was evil in the world, but to blame that evil on the wicked work of a malignant spirit was to evade the clear witness of Scripture that the evil in the world is the result of man's deliberate and free choice, his sin. He was not forced

Be deaf, therefore, when any one speaks unto you apart from Jesus Christ, who was of the race of David, the child of Mary, who was truly born, and ate and drank, was truly persecuted under Pontius Pilate, was truly crucified and died, before the eyes of those in heaven and those on earth and those under the earth; who also was truly raised from the dead, since His Father raised Him up, who in like manner will also raise up us who believe on Him— even His Father will raise us in Christ Jesus, apart from whom we have not true life.[1]

—Ignatius, *To the Trallians,* IX.

to this choice by the evil lusts of his material existence. He made it wittingly and freely. And so no phantom Christ could help him. Only a Jesus who came in a physical body, lived a material existence, died a real death, and rose again in a spiritual body could be his Redeemer.

That, in briefest terms, was the Christian case against Gnosticism. By putting the blame for evil on an evil spirit, it ignored the real cause of human misery. By making Christ a phantom, it robbed redemption of its reality. By making the world the work of an evil spirit, it denied the truth of God's good creation.

Though we cannot say definitely, it seems likely that as a result of this Christian battle against Gnosticism that statement of faith which we know as the Apostles' Creed came into being. Though it was not in the full form which we know today and though parts of it were known in Rome before the Gnostic controversy, many of its phrases seem to have been written with the Gnostics in mind. As you read through the Creed, can you spot the phrases that answer the Gnostic point of view?

> I believe in God the Father Almighty, Maker of heaven and earth. And in Jesus Christ, his only Son, our Lord; Who was conceived by the Holy Ghost, born of the Virgin Mary; Suffered under Pontius Pilate, was crucified, dead, and buried; He descended into Hell; The third day he rose from the dead; He ascended into heaven; and sitteth on the right hand of God the Father Almighty; From thence he shall come to judge the quick and the dead.
>
> I believe in the Holy Ghost, The Holy Catholic Church; The communion of saints; The forgiveness of sins; The resurrection of the body; And the life everlasting.

The Gnostics did not believe that God is the "Maker of heaven and earth," for they denied that the physical universe was his creation. Have you ever wondered why the Creed bothers to say anything as obvious as "I believe Jesus Christ was buried"? Well, here is your answer. All of those phrases about Jesus from "born of the Virgin Mary" on were inserted into the Creed deliberately to let the Gnostics know that the Christian faith held that Jesus Christ was a real man, subject to all the pains and pressures of human existence, not excepting death itself. Don't overlook the faith in the "resurrection of the body" in the last section of the Creed. That too has the Gnostics in mind with their teaching about the immortality of the soul once it has finally been released from the evil of its bodily prison!

Doubtless there had been a creed before this. It probably originated at Rome as the profession of faith made by those about to be baptized as new converts to the Christian faith.

Probably also it was little more than a statement of faith derived from Matthew 28:19. The candidate for baptism said, "I believe in the Father and in the Son and in the Holy Ghost." But by now it began to appear that that was not enough. Who was the Father and what was his relation to the world? Who was the Son? Was he really man? By forcing the church after the apostles to ask and answer questions like these, the Gnostics can be said to have given us what essentially is known today as the Apostles' Creed.

MARCION AND THE OLD TESTAMENT

We have said that Gnosticism had a variety of expressions and a number of interpreters. There is one whom we must notice in particular, for his interpretation was somewhat different from the rest and forced the church to another decision. Marcion had been brought up a Christian; in fact, the tradition is that his father was a bishop. A wealthy layman, he came to Rome in about 139 and became active in the church there.

Using the Gnostic pattern of two gods, Marcion applied it to the Bible. It was clear to him that the god in the Old Testament was very different from the God revealed by Jesus Christ. The Old Testament with its rigorous legalism, its bloodthirsty tales, its self-righteous chosen people is all the work of an evil god. Jesus Christ, who, following the usual Gnostic teaching, was a spirit only seeming to have a body, came to reveal the true God, to set men free from their bondage to the laws and sacrifices that had been the demands of the old god.

Marcion of Pontus . . . developed his school, advancing the most daring blasphemy against Him who is proclaimed as God by the law and the prophets, declaring Him to be the author of evils, a lover of war, inconstant in judgement, and contrary to Himself. . . . Besides this, he mutilates the Gospel which is according to Luke, removes all that is written respecting the generation of the Lord, and sets aside a great deal of the teaching of the Lord's discourses, in which the Lord is recorded as most clearly confessing that the Maker of this universe is His Father. . . . In like manner, too, he dismembered the epistles of Paul, removing all that is said by the apostle respecting that God who made the world, to the effect that He is the Father of our Lord Jesus Christ . . .[2]
—Irenaeus, *Against Heresies*, 1.25.1.

There is just enough in the letters of Paul about the insufficiency of the law to give some credence to Marcion's assertion that his point of view was also that of the great apostle. Accordingly he made up his own version of the New Testament. It included most of Paul's letters, although Marcion had to edit them to remove some things which did not agree with his point of view. These corruptions, he maintained, (thus beginning a practice which has been followed many times since) had been added by later authors. His New Testament also included a carefully edited version of Luke's Gospel since it contained the fewest Jewish references.

Of course it is not difficult to see that the church had to deal with Marcion as it did with the other Gnostics. For in spite of his peculiar use of Gnosticism in a biblical way, his basic ideas were no different from those which had been condemned. Once again we should notice how Marcion's ideas have lingered long after his time. Do you know anyone who thinks that the Christian church would be better off without the embarrassment of the Old Testament? Perhaps few people would be willing to say it out loud, but judging from the way in which many Christians ignore the Old Testament, many share Marcion's opinion.

The church had no difficulty dealing with the rejection of the Old Testament by Marcion. The Old Testament was the Bible, as far as the early church was concerned. And the church was the continuation of the chosen people, the new Israel, the instrument through which God works in the world. To turn its back on the Old Testament would be turning its back on its own history.

Marcion's proposed New Testament was a different matter. Clearly his suggestion that it should include only his edited versions of Paul's letters and Luke's Gospel was preposterous. But what should it contain? That may strike you as a very strange question for the church to be asking almost 150 years after the birth of Jesus Christ. The fact is that there had never been a decision as to just what books did belong in the New Testament. In Marcion's day it was still an open question.

That is not to say that Christians in the second century did not possess all the books which today are included in our New Testament. They had them and more besides. About many there was no question, but others had provoked some discussion. A great second century theologian, Irenaeus, tells us that John's Gospel had not won as rapid acceptance as the other three, though by his time it was no longer in dispute. But the Revelation of John, the last book in our New Testament, was long questioned by many, as were Hebrews, James, Second Peter, Second and Third John, and Jude. On the other hand there were books like the Apocalypse of Peter, the Epistle of Barnabas, the Shepherd of Hermas and some others which had strong supporters for inclusion in the New Testament.

It was a question which was not soon settled. In fact not until 367 did the canon of the New Testament finally take its present form of twenty-seven books. But with the exception of the books we have mentioned, from the time of Marcion on there began to be a New Testament containing the four Gospels, Acts, the letters of Paul, and some of the other apostolic writings. The exact books which the church included in the New Testament (or the Old, for that matter) are called the *canon*. The fact that there began to be a New Testament canon in the second century, a collection of Christian Scriptures included with the Scriptures of the Old Testament, is a debt that we owe to the heretic Marcion. It was his canon that forced the church to think about a canon of its own.

SPEAKING IN TONGUES

There was another type of heresy which developed in these years after the apostles which had nothing to do with Gnosticism. Its leader was a man named Montanus who came from Phrygia in Asia Minor. He lived at about the same time as Marcion. Montanus was a very simple man who was distressed by the fact that Christians no longer looked for the second coming of Christ with the same zeal that they had in earlier days. Reading the prophecies of that coming, he became what

. . . It is evident that these later heresies . . . are spurious innovations on the oldest and truest Church. . . . unity is a characteristic of the true, the really ancient Church, into which those that are righteous according to the divine purpose are enrolled. For God being one and the Lord being one, that also which is supremely honoured is the object of praise, because it stands alone, being a copy of the one First Principle: at any rate the one Church, which they strive to break up into many sects, is bound up with the principle of Unity. We say, then, that the ancient and Catholic Church stands alone in essence and idea and principle and pre-eminence, gathering together, by the will of one God through the one Lord, into the unity of the one faith, built upon the fitting covenants (or rather the one covenant given at different times) all those who are already enlisted in it, whom God foreordained, having known before the foundation of the world that they would be righteous.[3]
—Clement, *Miscellanies,* Book VII, chapter XVII.

today we should call a "premillennialist." He believed, in other words, that Christ would come and rule on earth for a thousand years before the final end of the world.

Montanus also took very seriously what the New Testament had to say about "speaking in tongues" and believed that he, with some of his followers, had the power to do it. He was also disturbed by what he considered the growing worldliness on the part of many Christians.

From this brief description we should be able to recognize Montanism for what it was, the first of many protests against too close an alliance between the church and the world, against too easy an accommodation of the Christian faith to its surroundings. What Montanus wanted must have found a responsive chord in many hearts for he converted to his movement no less a person than the great apologist Tertullian. A crude and uneducated person himself, Montanus was seeking to call the church back to the "old-time religion."

Why then was Montanus condemned as a heretic? It was not so much because of his teaching. As we shall see, there were to be many such attempts to return to the old-time religion in years to come, most of which met with the church's blessing. It was rather because of the attitude with which he taught it. Not only did Montanus make himself the center of his movement, he refused fellowship with other Christians who did not agree with him. Though it is hard to judge from this distance, it seems fair to say that to further his own position Montanus was willing to split the church. It was not so much his doctrine as his lack of charity, his refusal to take seriously the unity of the body of Christ, that took Montanus out of the fellowship of the church.

Unfortunately Montanus was the first of a type with which the history of the church has been filled, good men who take themselves and their ideas more seriously than they take the oneness of the church. Rather than surrender their ideas, they have been willing to start a new church, breaking the unity of Christ's body. What happened to Montanus ought to warn us that serious as was false doctrine like that of the Gnostics, in the thinking of the early church, schism, the splintering of Christ's family, was just as serious.

4

The Age of Creed-Making

Persecution came to an end in 313 when the Emperor Constantine recognized the Christian faith as one of the legitimate religions of the empire. Although he never abolished paganism (that came later) and did not make Christianity the official religion, his own inclination was so strongly that way (near the end of his life he was baptized) that thousands who had previously held back now became Christians. Some of them probably had been sympathetic but had been afraid to declare themselves because of the ever present threat of persecution. Others doubtless became Christians from no conviction but simply because it seemed the thing to do.

There has been continual discussion whether Constantine's official recognition of the church was a kindness or not. To be sure, the removal of the long nightmare of persecution meant that the church was now free to do its work without fear. To this day in Eastern Orthodoxy Constantine is regarded as a saint. But on the other hand, there can be no doubt that in favoring Christianity Constantine helped fill the ranks of the church with many persons whose interest was not sincere.

However you may choose to answer that question, Constantine's action did have one result which had not been expected. As long as the Christian faith remained an unofficial movement it could avoid much discussion and the necessity for precise formulation. There was no need for a believing Christian to explain to himself who Jesus Christ was; he knew Jesus Christ as the Redeemer of the world and that was enough. When Christians sought to persuade others to their faith, there was no need for them to become involved in lengthy theological discussions. Their preaching was based on experience, not on theological theory.

Once Christianity became an official religion all that was changed. Living openly in the world of other religions, of philosophy and science, Christians had to explain what they meant. They found themselves under the necessity of putting into precise statements and accurate formulas the faith which they professed. It was no longer sufficient to say that Jesus was the Redeemer. Now an enquiring world wanted explanations. Who exactly was he? God? Man? Or if both, how were they combined in a single person?

To be sure, Christians had given some attention to these questions before this. They had, for example, rejected the theory of Sabellius that

Jesus had been God the Father appearing and acting in human form. They had similarly rejected the explanation of Paul of Samosata, usually called "Adoptionism." Paul had argued that Jesus had been a man who became the Son of God when he was baptized by John. By these decisions the church had made clear its faith that the Son was distinct from the Father and that he had a divine nature as well as a human. There the matter had rested.

ARIUS

Apparently the first person to take up the challenge of the new situation and explain who Jesus was was a popular preacher in the church in Alexandria named Arius. His enemies had accused him of ambition and said that his real motive was to become bishop. In any event, he objected to certain statements which Alexander, his bishop, had made as sounding like those same Sabellian theories against which the church had already decided.

The theory which Arius proposed was that Jesus was neither fully God nor completely human. As the eternal Word he was quite literally the first created being. As such he became man for us men and for our salvation. By this theory Arius felt that he had avoided both the extreme of Sabellius, who had said that Christ and his Father were the same, and that of Paul of Samosata with his assertion that Christ was only a man until adopted by God at his baptism.

But Bishop Alexander was not without his defenders in Alexandria. Chief among them was a young deacon named Athanasius who was later to be his successor. To them it was a fatal mistake on the part of Arius to deny that Christ had been fully God. Let Arius put him as high as he could in the order of created things. Unless God himself and not an intermediary had been involved in man's redemption in the life, death, and resurrection of Jesus Christ, that redemption was not real. For what, after all, is the heart of the Christian gospel? Is it not that God himself came in the person of his Son? And now here is Arius saying that someone else came, the most important being in all creation, to be sure, but still not God himself.

Once started the discussion soon spread beyond the confines of Alexandria until it had become empire-wide. Families debated around the dinner table whether Christ was of the same substance as God or of like substance. The barber who cut your hair might ask whether or not you believed there was a time when Christ was not. Was Christ begotten or was he created? These were some of the popular forms which the argument took.

Both sides in the discussion found powerful supporters. Bishop Eusebius of Nicomedia became Arius' chief defender and maintained his point of view even after Arius' death. It is not likely that the emperor (Constantine) understood what the discussion was all about, but he quickly grasped its potential for trouble to his empire. In 325, therefore, he summoned a council of all the bishops at his summer home in the town of Nicaea. With Constantine himself in the chair, the council debated the question and the debate was often hot.

The decision finally went to the party of Alexander and Athanasius. The formula adopted by the Council forms the heart of what today is called the Nicene Creed. Though not so well known as the Apostles' Creed, it is still used in a slightly changed form in many churches. Here are its words about Jesus Christ: ". . . And in one Lord JESUS CHRIST, the Son of God, begotten of the Father, Light of Light, very God of very God, begotten, not made, being of one substance with the Father . . ." Such phrases as "begotten of the Father," "begotten, not made," "one substance" were all explicitly chosen to rule out any possibility of compromise with the Arian party.

ATHANASIUS AGAINST THE WORLD

The adoption of this Creed by the Council of Nicaea in 325 by no means settled the argument, however. Though his teaching was condemned and he himself was banished from Alexandria, Arius had powerful friends. It took but the death of Constantine to bring the Arians back to power and to secure the banishment of their great opponent Athanasius. There is not time to tell here how the contest seesawed back and forth almost for the rest of the fourth century. Athanasius was banished so often for the faith which he steadfastly maintained that he became known as "Athanasius against the world."

It is, of course, easy to dismiss all this history as nothing but a quibble over words. It certainly looks like it when you know that the slogan of either party differed by only one letter. The Arians said that Christ was *homoiousion,* of a similar substance with the Father, while the Athanasians said that he was *homoousion,* of the same substance as the Father. It is easy to sneer, as many have done, and say that Christendom was split into warring camps over a single *i*.

But as Baron von Hugel once remarked, if a man had promised to write him a check for 1,000 dollars and wrote it instead for 000 dollars, you could say if you like that he was becoming irritated over a single *1*. But the fact would be that this *1* changed the value of the check.

We must, therefore, understand what the single *i* represented to

Athanasius and his followers. From their point of view by that *i* the gospel was made worthless. If God did not send his Son into the world, "His very Self, and essence all-divine," as Cardinal Newman once put it, then, Athanasius maintained, there is really no gospel. Arius' theory may provide us with the most divine of instructors, with a teacher whose every word is spoken with the authority of heaven itself. But that does not answer our deepest need. Our deepest need is not for instruction but for redemption, for deliverance from the cruel bondage of our frustration and failure. And that only God and no one less than God can provide.

From that position Athanasius would not budge, even though his persistence meant repeated banishment and the possibility of death. And we may be grateful that he would not. For in objecting to that single *i*, he was insisting, so to speak, on the full value of the check. Long after their final condemnation the Arians completely disappeared from history. At one time they were a powerful group with extensive missions; in a few centuries they were as extinct as the dinosaur. Why? Not because they were persecuted out of existence; they were not. Arianism disappeared because in the long run, as Athanasius clearly foresaw, it really had no answer for the deepest need of the human situation.

There was another question at issue in this long dispute, though it does not come so clearly to the surface. It is symbolized in the fact that when the Council met in Nicaea in 325 it was the emperor who presided. Though it was not meant to be the issue, the Arian controversy raised the question of the authority of the emperor over the church. Whether from diplomacy or conviction, the Arians were pro-imperial in their policy. They believed that the emperor should have the final decision even in theological questions. The Athanasians, on the other hand, just as stoutly maintained that the church should be completely free to decide for itself any question relating to its faith.

We touch here for the first time the question of the relation of

Before the famous Council at Nicaea, Athanasius stated his reasons for believing that Christ must be God-made-man if he were in truth to be God's Revealer and man's Saviour. Here is his thinking:

We have, then, now stated in part, as far as it was possible, and as ourselves had been able to understand, the reason of His bodily appearing; that it was in the power of none other to turn the corruptible to incorruption, except the Savior Himself, that had at the beginning also made all things out of

church and state, a question which has left its effect on the life of the church right down to our own day, a question which will arise repeatedly in the course of our story. Here we meet it for the first time. Nor was it ever settled in the era of which we are speaking. In fact we can say that the close relationship between church and state began to be forged in the fourth century.

But it is to Athanasius' credit that he disapproved of the relationship even when his own safety depended on imperial favor. In fact, it is interesting to speculate how different the history of Europe might have been if Athanasius' views had prevailed and the church, from the very beginning of its legitimate life, had stood free of interference from or control by the state.

That very freedom of the church is, however, distressing to some people. The minutes of the Council of Nicaea, for example, do not make pretty reading. Here were the leaders of the church from all parts of the Mediterranean world gathered in a Christian assembly. But they often behaved like a convention of fishwives! Not only did they interrupt each other, call each other unpleasant names, but sometimes the discussions ended in violence as one reverend bishop pulled the beard of another! How, some people ask, can we accept the decisions of the Council of Nicaea when we know how they were reached, the cheap maneuvering and petty squabbling that lie behind them, the mean and uninspiring characters of many of the men who wrote them?

Such criticism forgets that almost the same thing was said about the Christian gospel in its earliest days. How can we accept the Christian message, it was asked, when it is offered by an illiterate and untrustworthy fisherman, a dishonest tax gatherer, a woman of questionable reputation? The very human side of the church as it was gathered in Nicaea (and as it would be gathered on many occasions in the future) is both the scandal and the glory of the Christian faith. It is not through angels but through men, with all of their imperfections sticking out in every direction, that God does his work in his world.

---

nought; and that none other could create anew the likeness of God's image for men, save the Image of the Father; and that none other could render the mortal immortal, save our Lord Jesus Christ, Who is the Very Life; and that none other could teach men of the Father, and destroy the worship of idols, save the Word, that orders all things and is alone the true Only-begotten Son of the Father.

But since it was necessary also that the debt owing from all should be paid . . . He next offered up His sacrifice also on behalf of all . . . Whence . . . the Word, since it was not possible for Him to die, as He was immortal, took to Himself a body such as could die, that He might offer it as His own in the stead of all . . .[1]

CONSOLIDATING THE FAITH

The close of the Arian dispute toward the end of the fourth century by no means brought to an end the questions which had to be asked about the person of Jesus Christ. It can be said that this chapter in the controversy was pretty well concluded by the theological work of three men who are known as the *Cappadocians* because they all came from the same area in Asia Minor. Two of them were named Gregory: Gregory of Nyssa and Gregory of Nazianzus. The third was Gregory of Nyssa's older brother Basil. Their work in explanation and defense of the position taken by Athanasius paved the way for the calling of another council at Constantinople in 381. The statement which had been drawn up at Nicaea almost sixty years before was now amplified into what we today know as the Nicene Creed. After the Council of Constantinople Arius' was no longer a permissible opinion in the Christian church.

Although the word can be found in earlier history, it was during this era of controversy that the followers of Athanasius generally began to use the term *catholic* to describe themselves. Since the word basically means nothing more than *whole,* they probably began to use it not simply to indicate that they were the universal church as opposed to the Arians, but even more importantly that theirs was the whole faith while Arianism was only partial in its understanding of the gospel.

Whatever lay behind the use of the word, it stuck. The *catholic* church and the *catholic* faith became the common way of describing the church as opposed to those who left it in pursuit of their own opinions. It is ironic that because the Roman Catholic Church has made exclusive use of the word in our time Protestants should be unwilling to use it. By denying that we are catholics we are saying that we have left the church in pursuit of our own opinions—which, incidentally, is the very case that the Roman Catholic Church would like to make against us!

Once the Council of Constantinople and the Cappadocian theologians had settled that Jesus Christ was true God and true man, the discussion shifted. How these two natures were related to each other in a single person became the new center of interest. There were those who said that he was a divine person with nothing human but his body. There were those who maintained that the two natures existed in him in parallel lines which never met. Council succeeded council and discussion followed discussion in the century after Constantinople. The best that can be said is that on this question no real decision was ever reached. Attempts were made but they succeeded in saying nothing more than that Christians must believe that their Saviour was truly God as he was truly human.

It is true that this kind of discussion, had it gone on, could easily have dissipated the Christian gospel into speculation and theorizing. The further the discussion went, the more removed it became not only from the understanding but from the needs of the average Christian. But before we condemn the theologians completely, we ought to remind ourselves that they had an important work to do. In a world which prided itself on its intellectual ability they had to make a case for the intellectual acceptability of the Christian faith. The case may no longer appeal to us who are not trained as Hellenistic philosophers. But before we condemn them we might ask what intellectual case for the Christian faith we could make in the world of space and missiles.

While the discussion about the relation of divine to human continued to occupy the attention of learned theologians in quiet studies for many years to come, it soon ceased to be of central interest to the church. Even during the latter days of controversy, the distant thunder of drastic events could have been heard. But with the dawning of the fifth century in many parts of the empire what had been distant thunder became a roaring tornado. As old landmarks were swept away in the storm which closed in on every side, the question increasingly became not "What is the person of Jesus Christ?" but "What are his power and his purpose in this world?" It was not a question asked by learned theologians in quiet halls but by countless men and women in the agony of a civilization's death.

PART II
THE CHURCH IN A BREAKING WORLD

•

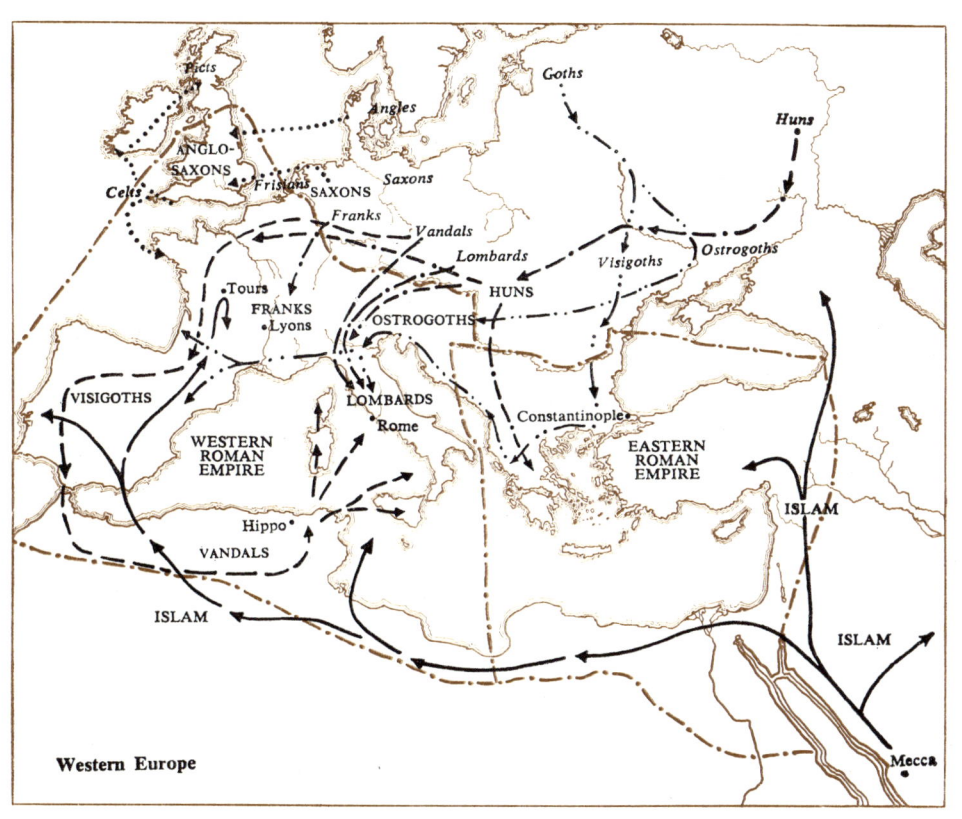

Western Europe

•

For Christmas Eve

O GOD, Who makest us glad with the yearly remembrance of our redemption, grant that, as we joyfully receive Thine only begotten Son as our Redeemer, we may also see Him without fear when He cometh as our Judge; even our Lord, Who with Thee and the Holy Spirit ever liveth, one God, world without end. Amen.[1]   —*Gelasian Sacramentary*, fifth century

For the Nativity of Christ (December 25)

THY NATIVITY, O Christ our God, hath revealed to the world the Light of wisdom: for in it those who worshipped the stars were taught by a star to adore thee, the Sun of Righteousness, and to know thee, the Dayspring from on high. Glory be to thee, O Lord.[2]
    —Greek Orthodox hymn

For Epiphany (January 6)

ALMIGHTY and everlasting God, the brightness of faithful souls, Who didst bring the Gentiles to Thy light, and made known unto them Him Who is the true Light, and the bright and morning Star, fill, we beseech Thee, the world with Thy glory, and show Thyself by the radiance of Thy Light unto all nations; through Jesus Christ our Lord. Amen.[3]
    —*Gregorian Sacramentary*, sixth century

5

The City of God

Thus far in our story it has almost seemed that nothing could stop this Christian movement. It had come back from every imperial persecution stronger than before. Instead of reducing its ranks the persecutions actually seemed to increase them. Finally the very empire which had sought to destroy the church became its conquered subject. Can you think of a more thrilling success story than this one of a despised minority which in less than three centuries became the most powerful single force in the Mediterranean world?

We have no diaries from the period, but it is not unlikely that Christians living in, let us say, 350 to 400 felt the same way themselves. In an earlier age Christians had lived in high expectation of the imminent return of their Lord and the end of the world. By this time that hope had faded. But it did not seem unreasonable to suppose that the Christian church would continue its work of penetration and conquest until the whole world had been won for Christ. Then the end would come.

But if there were such optimists, there were several realities on which they were not reckoning. For one thing apparently no one in the Christian movement realized the implications of being identified with the empire instead of being opposed to it. In the old days of persecution the fate of the empire had been no particular concern to Christians. Hunted and hated as they were, they were keenly aware that they were part of a kingdom which was not of this world, a kingdom the victory of which did not depend on the political history of any government.

CAN THE CHURCH SURVIVE?

All that was changed now. Not only was the empire their empire, its future was their future. They found themselves asking what would become of the church if anything happened to the empire, a question which a few years before would have been unthinkable. Just as many people in our own country seem to feel that the future of the United States and the future of Christianity are one and the same, that the American way of life and the Christian way of life are in no essential way different, so in that era many Christians felt that the preservation of the empire meant the preservation of the church. They even found themselves saying that God could not let anything happen to the Roman Empire for he would be destroying his church.

Yet the more sensitive, at least, knew that that empire had many internal weaknesses. The mere fact that it had become Christian had not done away with graft, corruption, political duplicity. Especially because so many Christians were only nominal Christians, there were plenty of scandals in government. What is more, the loyalty of many of the satellite nations in the empire was very shaky. It needed only some small occasion to turn to hate.

As early as 378 the first signs of trouble were there to be seen. In that year the Goths, a barbarian people living on the fringes of the empire, had defeated the imperial forces at the battle of Adrianople. It was the first sign that the empire had hard days ahead of it. But other signs were not slow in following. In the year 410 the city of Rome itself was conquered by the same Goths, plundered, and left a smoking ruin. In one place after another the barbarians hurled themselves savagely against the empire. And in most places they were successful.

To be sure, the empire had its successes in dealing with them, too. Its favorite device was to recognize the barbarian king as a satellite of the empire, leaving him complete jurisdiction over his own people while granting them definite territorial boundaries. In some instances the policy was a successful one. Not only did it quiet the barbarians but, in theory at least, it extended the sway of the empire.

But in other cases it was not successful for some of the invaders were not looking for stable places in the sun. They simply wanted blood and loot. When in utter disregard of the value of human life they flung themselves against the empire, the results were often disastrous. Many of the Gothic invaders were Christians, though it was the Arian version of Christianity to which they adhered. But many others had no religious faith. They simply wanted what they could get from the empire.

INTRODUCING AUGUSTINE

The man who saw more deeply than any other of his time into the meaning of this changing situation was the bishop of the little North African city of Hippo, Augustine. Converted to the Christian faith in 386 in a dramatic experience, he became a bishop in 395 and continued to be the Christian leader in Hippo until his death in 430.

Because of his own experience of conversion, Augustine's interest did not lie in the theological discussion about the person of Jesus Christ which was still going on when he became a Christian. Deeply aware of the great transformation which had taken place in his own life when he accepted the gospel, Augustine found his theological interest in the great realities of human sin and divine grace. Augustine the wild and careless student of philosophy had become a new man, with totally new attitudes and outlooks. It was his own experience of the reality of sin and estrangement from God, the terrible reality of the search for him that drives men to all kinds of desperate actions, followed by the reality of his grace and forgiveness in Jesus Christ that provided the center of Augustine's thinking.

It was not that he did not accept what the Eastern theologians had said and were saying about the person of Jesus Christ and his place in the Trinity. He did. But Augustine saw clearly how irrelevant to the human situation as he understood it that kind of theology could easily become. How did sin, failure, evil get into the world? What keeps it there? How can it be overcome and driven out? These were the questions in terms of which Augustine saw the relevance of the Christian gospel.

This is not the place to examine Augustine's theology of sin and grace in detail. The important thing to notice is that Augustine represented a real shift in emphasis in the history of Christian thought. We could put it one way and say that he re-centered Christian thought on the need of human nature and God's answer to it. But we could put it another way and say that Augustine was the first Christian thinker to take seriously the gospel as defined in the New Testament letters of Paul.

It should not surprise us that Augustine found Paul such a congenial spirit. Both were men of passionate nature; both had experienced a dramatic conversion; both had been bitter opponents of the faith they finally embraced; both felt sin as a radical flaw in human nature; both had experienced the re-creative power of grace. What is surprising is that Paul's interpretation of the gospel had meant so little in the years since his death. We have no answer to the mystery; we can only point out the strange fact that though his writings make up the bulk of the New Testament, Paul's interpretation of the gospel was almost completely ignored until Augustine's time.

But it would be a mistake to think of Augustine's re-centering of Christian theology in purely individual terms. For he lived through these days of increasing trouble of which we spoke earlier. He lived through the capture and plunder of Rome in 410. While he was still bishop of Hippo the Vandals (their very name has become a synonym for wanton destruction) were at the gates of his own city, letting the bodies of their dead pile up against the city walls until they could climb over them. And all of these events forced him to think of sin and grace not only in terms of individual need but in terms of history as well.

When Rome fell in 410 there were those who said that the city was receiving its just punishment for forsaking its ancestral gods for the strange new religion of the Christians. Nobody took them very seriously, least of all Augustine. But he was concerned by the common Christian opinion that the end of the empire would mean the end of the Christian church. Perhaps his greatest book, *City of God*, was written to interpret history, the history of his own time, from a Christian point of view.

A THEOLOGY OF HISTORY

It need not surprise us that Augustine saw history in the same terms of sin and grace which he had discovered in the individual situation. Far from being the necessary or essential guarantor of order and safety without which the Christian faith could not last, the empire was doomed because it was the organized representative of human pride. It had done many good things. But like the great empires of the past, Babylon, Egypt, Assyria, Rome was only the political organization of human sin, selfishness, and greed.

Against these earthly empires, there was the empire of grace, the heavenly city, the city of God. It was represented in the world by the church, though not all members of the church were necessarily part of the heavenly city. As each earthly empire dissolved in ruin, the heavenly city continued and grew. And this must be the pattern of history, the destruction of earthly empires and the growth of the heavenly city until finally it is all in all when the kingdoms of this world have become the kingdom of our God and of his Christ.

The fate of the city of God, therefore, is not bound up with the fate of the Roman Empire. Indeed, Christians ought to welcome the dissolution of that empire insofar as it witnesses to the further growth of the city of God. On a large canvas, history is the same story of sin and grace as the story of the individual under God's judgment and mercy. So the earthly empire, the representative and embodiment of human sin and pride, is judged and replaced by the city of God.

We must spend some time in considering the influence of Augustine upon later Christian history. But before we do that, it would be worth while to think about the implications of the thesis of his *City of God*. Naturally, when we think about them in terms of the time and place in which Augustine lived we have no difficulty whatever in agreeing with them. Augustine was certainly right in his theory of the two cities, especially as against those who were panicked because they felt that the destruction of the empire would mean the destruction of the church.

But what happens when we take Augustine's ideas and begin to apply them to the time and place in which we live? How does it strike you to read that the government of the United States of America is but one more form of organized human sinfulness? That like all such organizations it is doomed to disappear? That our loyalty must be not to these earthly cities but to that city of God which is coming to fulfillment through all the rise and decay of earthly empires? The question becomes a different one in these circumstances. And yet it is precisely in these circumstances that we have to think about the validity of Augustine's claim.

It is a commonplace thing for theologians to say that there is a great difference in theological emphasis today between the Eastern churches (represented by the various Orthodox communions) and the Western churches (represented by both Roman Catholicism and the various Protestant denominations). Not that they proclaim different gospels, but that they stress different aspects of the gospel.

This difference can be characterized in at least two ways.

1. In the Eastern churches the emphasis of the gospel falls on resurrection and immortality. The goal of the Christian faith is life everlasting. In the Western churches, on the other hand, though certainly they do not deny the resurrection, the emphasis is on redemption from sin, the experience of forgiveness and grace. In a general way the Eastern churches have always been concerned with the theology of Christ's person while the Western churches have stressed the theology of Christ's work, what it was that he did on the cross.

2. The second difference in emphasis is to be found in the passive way in which the Eastern churches have tended to accept the situations of their history contrasted with the active way in which the Western

The City of God and the City of Man

When the Gothic warriors under Alaric captured Rome, the eternal city, in 410, the old Roman empire was shaken to its foundations. Pagans blamed Christianity for the catastrophe, and Christians wrung their hands, crying, "Why did God let it happen?" Augustine undertook to answer both in City of God (De Civitate Dei), *which sought to show the rule of God in history. Two cities, the earthly and the heavenly, "are entangled together in this world and intermixed until the last judgment." Augustine describes the nature of these two cities midway in his book. Does this description have anything to say about the questions people were asking?*

churches have tried to influence and change their situations. While there have been, of course, distinguished exceptions, it is generally true that the Western churches have been active in social reform, in seeking to do something about bettering the human situation here and now, while in no way relinquishing their belief in the final victory of God's Kingdom.

Though it is usually the fashion to put these differences in emphasis down to that elusive thing called "temperament," we should consider to what a large degree Augustine can be called responsible for them. Whether he was expressing purely individual concerns or whether he was expressing the point of view of that part of the world in which he lived need not detain us. The point is that Augustine was the first great Christian thinker to set the directions for what have been the main interests of Western Christianity ever since.

For if it is true that Western Christianity has been mainly concerned with sin and forgiveness, it can be said that this was Augustine's favorite theme. Look in your hymnbook and see how many of the hymns there are concerned with this topic in one way or another, whether in terms of the cross of Christ, forgiveness, new life, or whatever. To jump down the centuries for a moment, this was the great theme at the time of the Protestant Reformation in the sixteenth century, the principal interest of men like Martin Luther and John Calvin. Small wonder that in many ways they felt that Augustine was their theological master. It is no exaggeration to say that here he set the main line down which Western Christian thinking was to go for centuries afterward.

At first sight it may seem less clear how Augustine influenced the Western church to social activism. After all, his *City of God* really insists upon the transience of all political systems. Would that point of view not lead to a passive acceptance of all social and political systems, good or bad, since all of them were doomed by the coming of the city of

> Accordingly, two cities have been formed by two loves: the earthly by the love of self, even to the contempt of God; the heavenly by the love of God, even to the contempt of self. The former, in a word, glories in itself, the latter in the Lord. For the one seeks glory from men; but the greatest glory of the other is God, the witness of conscience. The one lifts up its head in its own glory; the other says to its God, "Thou art my glory, and the lifter up of mine head." In the one, the princes and the nations it subdues are ruled by the love of ruling; in the other, the princes and the subjects serve one another in love, the latter obeying, while the former take thought for all. The one delights in its own strength, represented in the person of its rulers; the other says to its God, "I will love Thee, O Lord, my strength." And therefore the wise men of the one city, living according to man, have sought

God? That might seem to be true. And it would perhaps have been well if many of the social activists in Christian history had learned that lesson from the *City of God*.

But at the same time, Augustine's book represented the first real attempt (apart from the New Testament itself) to interpret history in a Christian way. It had almost been the thing to say that history made no difference since the ultimate destiny of the Christian is heaven. But Augustine could not admit that history made no difference; it was part of God's purpose. More than that, history was the theater in which God's purpose came to fulfillment.

Once history has been made part of God's purpose, however, then Christians must take the events and the power structures of this world seriously. Even when one believes that political and social structures are organized sin, one is still under obligation to see that they reach the maximum of goodness possible to them, that even though they cannot be redeemed, they at least live by divine law. Though it may seem a more indirect kind of influence, the facts entitle us to say that by giving the Western church a philosophy of history Augustine gave it a concern with social questions and political organizations.

Indeed the later histories of Eastern and Western Christendom bear this out. Eastern Christendom was to have its troubles, as we shall see. But until those troubles came, its history is almost exclusively a theological history. That is to say, we can write the history of what the Eastern churches thought, but there is little to write about what they did. Immobile in the face of a changing world, they refined the delicate points in Christology, trying to organize its subtleties.

Western Christianity in the next centuries presents a very different picture. Its thinkers were few and far between. In fact we must travel a good many centuries before we find another of the stature of Augustine. But, embattled on many fronts, it set forth resolutely to take history seriously and subdue it to the purposes of God.

---

for profit to their own bodies or souls, or both, and those who have known God "glorified Him not as God, neither were thankful, but became vain in their imaginations, and their foolish heart was darkened; professing themselves to be wise"— that is, glorying in their own wisdom, and being possessed by pride—"they became fools, and changed the glory of the incorruptible God into an image made like to corruptible man, and to birds, and four-footed beasts, and creeping things." For they were either leaders or followers of the people in adoring images, "and worshipped and served the creature more than the Creator, who is blessed for ever." But in the other city there is no human wisdom, but only godliness, which offers due worship to the true God, and looks for its reward in the society of the saints, of holy angels as well as holy men, that God may be all in all.[1]   —*City of God*

A church that a short while before had felt that nothing could stop its conquest of the world now found itself threatened on every side. But even while the skies were darkening, there were those who, following Augustine's inspiration, were preparing to brave the storm, knowing that their loyalty was not to a tottering empire but to a Kingdom that was coming in power.

6

The Monastic Movement

Even before the end of the age of persecution Christianity was becoming fashionable. Though there were outbreaks of imprisonment and martyrdom, whole generations passed not knowing the meaning of the words. After Constantine's decision favoring the church the fashion, of course, increased. We have already had occasion to notice some of the effects of this rise of what may be called nominal Christianity.

But one effect we have not yet mentioned. As nominal Christianity increased and Christian standards relaxed in severity, there were those who viewed the whole situation with alarm. They remembered the days when the Christian movement had been a highly disciplined group, visiting severe punishment on any lapses from Christian standards, carefully screening all who requested admission. But now more and more they saw an easy accommodation to the ways of the world, a winking at lapses, a lessening of requirements for admission to the Christian fellowship. Worst of all, even the leaders of the church seemed more anxious to avoid offending prominent laymen than to exercise Christian discipline.

Theirs was a steadily increasing frustration. One such person, an Egyptian layman named Anthony, was one day struck with a sudden answer. A young man of some means, he had obviously been bothered by the very problems we have mentioned. One Sunday in church he heard the verse from the gospel, "If thou wilt be perfect, go and sell that thou hast, and give to the poor, and thou shalt have treasure in heaven: and come and follow me" (Matt. 19:21 K.J.V.). How simple, Anthony thought. Without hesitation he disposed of his estate and distributed the proceeds among the poor. He retired to the country, earning what little was necessary for his keep by doing odd jobs. More and more he withdrew from society until finally, making himself a crude home in an abandoned fort, he lived a solitary life of prayer and meditation for almost twenty years. His only appearances in public were motivated by the report of some need, especially the needs of his brethren serving in prison or as mine slaves.

When Anthony died in 356 (at the age, so tradition says, of 105!) he had many imitators. Even in his lifetime others who felt his distress had joined him in his way of life, some living as hermits in the same neighborhood as Anthony, others in other parts of the Eastern world.

Their main motivation seems to have been a desire to practice the total discipline of Christian living, as they understood it, free from the influence of worldly clerics.

OVERCOMING INDIVIDUALISM

What might have been a purely individual movement and one subject, therefore, to all the whims and extravagances of individual taste was taken in hand and given form and organization in Anthony's lifetime by a younger contemporary named Pachomius. Perhaps the fact that he had served as a soldier in the imperial army made this young Egyptian realize the need for order and discipline. At any rate, after his military discharge Pachomius became a Christian. Almost immediately after his baptism he felt as Anthony had, but he was distressed by the possible dangers in the individualism of Anthony's withdrawal from society.

What Pachomius organized was a community for those who wished to leave the world and devote themselves wholly to the practice of Christianity. Instead of living alone in caves or holes in the desert, Pachomius' followers lived together in a secluded place. The rules of the community were very strict. Nor was it all prayer and psalm singing either! Manual labor for the support of the community formed part of the daily program. It seemed to Pachomius that an organized community of this kind was a much more effective instrument for those who wished to live apart from the world than the private retreat of a man like Anthony, however devout he may have been. Many communities organized after Pachomius' pattern sprang up in succeeding years. Basil, one of the great Cappadocian theologians whose name we have already met, made adaptations of Pachomius' rule.

For reasons which are not hard to understand this way of withdrawal did not find an immediate response in the Western church. To be sure, there were plenty of Christians who were just as distressed by the growing worldliness of the church as Anthony and Pachomius. But they did not see any reason for withdrawal from society in order to live a disciplined Christian life. Their first reaction was to accept the full requirements of Christian living while remaining at their tasks, whether those tasks were in the church or in the secular world.

Anthony's earliest and most famous admirer in the West seems to have been Jerome. Much better known in history as the man who performed the prodigious feat of translating the Bible from Hebrew and Greek into Latin (his version forms the basis of the Vulgate, to this day the official translation of the Roman Catholic Church), Jerome was an impressionable young Italian layman who was won to the solitary life by stories of Anthony's religious heroism. He tried it for a time in his native town and then went to the Middle East where he lived as a hermit for three years. Eventually, however, he returned to Rome where he attempted to live the life of a hermit while mixing in high Roman society. The compromise was, of course, a failure. In 386 he left Rome for good. Taking with him a number of converts, including a Roman noblewoman, Paula, he went to Bethlehem where they founded two communities, one for men and the other for women who wished to withdraw from the world. There Jerome labored with his books and his studies until his death in 420.

Even though it was slow in starting, the monastic movement (the technical name of the trend we have been describing) did finally make its way west. Especially as the political future of the Western empire grew more and more uncertain and the ravages of the barbarian hordes grew more and more violent, an increasing number of people sought to leave what seemed to be a decaying society and live a "religious" life.

The early growth of monasticism in the West seems to have been a sporadic thing as communities sprang up here and there, probably under the inspiration of some local leader whose name has long since been forgotten. In some places it was popular; in others there was little trace of it. Apparently the most popular place for the movement was way out on the fringe of the empire in Ireland. There almost the entire church was monastic in life and organization, and the head of the monastery seems to have been a much more important person than the bishop.

THE MONASTIC ORGANIZER

The man who gave Western monasticism its lasting shape, and organized it effectively was Benedict of Nursia. Born about 480, as a

From the Rule of Benedict

The rule which Benedict of Nursia developed in the sixth century became a standard for monasteries. Here are a few of its characteristic regulations:

And so we are going to establish a school for the service of the Lord. In founding it we hope to introduce nothing harsh or burdensome. But if a certain strictness results from the dictates of equity for the amendment of vices or the preservation of charity, do not be at once dismayed and fly from the way of salvation, whose entrance cannot but be narrow. . . .

young man Benedict felt disgusted by the world around him and adopted the life of the hermit. Several little communities in the hills around Rome where Benedict lived invited him to come and direct them. But his requirements were too strict and Benedict went back to the hermit's life.

It was not until about 528 that Benedict decided to establish his own community. He chose Monte Cassino as its location, destroying a pagan temple which had stood there for centuries. A dreamer of great dreams, Benedict also proved to be a master at organization. The community which he founded (others were soon to follow) was completely self-contained and self-supporting. Idleness was the one sin which could not be tolerated. Whether in prayer or in work (and Benedict saw little difference between the two) the whole day was usefully provided for. Laymen as well as priests were welcome; butcher, baker, shoemaker—everyone's skill would be put to use.

Benedict's communities were in reality little communistic societies in which everyone shared alike. Whatever a man had, had to be turned over to the community upon his entering it. Whatever he produced was used for the support and welfare of the community. We do Benedict a great injustice if we think of a monastery simply as a place in which people were able to pray all day. Prayer was certainly an important part of monastic life to him, but by no means the only part. His monasteries were new social orders, complete communities within the framework of the old society. Perhaps Benedict himself did not realize what an important role these communities would play in coming years as the old social order increasingly fell apart.

For that is exactly what happened. As the old imperial government and society began to go down in the blood and smoke of barbarian

Chapter 5. On Obedience. The first degree of humility is obedience without delay. This is the virtue of those who hold nothing dearer to them than Christ . . .

Chapter 16. How the Work of God Is to Be Performed During the Day. "Seven times in the day," says the Prophet, "I have rendered praise to You." Now that sacred number of seven will be fulfilled by us if we perform the Offices of our service at the time of the Morning Office, of Prime, of Terce, of Sext, of None, of Vespers and of Compline . . . and in the night let us arise to glorify Him.

Chapter 33. Whether Monks Ought to Have Anything of Their Own. This vice especially is to be cut out of the monastery by the roots. Let no one presume to give or receive anything without the Abbot's leave, or to have anything as his own . . . since they are not permitted to have even their bodies or wills at their own disposal . . .

invasion, as one landmark after another was swept away in the flood, these little islands remained. Not really having been part of the old order, they did not disappear with it. And when the destruction of the old order might well have meant complete chaos, the monasteries were there to provide some kind of continuity with the past and organizing center for the future.

That does not mean that the monasteries were anxious to put a dead empire back in business again. But it does mean that in their libraries the literature and philosophy of a dying civilization was still available. It does not mean that the new social order in Western Europe took its pattern from the monasteries. But it does mean that centers of stability remained to influence the shape of the age that was being born.

EVALUATING MONASTICISM

It is too bad that most of us think of monasticism as it was at the time of the Protestant Reformation. By that time the monasteries had become places of rich privilege with large holdings of land and fat endowments. Too often they were easy berths for lazy people. They had been so before but had always been able to reform themselves. But by the time of Luther and Calvin, apparently, they had lost the energy to reform.

At this earlier stage of the story, however, they represented something quite different. Not only were they able to attract some of the finest men and women in society, they performed the function of college and university as well as being centers for prayer and meditation. In the troubled times of the breaking of the empire, it was the monastery libraries, in which the brothers worked laboriously copying books by hand, that preserved the historic culture of Greece and Rome, to say

---

Chapter 48. On the Daily Manual Labor. Idleness is the enemy of the soul. Therefore the brethren should be occupied at certain times in manual labor, and again at fixed hours in sacred reading. . . .

Chapter 73. On the Fact That the Full Observance of Justice Is Not Established in This Rule. Now we have written this Rule in order that by its observance in monasteries we may show that we have attained some degree of virtue and the rudiments of the religious life. But for him who would hasten to the perfection of that life there are the teachings of the holy Fathers, the observance of which leads a man to the height of perfection. . . .

Whoever you are, therefore, who are hastening to the heavenly homeland, fulfil with the help of Christ this minimum Rule which we have written for beginners; and then at length under God's protection you will attain to the loftier heights of doctrine and virtue which we have mentioned above.[1]

nothing of the Holy Scriptures. It was the monastery school that often provided the only available form of education. As a little society within society, the monasteries were able to do many essential tasks which a beleaguered and dying society could not begin to undertake.

Even while we must admire these early monastic societies and their work, we must face up to the question they raise. For presumably there were many devout and sincere Christians who did not go to the monasteries, but who stayed in the threatened cities of the Western empire. What about them? While the motive may have been entirely devout, did not this wholesale withdrawal from the world begin a double standard in Christianity? Benedict and his followers may not have intended any such thing. But their actions were certainly saying that it is impossible to be a full Christian and live in ordinary society.

That this was the result of their movement can be seen from the fact that Christians who left the world were called "religious" while those who remained were termed "secular." No one maintained that it was impossible to be saved if one remained as a butcher or baker in his native village. But the clear implication was that it was impossible to live as a Christian in such a situation, that to remain was to settle for a lesser standard, a softer requirement than that demanded by the New Testament.

Believe it or not, we still have a lingering of this idea even in Protestantism. Ask the average Protestant and he will tell you without any hesitation that there is something holier, yes, something more religious about being a minister or a missionary than there is in being a banker or a farmer. We still talk about "full-time Christian service" as though that kind of Christian service were impossible except in those professions directly related to religion.

As we shall see, this was an issue which came to the fore in the time of the Reformation. But because it has had such a long history in the Christian church we must look at it here where it began. Must a man leave society if he wishes to take Jesus Christ seriously? There is the question in simplest terms. Anthony, Benedict, and all of the monastic leaders would have replied Yes. If we remain in society there are too many compromises, too many accommodations, too many relaxations to allow us to follow the pure light of the gospel.

To be sure, the New Testament knows nothing of any such withdrawal. Hostile as the society was in which that community had to exist, there is no hint in any books of the New Testament of a separate and withdrawn community. That fact should be conclusive for us.

But the mere fact that we are prejudiced against their solution should not prevent our serious consideration of the problem which they were trying to solve. We say it is not necessary to leave the world in order to follow Jesus Christ. And we are right. But before we dismiss Anthony and Benedict as completely wrongheaded, we should let them speak, prodding our consciences to ask ourselves to what extent we allow the world to compromise our Christian witness. This is not to say that monasticism is the solution. But it does raise some serious questions.

1. We all complain about the hypocrisy of Sunday religion. But does not the widespread popularity of Sunday religion show that taking Jesus Christ seriously in the world is not the simple thing we should like it to be? Whether we are businessmen or high school students we have to ask ourselves to what extent we appease the world in order to remain comfortable. If we were to take Jesus Christ seriously would we lose our friends, our business, our status? Are Anthony and Benedict right after all?

2. A second question which Anthony and Benedict force us to consider is the extent to which the congregation of which we are a part really presents to the world a demonstration of fellowship in Christ. The communism of the early church or of the monastic community is not the point. Do we as Christians display the concern for each other's welfare, the responsibility for our brother's need that makes Christian community a striking reality? To what extent is such community really possible in our society? Are Anthony and Benedict right after all?

But perhaps in asking about the "rightness" of the monastic movement we are really asking the wrong question. For right or wrong, there can be no question that at the moment that it came upon the scene in the Western world it had a very necessary role to fill. What that role was we have tried to describe. Still there was another aspect to it which was to become of increasing importance, even though it is doubtful that any of the early monastic leaders had it in mind.

Western Christendom found itself increasingly encircled by the barbarians. Some of them were Arian Christians; others were still worshiping their tribal gods. It was clear, however, that the future lay with these same barbarians, whether they were in some way incorporated into the empire or whether they smashed it and sat triumphant upon its ruins. Christian leaders in the West saw how imperative it was that the gospel should be taken to these same barbarians. Future or no, they too were souls for whom Christ had died.

The evangelizing of hordes of pagan peoples all the way from the borders of Italy to the far reaches of Scandinavia, however, was a staggering task. Who would go and how would he get there? How would he be supported once he had arrived? Great as our missionary task is, that faced by the church at that time was enormous, because of the lack of transportation and communication and the hostility of the tribes to which the gospel had to be brought.

But here in the Benedictine communities were the shock troops ready for the task. Already detached from the world and devoted wholly to the gospel, they had no responsibilities to keep them at home. Without realizing it, Benedict had formed almost the perfect instrument for the propagation of the Christian faith among the barbarian tribes from whom modern Europeans descended. And so one of the greatest paradoxes in history came to pass. That same group of men who had left the world became the primary means by which the world, in a larger sense than they had ever dreamed, heard the gospel.

7

The Monks March
TO SCOTLAND

In the year 563 a little boat, called a coracle, landed on the island of Iona, just off the west coast of Scotland. Its chief passenger was an Irish nobleman named Columba. With him in the coracle were twelve carefully chosen helpers. His parents had been of Irish royal blood and Columba himself had been one of the rising young stars in the Irish ecclesiastical firmament. A pupil of the famous Finnian of Moville who had brought the Scriptures to Ireland, Columba had attracted much notice even as a young monk.

Partly because of the influence of his family but even more because of the strength of his own personality, he soon became a powerful force in Irish church life. New monasteries, including a famous one in Derry, were started by him. He seemed to have a brilliant career as the leader of the Irish church before him. But, high-spirited as he was, he became involved in a quarrel with his old teacher, Finnian. Since neither Finnian nor Columba would give an inch, the question had to be decided by the High King. When the decision was given against Columba, even though he was a monk, his royal blood asserted itself and he led his clan in a rebellion.

In the eyes of his fellow Irish churchmen such conduct had destroyed his usefulness as a religious leader in his native country. There is reason to believe that Columba also, once his temper had cooled, was ashamed of what he had done. In any event, he wanted to resume his monastic way of life but he realized the impossibility of continuing in Ireland as anything but a nameless brother in some remote monastery. Penitent as he was, the desire for leadership was in his blood. And that was why his coracle was anchored off the island of Iona that day in 563.

Three Whom Christ Sent Forth

What made the early missionaries go out among unfriendly Celtic and Germanic tribesmen? Early accounts tell something of the beginnings of their missionary labors. Even in the sometimes fanciful legends related by these early writers we catch the picture of faithful servants of Christ who heard his call and answered. In this chapter you will find quotations from three such accounts.

55

For the situation in Scotland was one which cried for attention. For more than half a century immigrants had been arriving in Scotland from Ireland. Settling along the west coast, they had pushed steadily eastward in their expansion. But just three years before Columba's arrival, the Picts, whose kingdom was being threatened, had beaten the immigrants and reduced them to a second-class status. What was of greater concern to Columba, however, was the fact that these immigrants were without church or gospel. This was the need that brought him from Ireland to Scotland as an act of penance.

For more than thirty years Columba made the island of Iona his base of operations. Building a church and monastery there, he used it as a center from which the Christian gospel was planted all over the west of Scotland. Traveling in their coracles, Columba's followers went up and down the mainland and visited all the islands, leaving Christian congregations behind them wherever they had been. Not content with limiting himself to this territory, Columba looked farther afield as the strength of his movement grew. Monks from Iona were soon found in the north of England, preaching the gospel to the Anglo-Saxons. When he died in 597, Columba had been one of the most effective missionaries of the gospel in the British Isles and his center in Iona had become a lasting home of missionary power. All this because a hot-tempered Irishman felt called upon to do penance for his reckless defiance of authority!

TO HOLLAND

Less than a century after Columba's death, in that northern part of what is now England which Columba's monks had Christianized, there was a young man named Willibrord. Born in 658, he had received almost his entire education in the monastery. But since the facilities for advanced study were meager in a country so recently become Christian, Willibrord went to Ireland in 678, for at that time that country was considered almost the leader in scholarly and intellectual Christianity.

The Venerable Bede (c. 673–735) Writes of Columba

In the year of our Lord 565, when Justinian the Younger had succeeded Justinian and ruled as Emperor of Rome, a priest and abbot of outstanding life came from Ireland to preach the word of God in the provinces of the northern Picts, which are separated from those of the southern Picts by a range of steep and desolate mountains. . . .

The next twelve years of his life were spent there in study and meditation.

But study and meditation were not enough for Willibrord. A fellow countryman of his whom he had met in Ireland, Egbert by name, had fired his imagination with the need for the gospel among the tribes of Northern Europe. The more he thought about Egbert's vision of help to them, the more restless he became among the books and manuscripts of the monastery library.

Finally he could resist no longer. In the year 690, with twelve companions, Willibrord made his way to the mouth of the Rhine river in what today we should call Holland. A tribe called Frisians inhabited this region and they were still pagans. Rathbod, their chieftain, however, was a vassal of Pepin, who was a Christian. With his support, Willibrord undertook his work, building a church and monastery just outside the present city of Utrecht.

For the rest of his life Willibrord made this his home. Having achieved considerable success in the conversion of the Frisians, he was not content to rest on his laurels but sought to extend his work into Denmark and northern Germany. When he died in 739, the fact that what we today call Holland was a Christian country was largely the work of Willibrord—that studious British monk who could not resist the call to conquer fresh territory for his Lord.

MISSION PRODUCES MISSION

In 716 a volunteer came to Willibrord's mission in Utrecht. An Englishman whose name had originally been Winfrith but had been changed to Boniface, he had been offered all kinds of opportunities in his own country. Born in 680 in the town of Crediton, Boniface had attracted attention as a brilliant student. But he too found himself restless in a situation that seemed to afford such little challenge. He wanted to do missionary work and the nearest missionary frontier was that being held by Willibrord in Holland. So to Holland he went.

>Columba arrived in Britain in the ninth year of the reign of the powerful Pictish king, Bridius, son of Meilochon (Mailcuin); he converted this island to the Faith of Christ by his preaching and example, and was granted the island of Iona on which to found a monastery. . . . Before he came to Britain, he had founded a noble monastery in Ireland known in the Scots language as *Dearmach*, the Field of Oaks, because of the oak forest in which it stands. From both these monasteries Columba's disciples went out and founded many others in Britain and Ireland; but the monastery on the island of Iona, where his body lies, remains the chief of them all.[1]

He came at a bad time, however, for the mission in Utrecht was at a standstill. Political difficulties had forced Willibrord to give up any plans for further advance. All he could do at the moment was to hold the line. For that work he needed no new recruits, and Boniface was not looking for that kind of job anyway.

It was a disappointed young man who had to return to England. Someone with less enthusiasm would have interpreted this rebuff as an indication that his action had been visionary. After all, he had tried to volunteer! Why not accept the fact that he was not needed and settle down to the brilliant future that awaited him in the English church?

But the vision which Boniface had seen would not disappear that easily. Two years later he was anxious to give it another try. But this second trip went by a different route. Boniface traveled to the missionary frontier by way of Rome. Gregory II, the pope who interviewed him, was much impressed with the ability and enthusiasm of this young monk from England. At his suggestion, Boniface set out for a new missionary frontier in Germany. For a time he worked with Willibrord in Frisia when conditions in his mission had improved. But having seen the possibilities for Christian work in Germany, Boniface made that his principal field of endeavor.

Within four years he had achieved sufficient results to impress Pope Gregory II. Summoned to Rome by Gregory, Boniface returned afterward to his German mission field as a bishop. Some sentences from Gregory's commissioning letter are interesting:

> There are some races in the parts of Germany and on the east side of the Rhine, who, under the suasion of the old enemy, live in error, in the shadow of death. We have learned that some, under cover of the Christian religion, worship idols. Others, not as yet having knowledge of God, nor washed in the water of holy baptism, do not recognise their Maker. For the illumination of both, we have thought it right to send the bearer of this letter, Boniface, our most reverend brother bishop, to preach the word of true

Alcuin (c. 735–804) Writes of Willibrord

... in the thirty-third year of his age the fervour of his faith had reached such an intensity that he considered it of little value to labour at his own sanctification unless he could preach the Gospel to others and bring some benefit to them. He had heard that in the northern regions of the world the harvest was great but the labourers few. Thus it was that ...

faith in these parts, so that by preaching the word of salvation he may provide for them eternal life . . .[2]

The rest of Boniface's story is a somewhat tragic one. A powerful and fearless preacher of the gospel, he made an enormous impression in the German mission field. But as his work grew by leaps and bounds, he discovered two things. Even though the pagan Germans were baptized by the thousands, their Christianity still contained many of the old pagan superstitions. Not even so dramatic a gesture as his cutting down of the sacred oak tree at Geismar could root out the superstitions which still lingered. Worse still, how could he preach the purity of the gospel to the Germans when he knew that there was just as much pagan superstition among the Christians in Rome? "If only your paternity would prohibit these paganisms in the city of Rome," he wrote to Pope Gregory, "it would be a gain to you, and a wonderful help to us in our church teaching."[3]

Boniface's second problem arose from the fact that the more successful his mission work among the Germans was, the greater need there was for organization. Rome looked to him for it. But that meant less time for preaching. New bishoprics had to be organized and supervised with schools and monasteries. It was a necessary job which Boniface was expected to do, even though he would far rather have been out in the forests preaching. He wanted more time, too, to devote to the development of his monastery in Fulda which he had planned as the great Christian center for Germany.

Was it the frustrations or was it the inescapableness of the call that brought Boniface, now an old man of 74, out of his episcopal work and out of his monastery in Fulda in 754? In his old mission in the Netherlands was a pagan tribe of Frisians to whom it now seemed that a Christian approach could be made. Boniface leaped at the chance and, taking a group of devoted young missionaries with him, set out for Frisia.

At first it seemed as though the information had been correct and that this Frisian tribe was indeed ready for the gospel. Large numbers

---

Willibrord, fully aware of his own purpose but ignorant as yet of divine preordination, decided to sail for those parts and, if God so willed, to bring the light of the Gospel message to those people who through unbelief had not been stirred by its warmth. So he embarked on a ship, taking with him eleven others who shared his enthusiasm for the faith. . . .

So the man of God, accompanied by his brethren, as we have already said, set sail, and after a successful crossing they moored their ships at the mouth of the Rhine.[4]

responded to the preaching of Boniface and his associates and the date was set for their confirmation by the aging archbishop. But on that very day a pagan army appeared without warning and massacred the entire mission. So Boniface died in 755, doing the thing he had always wanted to do among the very people with whom he had first tried to do it as a young volunteer years before.

Columba, Willibrord, and Boniface are but three of the monks who marched. During these centuries Western Europe was filled with devoted men, mostly from Ireland and Britain, who were anxious to bring the gospel. Especially as the political authority of the Frankish kingdom grew and included more and more pagan tribes within its borders, there were continually new frontiers for missionary endeavor.

It may strike us as strange that it was the monks who answered the call, that a movement which had begun as an escape from the evils of the world should now become a movement which fearlessly sought to bring the gospel back to that same world. But such was indeed the case. We have a very false picture of monasticism in those days if we think of the monk as a recluse, singing his hymns, saying his prayers, reading his manuscripts behind a monastery wall. There may have been some like that. But there were many more who saw their monastic vocation as an invitation to adventure, as a summons to go out and conquer in the name of Christ. The fact is that most of our ancestors in Western Europe were converted by the monks. Christian Holland, France, Germany, Scotland are all the result of the missions of these monks who marched.

MISSIONARY STRENGTH AND WEAKNESS

If we stop to think about it, monasticism had certain great advantages as a missionary movement. For one thing, it provided the missionary with a community. Notice that when Columba went to Scotland or when Willibrord went to the Netherlands, neither went alone.

Willibald (700–786) Writes of Boniface

Now when the winter season was over and the summer was well advanced he [Boniface] called to mind his intention of the previous year and carefully set about preparing the journey which had been deferred. Provided with letters of introduction from Bishop Daniel, of blessed memory, he tried to set out on his way to the tombs of the Apostles. . . . And when at last, through the prayers of the saints

They took twelve associates with them. Whether they knew it or not, there were good psychological reasons for this method of operation. Necessary as a leader was, a community was even more necessary. In all the loneliness of a strange and often hostile country, these men needed each other in close fellowship.

If there were good psychological reasons for this mission in community, there were even better theological ones. All too often we Protestants think of missionary work in the words of the old gospel hymn, "Win them, win them, one by one." In other words, we think in one-to-one terms, the individual missionary winning individual converts. But this is to forget that the Christian movement is a church, a fellowship. This was something that could never be forgotten by the monastic mission. For while individual monks might have their individual assignments and responsibilities, this mission was one of community to community, the new community of Jesus Christ meeting the old community of the pagan tribe.

This mission in community had the further advantage of planting a new community right in the midst of the old one. When individuals or parts of a tribe became Christian, they were not left in isolation, as is so often the case with us. For right there in their midst was a new community, a new family, in which they could share. Part of the effectiveness of these marching monks was in the fact that they were a complete community. From the moment they arrived, schools, hospitals, industry, as well as churches, came with them.

Yet we must face the fact that this community-to-community kind of evangelism had one great disadvantage. It was the one which troubled Boniface so deeply. In too many cases the approach was made to the tribal chief. If he chose to become a Christian, the rest of his people often had no choice but to follow suit. If the chief could be converted, the chances were high that the mass conversion and baptism of an entire tribe would be the result.

---

and the providence of God, the saint and his whole retinue had reached the tomb of St. Peter the Apostle unharmed, they immediately gave thanks to Christ for their safe journey. . . . Now after several days had passed, the saint had audience with His Holiness Pope Gregory the Second . . . When the Pope had read the letter and examined the note of introduction he discussed the saint's project with him every day until the summer season, in which he had to set out on the return journey, was near. When the end of April had passed and it was already the beginning of May the saint begged and received the apostolic blessing and was sent by the Pope to make a report on the savage peoples of Germany . . . to discover whether their untutored hearts and minds were ready to receive the seed of the divine Word.[5]

To be sure, the monks believed that they were giving careful instruction. They did not approve of overnight reception into the Christian church. They set up long hours of study and instruction before confirmation, as we have seen in the case of Boniface's murder. Still, what good is instruction to a man who is not really interested but has simply followed the leadership of his tribal chieftain? What value is study of a subject about which there has been no real inner persuasion?

In other words, the success of the monastic missions was also their weakness. Western Europe became Christian under their heroic efforts, but the number of nominal Christians was staggering. This was the reason for the continuation of those superstitions against which Boniface battled so valiantly. The men who practiced them too often had become Christian not from any conviction but merely from a desire to please and obey their leader. Consequently they brought over into their Christian faith most, if not all, of their old pagan customs and simply baptized them.

Sometimes, to be sure, the church encouraged this. Wherever pagan practices seemed innocent or in any way patient of a Christian interpretation, church leaders tried to encourage their preservation. Our Christmas tree is an outstanding case in point. Originally a pagan German custom, it has become an almost inseparable part of the celebration of the Christian Christmas. But other customs, less desirable, came too, despite the efforts of men like Boniface to keep them out.

We may pause here long enough to notice that this problem is one for which a satisfactory solution has never been reached in all the long history of Christian mission. It is still with us today. When an African chief is converted today, must he give up his four wives, a custom which in his former religion is perfectly admissible? If so, who is to provide for them economically? Questions like these are still live ones in our modern missions.

The still deeper question is the one which asks to what extent the Christian gospel can be mingled with local religions. The technical name for this mingling is *syncretism*. If we stopped to analyze, there is a surprising amount of syncretism in American Protestantism; the American way of life and the Christian gospel are almost indistinguishable in the minds of many people. Obviously the gospel cannot be an abstraction. It has to be preached to people where they are and in terms which they understand. That means using thought patterns and pictures which come from their situations. But when is such syncretism right and when does it become dangerous? For the fact that it can become dangerous is amply demonstrated in the later history of the church. At least a part of the work of the Reformation consisted in rooting out of Christian usage many of the baptized paganisms which had found their way in during the very era we have been discussing.

One final point deserves our attention. The three marching monks we have discussed come, roughly, from three succeeding centuries—Columba from the sixth, Willibrord from the seventh, and Boniface from the eighth. Did you notice one growing difference as the story unfolded? Columba went to Scotland on his own; he had a compulsion to go and he followed it. Willibrord was also answering a call, but when he got in trouble he called for royal help and got some support from the pope. While Boniface's call was just as sincere as theirs, when finally he arrived in Germany as a missionary it was with the pope's commission and blessing.

That says much for what was happening to the church during these centuries. Increasingly its life, its direction, and its expansion, which had largely been local up to this point, was coming under the control of the bishop of Rome. So significant did he become for the life of the church in the coming centuries that we need to examine how this concentration of power began.

8

The Two Swords

In the year 590 affairs in the land of Italy generally and in the city of Rome in particular were in a sorry state. Flood, famine, and pestilence had all ravaged the countryside, taking their toll in human life and welfare. And as though these natural disasters were not bad enough, the political fortunes of Rome had not been at so low an ebb in more than a century. A new barbarian horde, the Lombards, threatened the safety of the city. The Eastern emperor from Constantinople had planted a beachhead at Ravenna in northeastern Italy. The economic life of the people was depressed, because of the hordes of refugees who flooded the city in their flight from the Lombards.

Nor was the church situation any better. The bishop of Rome had always thought of himself as the senior bishop of the entire church. But Christian initiative had passed into other hands. To the east the bishop of Constantinople had shown himself much more aggressive. That same city of Ravenna which the Eastern emperor had conquered in 540 had become the headquarters for missionary representatives from Constantinople. To the north and west it was representatives of the Celtic church in Ireland who were invading the barbarian countries of Europe in the name of Christ. Neither Constantinople nor the Celts owed any allegiance to the bishop of Rome or consulted him in any of their moves. Even within his own territory the life of the church was stagnant and sterile.

THE FIRST POPE

That same pestilence which had killed thousands of Romans took the life of the bishop of Rome in 590. His successor by almost universal acclaim was a Roman nobleman named Gregory, then just fifty years of age. The son of a Roman senator, Gregory had himself begun a political career. But then, greatly influenced by the monastic movement as a young man, he had given it up, sold his large properties, and become a monk. With the money he realized from his estates he founded seven new monasteries.

Because he came from such a well-known Roman family, Gregory's acceptance of the monastic life did not escape the attention of Pelagius, the bishop of Rome. Within four years he compelled the young nobleman to leave the monastery which he had founded and appointed him as one of the seven deacons of Rome. Although he would have preferred the life which he had chosen for himself, Gregory pursued his new duties with such vigor that the bishop soon appointed him as his special representative to the bishop of Constantinople with whom, as we have noticed, the Roman bishop was having some disagreements.

Returning to his beloved city of Rome in 585, Gregory retired to his monastery of St. Andrew's which was housed in his family's former palace. His brethren there chose him for their leader soon afterward. But if Gregory had imagined that he could now spend the rest of his life in quiet retirement as abbot of St. Andrew's, he was soon to find that he was mistaken. For when the bishop died in 590, there was no hesitation as to the choice of his successor. Gregory was everybody's choice.

Because the bishop of Rome was also virtually the political leader of the city, the new bishop faced great problems in the disorganized state of affairs in the town. We can only mention here his masterful reorganization of the city administration, his program for the thousands of refugees who had come flooding into Rome to escape the Lombards, his skillful use of church funds to feed the victims of the famine, his careful investment of these same funds to secure a large and steady income for the Roman church.

Had things like these been the sum of Gregory's achievements he might well have been remembered as one of the finest bishops ever to govern the Roman church but as nothing more. He had much greater ambitions, however, and he had the will and the ability to achieve them. Before we have a look at them we must take time out for a brief study of the organization of the church at this time.

Soon after the era of the New Testament the life of the church in every place began to center in the person of one man, the bishop. He became the pastor of all the people in a given area, even though there were many pastors in individual congregations as the church grew. Because of history and prominence the bishops of cities like Jerusalem, Antioch, Alexandria, Constantinople, and Rome enjoyed a certain preeminence and their authority was respected over a wider area than their own immediate territory. But in theory each bishop was fully independent and only all the bishops assembled together in council (as at Nicaea) could make decisions affecting the life of the church as a whole.

Because the bishop was in a real sense the father of all the Christians in his territory the custom developed of referring to him as "papa" or, to use our version of the same word, "pope." Thus in the fourth or fifth centuries the church had many popes ranging all the way from those who served in small, backwater places to those who served in great centers like Alexandria or Constantinople.

Roman tradition claimed that the bishop of Rome was the senior bishop of all Christendom because, according to that tradition, the Apostle Peter was the first Roman bishop. Yet in actual fact the senior bishop in Christendom was ignored by those who should be his subordinates. This distressed Gregory. Added to this, the pope of Constantinople, a much younger church than Rome, was establishing outposts in Gregory's backyard. And the Irish monks, who probably had never even heard of the bishop of Rome, were conducting missionary work as close as France. It was Gregory's dream to make the Roman bishop head of the whole church not in theory but in fact. But he was astute enough to realize that to achieve this he had to demonstrate his claim not with words but with deeds.

No small part of Gregory's greatness was in the fact that he saw that the real future of his church lay not in the East but in the West. The bishop of Constantinople seemed an awesome and powerful figure. But Gregory had spent enough time in that imperial city as Roman ambassador to realize how much decadence and corruption lay beneath the magnificent surface. He quietly but firmly asserted his authority over the religious life of the city of Ravenna and though he was fought by devious means, his persistence finally won.

Having established that authority, he was content to let his quarrel with Constantinople rest. His real ambition was to win the West to Roman obedience. Once while still abbot of St. Andrew's he had seen

Gregory the Great Sees His Role as Bishop

The conduct of a prelate ought so far to transcend the conduct of the people as the life of a shepherd is wont to exalt him above the flock. For one whose estimation is such that the people are called his flock is bound anxiously to consider what great necessity is laid upon him to maintain rectitude. It is necessary, then, that in thought he should be pure, in action chief; discreet in keeping silence, profitable in speech; a near neighbour to every one in sympathy, exalted above all in contemplation; a familiar friend of good livers through humility, unbending against the vices of evil-doers through zeal for righteousness; not relaxing in his care for what is inward from being occupied in outward things, nor neglecting to provide for outward things in his solicitude for what is inward. . . .[1]

—Gregory I, Pastoral Rule, Part II, chap. 1.

some young men in the Roman slave market. Impressed by their appearance, he asked the slave dealer about their origin. "They are Angles," was the reply. "No, not Angles but angels," said Gregory.

Whether that rather romantic story was the reason or not, the fact is that Gregory made the Anglo-Saxons in Britain his first target. Though there was a Christian church in Britain, Gregory was determined to make it an outpost of Rome. The army which he chose for the conquest was made up of his own monks. To lead the group he selected his successor in St. Andrew's, Augustine (not to be confused with the great bishop of Hippo whom we have already studied), and about forty monks. Every move that they made in Britain was directed by Gregory from his headquarters in Rome. Augustine sailed for England in 596 and within eight years he had succeeded in bringing all of British Christianity under Roman obedience.

But long before that time Gregory had dispatched the second wave of his invasion. He had made a treaty with the Lombards in 593, halting the threat of their invasion. Now he directed his attention to bringing their land of northern Italy under Roman control. For the most part the Lombards were Arians, though many were still pagan. But employing the political influence which he had gained through his treaty-making, Gregory converted the Lombard queen, Theodelinda, to the Roman faith and through her gained access to another nation.

Nor was that the end. Missionaries were sent to the Arian Visigoths in Spain and they too were brought into the Roman fold. But his chief efforts were directed to the Franks in Gaul. Missionaries from Ireland had been at work among them, though on a rather hit-and-miss basis. Some of the Franks were sincere Christians, some were still pagan, while many were Christian in name only. Indeed, in many of the independent Christian churches in Gaul the bishops were ignorant thieves.

As in the case of Britain, armies of carefully trained and carefully directed monks from Rome flooded the country, their mission to bring the gospel where it had not been heard or to bring the independent churches into conformity with Rome. Everywhere they were successful because they represented order and responsibility in a situation which had largely been dominated by chaos and confusion. When Gregory died in 604 the neglected and feeble church of Rome controlled a territory which stretched across Western Europe from Britain to southern Italy. Small wonder that he soon became known as Gregory the *Great* and that historians reckon him as the first *pope* in our sense of the word.

The instrument by which Gregory achieved his goals is worthy of attention. Monasticism had begun as a retreat from the world. Individual monks, like Columba, had done missionary work. But Gregory was apparently the first to see the real possibilities in monasticism as an invasion of the world. The missionary movement under Gregory was not a matter of individual whim or fancy. It was a carefully directed campaign under his own skillful direction. It was Gregory who made the Benedictine monks the church's task force.

THE GREATNESS OF GREGORY

Still more important is Gregory's legacy. Upon his death in 604, while there were still small pockets of resistance, Britain, France, Spain, and most of Italy were one church. As nations they were still divided into many tribes and factions. But they had one religious leader, the bishop in Rome. And not only was he their acknowledged leader, but their practices and policies were all directed from Rome. Gregory had been ruthless in attempting to eradicate local customs in worship or even in local celebrations, such as the date of Easter. Everything was standardized to conform to the worship and usage of the church in Rome, matters in which Gregory took no small interest.

This rapid extension of Roman influence and control in the West had two principal results. For one thing it put the Western church in a very different position from the church in the East where the bishops of Antioch, Alexandria, and Constantinople still considered themselves rivals, each resentful of any attempted invasion of his jurisdiction by another. While Eastern Christendom still had a number of popes, Western Christendom after Gregory had only one. The importance of this development was to be seen in the time of testing which lay in the not too distant future.

Of even greater significance was the way in which Western religious unity prepared the way for Western political unity. Perhaps Gregory himself did not fully foresee what his conquest of Western Europe for the Roman church would eventually lead to. Indeed, it was almost two centuries in coming and those centuries included many apparent setbacks. None of Gregory's immediate successors was his equal in vision or ability. One of the popes in the seventh century died a prisoner in exile, while in the next century another Pope Gregory found himself caught in the old battle with Constantinople which the first Gregory had tried to neutralize.

Yet none of these temporary setbacks could alter the fact that in creating a religious empire in Western Europe Gregory the Great had made the papacy a political force to be reckoned with. Those very Lombards who had once been such a threat to Rome had become the pope's principal political support. The archbishops, bishops, and abbots throughout the West, no longer independent officials but now, for the most part, appointees of the Roman pope and responsible to him, gave him effective support in every Western country. For the most part, when any issue was at stake their loyalty was to him and not to the monarch in whose realm they were serving.

In the eighth century, however, a new pattern of alliance began to develop. Those same Lombards who had for so long been the pope's chief allies began to threaten certain areas of papal domination. But the situation was now very different from what it had been in Gregory's time. Thanks to Gregory's statesmanship the pope was not without friends. Making a dangerous journey across the Alps, Pope Stephen II appealed to Pepin, king of the Franks, for his help. In two campaigns, the first in 754 and the second in 756, Pepin's forces crushed the Lombard power and with the papal blessing Lombardy ceased to exist as a separate nation and became annexed to the kingdom of the Franks.

The next step was not difficult to foresee. Pepin's eldest son, Charles, was a man of great ambition and ability. Though his father had divided the kingdom between his two sons, when his younger brother died, Charles took his half and added it to his own. He crushed the last remains of Lombard strength in Italy. Having secured his southern flank in this way, he then conquered the German provinces of Saxony and Bavaria and added them to his realm. Though Spain by this time was largely in Arab hands, he drove the Arabs as far south as he could and made northern Spain another part of the kingdom of the Franks.

Clearly Charles was a man to be reckoned with. In fact the *Great* became so inseparably part of his character that it became part of his name, Charlemagne (Carolus Magnus). During most of Charlemagne's rise to power the pope was a Roman nobleman named Hadrian. While he could not help welcoming this powerful new ally of the church, Hadrian also had occasion to discover that the new alliance had its dangers too. When Charlemagne disapproved of a policy of the church, he was not afraid to say so—and he always had his way. Charlemagne, by extending the Frankish kingdom, had gained the political unity and strength which Gregory had gained for the church two centuries earlier.

THE FIRST EMPEROR

The final chapter took place on Christmas Day in the year 800. Leo III was now pope and he had been the victim of nasty intrigue by friends of his predecessor (Hadrian I) who had opposed his election. It is significant to notice that Leo's final appeal from the charges which had been brought against him (charges which most historians believe were false) was not to an ecclesiastical court, though the ecclesiastical court had made an investigation, but to the Frankish king. Charlemagne came to Rome, heard the report of the investigation, and on December 23 publicly declared that he found Leo innocent.

Two days later in St. Peter's Church in Rome Leo, without any previous public announcement, crowned Charlemagne as Roman Emperor. To this day the full story behind his action remains hidden. Whether he acted out of a sudden impulse of gratitude or as the result of a long-secret agreement between himself and Charlemagne no one knows and probably no one will ever know. The fact remains that after Christmas Day, 800, following long centuries of political chaos, there was once again a Roman Emperor in the West. Gregory the Great had given the world the figure of Roman pope; Charles the Great gave it the figure of Roman Emperor.

And, of course, the history of Western Europe for the next several

Charlemagne Sees His Role as King

Karl, by the grace of God king of the Franks and Lombards, and patricius of the Romans, to his holiness, pope Leo, greeting. . . . Just as I entered into an agreement with the most holy father, your predecessor, so also I desire to make with you an inviolable treaty of mutual fidelity and love; that, on the one hand, you shall pray for me and give me the apostolic benediction, and that, on the other, with the aid of God I will ever defend the most holy seat of the holy Roman church. For it is our part to defend the holy church of Christ from the attacks of pagans and infidels from without, and within to enforce the acceptance of the catholic faith. It is your part, most holy father, to aid us in the good fight by raising your hands to God as Moses did [Ex. 17:11], so that by your intercession the Christian people under the leadership of God may always and everywhere have the victory over the enemies of His holy name, and the name of our Lord Jesus Christ may be glorified throughout the world.[2]

—Charlemagne, "Manifesto to Pope Leo III"

centuries was to be dominated by these two officials, sometimes acting in unity, sometimes struggling with each other for the mastery. As in the case of Gregory's ambition, Charlemagne's dream also had to undergo some trial and difficulty before it became a fully established reality. But the pattern had been set, even though the details might be a time in developing.

The consequences for Christian history were enormous. For when, as was most often the case, pope and emperor worked in harmony, the church had tremendous political and economic power. With few notable exceptions papal policies were always carried out by imperial power. No longer was it necessary to persuade men to the Christian faith by preaching or by missionary endeavor; now they could be made Christian by imperial decree. The heroic stories of missionary pioneers like Boniface or Willibrord now begin to disappear from church history. Conversion was now a simple matter of choosing between baptism or the sword.

In such an alliance there were to be moments when the church dared to stand out and say No to the power of the state. But for the most part the church became simply a department of the state, supported by its revenues and in return supporting its decisions. Though neither Leo nor Charlemagne could have predicted the consequences of that most important Christmas Day in history, they are still with us.

Veni, Veni Emmanuel

The familiar Advent hymn, "O come, O come, Emmanuel," is a translation of these Latin words. They, in turn, are simply a verse form of a series of responses called "The Great O's," sung in the vesper services of Western monasteries the week before Christmas as early as the ninth century. The music which we use, too, is based on Gregorian chant. You may enjoy singing the familiar hymn in its original language:

Veni, veni Emmanuel!   Veni, veni o oriens!
Captivum solve Israel!   Solare nos adveniens,
Qui gemit in exilio,   Noctis depelle nebulas,
Privatus Dei Filio.   Dirasque noctis tenebras.

Veni, o Iesse virgula!   Veni clavis Davidica!
Ex hostis tuos ungula,   Regna reclude coelica,
De specu tuos tartari   Fac iter tutum superum,
Educ, et antro barathri.   Et claude vias inferum.

Refrain
Gaude, gaude, Emmanuel
Nascetur pro te, Israel.[3]

The identification of church and state, which was as much a part of Protestant history as of Roman Catholic and which provided (and still provides in some places) such fertile soil for Communism, began right here. The Christian faith was no longer necessarily a matter of personal conviction but of good citizenship. Charlemagne's legacy to the Western world was indeed a lasting one.

But even while Charlemagne's coronation as emperor took place there was another Roman emperor sitting on his throne in the Byzantine capital of Constantinople. His position was threatened and insecure because of the great success of a new religion from the Middle East. Before we continue our story in the West we must pause to have a look at developments in this other empire.

9

The Cross and the Crescent

At almost the same time that Gregory's missionaries were moving through the lands of Western Europe, the missionaries of a new religion from the East were spreading their gospel with an even greater vigor. The prophet of this new religion, Mohammed, was born about 570. By the time of his death in 632 his forces had spread from their native Arabia to conquer Egypt and Syria. Exactly a century later in 732 they were stopped in France by Charles Martel. In that century Mohammed's men had taken all of North Africa, crossed the Strait of Gibraltar, established themselves in Spain, and were threatening to conquer France when they were turned back.

This is not the place to discuss Mohammed's gospel except in a summary kind of way. Commonly known as *Islam* (which means "submission to the will of God"), the new religion of Mohammed was a strange mixture of Hebrew and Christian elements together with ancient Arabian ideas and practices. Mohammed obviously knew a good deal about both Judaism and Christianity. In fact he thought of himself as restoring the true religion of Abraham, while Jesus figures in Mohammedan scriptures (known as the *Koran*) as one of the great prophets. The heart of Islam is the proclamation of the greatness of the one true God, Allah, and of the necessity of a complete surrender to his will which is the sole cause of all things.

The Eastern empire into which this dynamic new religion came was in many ways healthier than it had been in a long time. For almost forty years it had been under the administration of an exceedingly capable emperor, Justinian, who had not only extended the borders of the empire but had done a good deal to stabilize its complicated legal and administrative structure. He had taken an active part in the effort to bring theological peace to the Eastern churches which were continuing to argue the fine points of Christology. Though the emperors who succeeded Justinian after his death in 565 were not so able as he, the legacy of empire which he left them enabled them to withstand the shock of the Mohammedan invasion.

For we must not forget that in spite of the great success of Islam, the Eastern empire did resist and did survive, though on a greatly reduced basis. The possession of places like Jerusalem or Alexandria changed hands several times before the Mohammedans could finally

74 THAT THE WORLD MAY KNOW

claim them. Though the forces of Islam hemmed in the empire on all sides, they were unable to capture its real heart, the holy city of Constantinople. Not till 1453 did that city pass into Islamic hands and the history of the Eastern empire finally come to an end.

THE EASTERN CHURCH

Our concern is not with the political history of the Christian East but rather with the life of the church during the Mohammedan invasion. While it is always dangerous to generalize about the life of so large a community as the Christian East, we may notice three characteristics which distinguished it from the Christian West.

1. Theological controversy, especially about the person of Christ, continued for a much longer time in the East than in the West. As far as the West was concerned, the Council of Chalcedon, which had in 451 declared the necessity of believing in the full deity and the full humanity of Jesus Christ, had settled the question. But as far as the East was concerned, Chalcedon had only raised new questions to be debated. The next two centuries were filled with angry debates between the Orthodox, who accepted and defended the formula of Chalcedon as final, and the Monophysites, who argued that the two persons were united in a single nature. Then when the Monophysites had finally been expelled from the church, a new party arose called the Monothelites. Their position was that though Jesus was fully human and fully divine, he had a single divine will and no human will at all. Needless to say, this position was also finally declared heretical. But in each case those who had been expelled by the Orthodox church formed separate churches, some of which continue to this very day.

No one wants to maintain that the questions which kept Eastern Christianity in a turmoil were trivial ones, though it might be argued that after a certain point they were questions which human reason is simply incompetent to answer. The point to notice is that as more energy was spent in pursuing these theological disputes, less attention was devoted to the mission of the church. At one time Eastern Christianity had been as vigorous in spreading the faith as Western Christianity. There is still a Christian community in India to testify to the fact that Eastern Orthodoxy had originally taken its missionary responsibility seriously, and there is evidence that one branch of Eastern Christianity had at one time penetrated China.

Yet by the time of which we are speaking Eastern Orthodoxy had become territorially frozen. The only significant addition to its forces was made not by missionary endeavor but by political fiat when in 988 the Emperor Vladimir, after having investigated various possibilities, made Russia an Orthodox country. In short, a church which had lost its crusading zeal was suddenly confronted by a new religion, relentless in its determination to conquer the world.

Nowhere does this contrast between West and East become more apparent than in the different directions taken by monasticism. In the West, as we have seen, monasticism became a disciplined army that marched through Europe to take it for Christ. In the East, however, the monasteries became places for study and contemplation, completely isolated communities in which men might devote themselves entirely to the mystical contemplation of God.

2. We have already noticed the fact that the ecclesiastical structure of Eastern Orthodoxy developed many "popes," each one independent in his own territory. Because Constantinople was the capital city, there was a natural tendency to regard the bishop there with special honor. But that gave him no real authority over his brother bishops of Antioch or Alexandria.

This division of spiritual responsibility was not the whole story. Ever since the days of Constantine himself there had been a strong tradition in the East that the true head of the church was the emperor. It was the great Justinian who in his codification of Byzantine law made the tradition into a rule. From his time on the emperor, whose coronation was a religious ceremony of great significance, was the accepted head of the church whose word in all matters was final. Not only ecclesiastical policies but even theological discussions could be settled by a single stroke of the imperial pen.

The Great Entrance

The worship of the Eastern churches is old in tradition and rich in symbolism. Singing by the choir plays a very important part. The Great Entrance is that moment in the liturgy at which the sacred elements of bread and wine are carried into the sanctuary in solemn procession and placed on the altar. The Cherubic Hymn is sung as the Great Entrance occurs, the first part in anticipation, the last part in celebration of the event.

We who mystically represent the Cherubim,
   and sing with them the thrice-holy hymn
   to the life-giving Trinity,
Let us lay aside all earthly care:
For we are to receive the King of all,
   invisibly attended by the angelic hosts:
   Alleluia! Alleluia! Alleluia![1]
              —*The Liturgy of St. Chrysostom*

Once again a contrast with the development in the West is instructive. The situation there took much longer to work out because of the relatively greater chaos in Western Europe. When it did work out, as we have seen, it resulted in two heads, a political sovereign and an ecclesiastical one, an emperor and a pope. While often they worked in such close harmony that church and state were virtually one, still at least the possibility for independent action by the church was there and sometimes it was effectively used. But in Eastern Orthodoxy after Justinian's time (and probably before) there was not even that possibility. Church and state had one head in the person of the emperor.

What may have seemed like a very effective arrangement was in fact a disastrous one for the life of the church. Having become a virtual department of the empire, the church had no real independence of thought or action. And having lost its independence, it soon began to lose its creativity. As new challenges arose and new situations came up, Orthodoxy was almost powerless to meet them. Its fortunes were entirely identified with the empire and the empire, of course, wanted nothing more than the preservation of the *status quo*.

One strange result of this identification of church and state was a sharp decline in the importance of preaching. There had been a time when Orthodoxy had produced some of the greatest preachers in Christendom. John Chrysostom, for example (his second name means "golden mouth"), had not only been a magnificent orator, but a fearless prophet. His preaching drew great crowds in Constantinople. When in his prophetic calling he had to point the finger at the Empress herself, he did not hesitate to do so, even though it meant banishment and ruin.

That was the kind of tradition that began to disappear. Possessed of a magnificent liturgy and splendid ceremonial, Orthodoxy began to interpret the Christian faith increasingly as preparation for the life of the world to come, with little or nothing to say to the questions of life in this world. The social thrust which was never quite lost in the West, even though it was often threatened, almost disappeared in the East. A church which had lost its creativity and independence was suddenly confronted with a deadly serious rival in Islam.

3. Although it cannot be put down entirely to the Eastern frame of mind, the years about which we have been speaking saw a steadily increasing rift between the Western and Eastern churches. The final break between Eastern Orthodoxy and Western Catholicism did not come till much later. But when it came, it was merely the last stage in a development which had been going on for centuries.

One of the great reasons for the growing divergence was, of course, Eastern suspicion of the growing power of Rome. After all, that same Council of Chalcedon which had decided about the person of Christ had also decided that "the See of Constantinople shall enjoy equal privileges with the See of Old Rome ... and second after it." Yet with the expansion of Roman authority begun by Gregory the Great and continued by his successors, to say nothing of the haughty way in which Rome dealt with Constantinople, the Eastern Orthodox began to suspect that they too, like the ancient church of Britain, were to be made provinces in a new Roman ecclesiastical empire. The mounting claims of the bishop of Rome were one of the great reasons for Eastern withdrawal.

The Orthodox also complained that the rising Roman authority was introducing many new customs in the life of the church and insisting upon their observance. While Orthodox monks remained single, for example, Orthodox clergy had always been permitted to marry (as they are to this day). But here was an upstart Western bishop ruling that no clergy could be allowed to marry. Not only was he upsetting tradition (a thing very precious to the Orthodox), but the implication was that the bishop of Rome's will should be law for the entire church.

Another reason for the growing separation was simply that two different temperaments were involved. Eastern Orthodox piety tended to be speculative and mystical; the Western mind was practical. Latourette, the great church historian of our day, has suggested that the difference may have been because Eastern Orthodoxy was possessed by the old Greek idea that salvation consisted in being free of the flesh whereas Western Catholicism reflected the Roman regard for practical administration and ordering of events here and now.

However that may be, the fact remains that it became increasingly difficult for East and West to understand each other as the years went on. To the Eastern mind the Western approach was too much immersed in the problems and concerns of this world; the West felt that the Eastern attitude was unrealistic and impractical. At that very time when the Western church was looking for new worlds to conquer, the Eastern church was withdrawing into liturgical mysticism rather than facing an enemy it felt powerless to resist.

The West could also point out that once it had exhausted itself in christological disputes, the Eastern church virtually abandoned theological thinking. Its last great theologian, John of Damascus, simply summarized all that had been decided in Eastern Orthodoxy and thereafter there was silence. New challenges to Christian faith which the West tried to meet creatively were never answered in the East. Orthodoxy was content simply to repeat the holy tradition to which nothing could be added and from which nothing must be taken away.

This Orthodox Church was to bear the brunt of Mohammedan fury when it came storming out of the East. By contrast the Western church had little contact with it, except for one or two significant battles. As we have described the temper of Eastern Orthodoxy, the surprising thing is not that Islam inflicted serious losses upon it; the surprising thing is that it survived at all!

In some places it did not. The worst defeat suffered by the Christian forces was in North Africa, which from Egypt westward to Carthage had been a Christian stronghold. Part of the reason for this collapse was the fact that Italy, Greece, and Sicily were within easy reach and to them as many Christians as could fled for refuge. Small pockets of Christians were left, but under such handicaps and in such isolation that within a few centuries the Christian cause had entirely disappeared from the northern coast of Africa.

THE CHURCH BEHIND THE CURTAIN

In other places such as Syria or Palestine the Christian church survived, though as a greatly reduced minority. Many of these schismatic groups actually enjoyed greater freedom under their Mohammedan conquerors than they had under the empire which had tried to persecute them into the Orthodox Church. But the Orthodox Church itself was allowed to continue, though under severe restrictions. Being a Christian involved paying large extra taxes. Those who were born Christians might continue, but any attempt to make new converts was strictly forbidden. While the Mohammedans seized certain churches and transformed them into mosques, they left certain others for Christian use. But no new church buildings could be built. Christians were even required to wear a special garb on the streets.

When we consider the total impact of such restrictive legislation we ought not to dwell on the fact that thousands of Christians took the easy way out and gave up their faith. The thing to be noticed is the fact that there were just as many thousands who did not, who accepted all that their new situation involved rather than surrender their faith in Christ. Except for North Africa, the Orthodox witness never died, even though it had to live for centuries under the shadow of the crescent.

To be sure, this kind of church life was very limiting. Given the innate temperament of Orthodoxy and the hostile and restricted environment in which it had to live, it is not difficult to see why these churches became extremely conservative and suspicious of any change, why they clung so tenaciously to the traditions of their fathers. Not only would change threaten their Christian integrity, as they saw it, but it might bring down the full wrath of their Islamic overlords and make further survival an impossibility.

In a time like ours when much of the Christian church again lives under a strange banner, this time not the crescent but the hammer and sickle, the story of the Eastern church under Islam has a strangely modern ring. Ours is not the first time in history when the Christian church has had to live behind a curtain and it may not be the last. When many foolish things are said today about the impossibility of being a Christian in a Communist country, we ought to remember that many foolish things were probably said a thousand years ago about the impossibility of being a Christian in a Mohammedan land.

Certainly we can recognize the serious limitations which this kind of situation puts upon the life of the church. No one would pretend that these are ideal conditions. But if the Christian church could survive a thousand years of Islamic domination, why should we despair at the prospect of less than a century of Communist rule?

An even more significant thing to notice is the pattern of history which is involved here. The Western church had been a threatened

"There Is No God but Allah . . ."

This was the cry which brought terror to Christians in the seventh century, through Western Asia, across North Africa, into Europe. The conquering army of Islam had a simple creed: la ilaha illa'llah; muhammad rasulu'llah—*"There is no God but Allah: Mohammed is the Messenger of Allah." Five times daily, when the muezzin called to prayer, they knelt facing Mecca and recited what is often called "the Lord's Prayer of Islam," the opening* sura *or section of their sacred book, the Koran:*

In the name of Allah, the Beneficent, the Merciful.
1. Praise be to Allah, the Lord of the Worlds,
2. The Beneficent, the Merciful.
3. Owner of the Day of Judgment,
4. Thee (alone) we worship; Thee (alone) we ask for help.
5. Show us the straight path,
6. The path of those whom Thou hast favoured;
7. Not (the path) of those who earn Thine anger nor of those who go astray.[2]

and insecure group, face-to-face with the challenge of hordes of barbarians. The Eastern church had been a secure and stable community, totally identified with the world's most powerful empire. If we were to compute the future of the church purely in terms of military might and economic strength, then by anybody's prediction it was Western Christianity that ought to have disappeared and Eastern Christianity that should have survived in strength.

But the life of the church is not subject to such standards of computation because the church is the people of God. It was, therefore, the church that felt strong and secure, that almost said "I have need of nothing," that almost died, that saw itself reduced to an impotent remnant. The time of similar testing for Western Christianity was to come. Still the lesson of Eastern Orthodoxy is clear. The church which loses its sense of dependence and its missionary impulse must die in order to live.

PART III
THE CHURCH SEEKS TO CONTROL THE WORLD

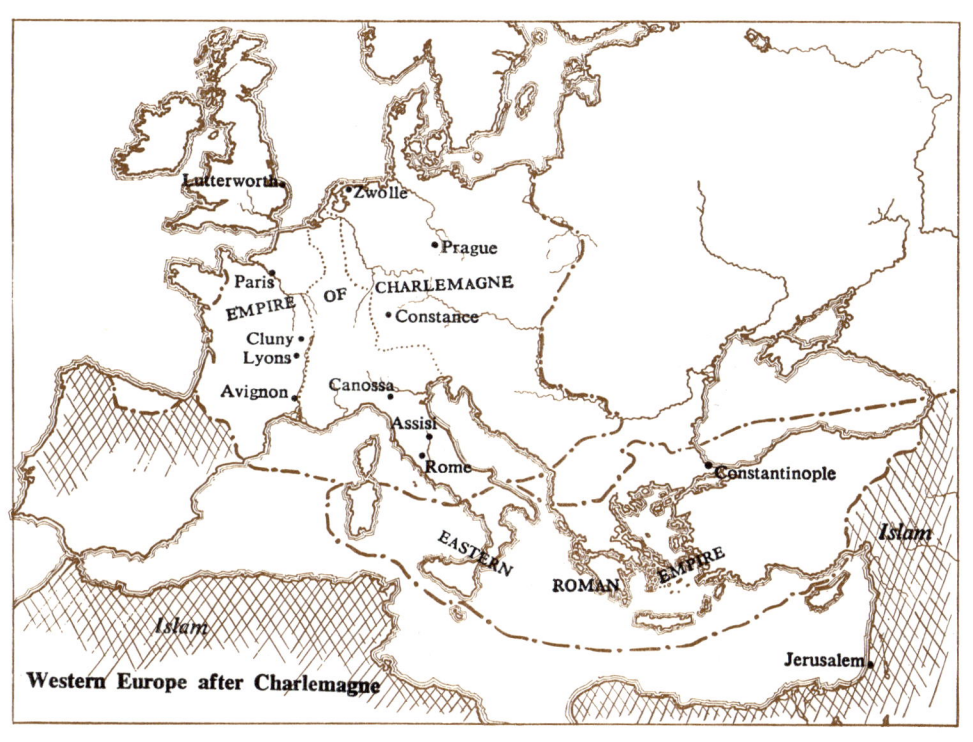

THOU art good, O Lord, to the soul that seeketh thee; if to it, how much more to that which findeth thee! If the anticipation is so sweet, what must the reality be! If honey and milk are sweet under the tongue, what must they be on the tongue![1]
—Bernard of Clairvaux (1090–1153)

GOD Almighty, Eternal, Righteous, and Merciful, give to us poor sinners to do for Thy sake all that we know of Thy will, and to will always what pleases Thee, so that inwardly purified, enlightened, and kindled by the fire of the Holy Spirit, we may follow in the footprints of Thy Well-Beloved Son, our Lord Jesus Christ. Amen.[2]
—Francis of Assisi (1182–1226)

GIVE me, O Lord, a steadfast heart, which no unworthy thought can drag downward; An unconquered heart, which no tribulation can wear out; An upright heart, which no unworthy purpose may tempt aside. Bestow upon me also, O Lord my God, understanding to know thee, diligence to seek thee, wisdom to find thee, and a faithfulness that may finally unite me with thee; Through Jesus Christ our Lord. *Amen.*
—Thomas Aquinas (1225–1274)

O LORD JESU! forasmuch as Thy Way is narrow and is also much despised in the world, give me grace to bear gladly the despisings of the world. There is no servant greater than his Lord, nor any disciple above his Master. Let Thy servant therefore be exercised in Thy ways, for therein is health and the very perfection of life; whatsoever I read or hear beside that Way, it refresheth me not, nor delighteth me fully.[3]
—Thomas à Kempis (1379–1471)

10

The Dark Ages

On Christmas Day, 800, the situation for both church and state in Western Europe seemed brighter than it had for many years. In pope and emperor there were now responsible political and religious heads, both of whom could bring unity to the life of the Western world. Ideally that should have been the case; actually it turned out far differently.

It was the newly formed empire which first ran into trouble. Charlemagne died in 814, leaving his crown to his son Louis the Pious, a good but ineffective ruler who barely held things together until his death in 840. The empire was then divided among Louis' three sons, one of whom retained the title of emperor. Incidentally, the Treaty of Verdun by which this division was made in 843 is usually regarded as the beginning of the division between France and Germany which hitherto had been together as part of Charlemagne's realm.

The division was not a happy one. Political unity was weakened, especially by the fact that there was great rivalry between the three newly created kingdoms. Yet unity was a desperate necessity, for on almost every side Western Europe was under attack. To the north the Scandinavians were a continual threat; on the east the Hungarians kept up their pressure; Italy was the victim of frequent Mohammedan raids, one of which resulted in the plundering of St. Peter's itself.

Not only was the division of the empire into three parts an unhappy arrangement, but very often those who sat on the royal thrones were such weak and ineffectual sovereigns that the kingdoms themselves tended to break down into smaller and smaller units of authority. Local nobles and petty barons, having learned that they could safely defy the royal power with perfect safety, did so increasingly until finally each kingdom was in reality little more than a loose federation of petty sovereignties. If ours were a political history of Europe we should have to spend a good deal of time at this point tracing the origins of the whole feudal system which became so characteristic of medieval Europe, for its origin is to be found in the almost complete breakdown of national authority.

An even more significant result of this political collapse was to be found in the swift decline of education and learning. This development more than any other gave this period its common title, the *Dark Ages*. Though Charlemagne himself had been barely able to read and write, he had recognized the importance of learning and had been the patron of its revival in Western Europe. Greatly impressed by the education which had survived in the British Isles, Charlemagne had imported the British monk Alcuin to be his minister of education, so to speak. Preaching, which through ignorance had been neglected, was revived; books of sermons were carefully copied and circulated. The emperor was anxious that every Christian should be able to repeat the Lord's Prayer and the Apostles' Creed. That may seem like little to us, but in that age of sheer barbarism it represented a great deal.

Yet within a century everything that had been done to develop education and learning had about come to an end. Lacking an imperial patron, the renaissance which Charlemagne had begun languished. The robber barons whose principal interest lay in extending their own wealth had no concern (nor would they have spent their money); the kings were too weak to provide effective leadership. There were occasional bright spots like the kingdom of Alfred the Great in England. But for the most part the clergy returned to ignorance and the population to illiteracy. Schools were almost unheard of save in a few monastic centers.

FILLING THE VACUUM

Into the vacuum created by the collapse of political leadership the power of religious leadership came. During this time of political chaos the papacy increasingly assumed political as well as religious mastery. In some ways it was a natural development. The bishops and priests, many of them sincere men, resented the interference of their archbishops, most of whom were nothing but the puppets of the local sovereigns. It became increasingly common for bishops to appeal over the heads of local authorities to Rome for support.

We can spend a lot of time debating whether it was fortunate or unfortunate that at the very time that political authority was in such a state of collapse a succession of strong men sat on the papal throne in Rome. Probably the ablest was Pope Nicholas I who reigned from 858 to 867. Like his great predecessor Gregory, Nicholas was a Roman nobleman, a man of fearless integrity. In a series of confrontations he challenged the power of the local archbishops and in every case won. A few examples of his courage will help illustrate how he increased the power of the papacy.

Lothair II, king of Lorraine (one of the three kingdoms into which Charlemagne had divided his empire), had grown tired of his wife, Thietberga, and desired to marry another woman. He applied to the archbishops of Trier and Cologne, who were of course his willing servants, for a divorce which was readily granted and confirmed by a special synod held at Metz in 863. When word of all this reached Nicholas' ears, he moved with great speed, declaring the divorce null and void and throwing out the two archbishops who had sanctioned it. In doing so he risked retaliation from an outraged king and two angry archbishops. But that did not in the slightest deter him.

A similar case occurred at almost the same time when Hincmar, the archbishop of Rheims, deposed Rothad, one of his bishops who had been critical of him. Again Nicholas moved with dispatch, ordering the archbishop to restore the bishop or face removal himself. There was also a similar tussle with the archbishop of Ravenna which had a like result. In every case the result was the establishment of Rome as a final court of appeal in all matters ecclesiastical. Nicholas' theory was a very simple one. To use the words of one of our great American church historians, Williston Walker, "In his thought, the church is superior to all earthly powers, the ruler of the whole church is the Pope, and the bishops are his agents."[1]

But after all Rome itself was a city with a nobility that was greedy for power. Once a pope like Nicholas had made them realize what power lay in the papacy it became a prize which they were eager to capture for themselves. It was not too long after Nicholas' death, therefore, that the papacy became the plaything of Roman nobility and soon followed the empire into eclipse. Papal elections became contests between rival Roman factions; riots and even murder accompanied them. In the fifty-eight years from 897 to 955 there were no fewer than seventeen popes, many of them the creatures of two notorious Roman women, Marozia and Theodora. The age seemed a dark one indeed when both political and religious leadership had failed and Europe was left to flounder aimlessly.

In the century of confusion which followed there is one episode which sheds some light on the situation. Since the line of Charlemagne had come to an end in Germany, the nobles had to choose a new king. Their first choice having proved a disappointment, they finally selected the Duke of Saxony in 919. It was his son, Otto, who came to the German throne in 936, who began to lay the foundations for the re-creation of the empire. His first task, of course, was the consolidation of his own country, splintered as it was into little semi-independent factions. Because the papacy in Rome was at the time extremely feeble, Otto was able not only to make sure that all the political appointments were loyal to him but even to secure the right of ecclesiastical appointments for himself. In less than twenty years he had not only unified Germany but extended its borders into Denmark on the north and the Slavic countries on the east.

Not content with these accomplishments Otto next turned his attention toward Italy. After some interruptions he made his final invasion in 961. His able ally in this campaign was one of the strangest popes in all history. The grandson of the notorious Marozia, John XII had become pope in 955 when he was only eighteen. His private morals were a scandal to the whole community but that made no difference. He belonged to the right political faction. It was to prop up his tottering regime that John invited Otto I to come to his rescue. And when Otto had taken Rome, John rewarded him by crowning him emperor in 962. The empire created under these rather curious circumstances was, however, to prove more lasting than that created by Charlemagne. On paper, at least, it lasted till 1806!

The rest of the story is one of alternating mastery between pope

Henry, king not by usurpation, but by the holy ordination of God, to Hildebrand, not pope, but false monk.

This is the salutation which you deserve, for you have never held any office in the church without making it a source of confusion and a curse to Christian men instead of an honor and a blessing. . . . All this we have endured because of our respect for the papal office, but you have mistaken our humility for fear, and have dared to make an attack on the royal and imperial authority which we received from God. . . . Our Lord Jesus Christ has called us to the government of the empire, but he never called you to the rule of the church. . . . St. Peter himself said: "Fear God, honor the king" [1 Pet. 2:17]. But you, who fear not God, have dishonored me, whom He hath established. . . . Come down, then, from that apostolic seat which you have obtained by violence; for you have been declared accursed . . . for your false doctrines and have been condemned by us and our bishops for your evil rule. Let another ascend the throne of St. Peter, one who will not use religion as a cloak of violence, but will teach the life-giving doctrine of that prince of the apostles. I, Henry, king by the grace of God, with all my bishops, say unto you: "Come down, come down, and be accursed through all the ages."[2]   —from Henry IV's letter

and emperor, much depending on the strength of the man who sat on either throne. While it is too complicated for us to study, there was one occupant of the papal throne who deserves our attention. Indeed in a real sense the great crisis in his story was the result of the legacy left by the new emperor, Otto. In the eleventh century the papacy underwent considerable reform. There was a succession of popes who were determined to root out the indifference, weakness, and corruption which for too long had been associated with the Roman see. Behind each of them it is easy to trace the hand of a little peasant from Tuscany who was completely dedicated to the purity and independence of the church.

Hildebrand had served as administrator of papal affairs for almost twenty-five years when he was made pope in 1073. Taking the name of Gregory VII (was he consciously thinking of the first Gregory?) he was merciless in his efforts to destroy immorality of any kind within the church. But though he could not have realized it at the time, his greatest struggle was to be with no one less than the emperor himself.

Otto had taken advantage of the weakness of Rome to claim for himself the right of ecclesiastical appointments. However desirable a

St. Peter, prince of the apostles, incline thine ear unto me, I beseech thee, and hear me, thy servant, whom thou hast nourished from mine infancy and hast delivered from mine enemies that hate me for my fidelity to thee. Thou art my witness . . . that thy holy Roman church called me to its government against my own will, and that I did not gain thy throne by violence . . . It is by thy grace and as thy representative that God has given to me the power to bind and to loose in heaven and in earth. Confident of my integrity and authority, I now declare in the name of omnipotent God, the Father, Son, and Holy Spirit, that Henry, son of the emperor Henry, is deprived of his kingdom of Germany and Italy; I do this by thy authority and in defence of the honor of thy church, because he has rebelled against it. . . . He has refused to obey as a Christian should . . . he has despised the warnings which, as thou art witness, I sent to him for his salvation, he has cut himself off from thy church, and has attempted to rend it asunder; therefore, by thy authority, I place him under the curse. It is in thy name that I curse him, that all people may know that thou art Peter, and upon thy rock the Son of the living God has built his church, and the gates of hell shall not prevail against it.[3]

—from Pope Gregory's reply to Henry

thing this may have been then, in the long run it proved to be a bad thing for the life of the church. As had been the case earlier, religious leadership tended to pass into the hands of political hacks and princely puppets. Hildebrand was determined to put a stop to it. One of his first moves after his election as pope, therefore, was to issue a decree forbidding lay investiture, or the appointment to ecclesiastical office by political leaders.

The decree met with varying reactions, but the emperor, Henry IV, was just as determined to ignore it as Hildebrand was to enforce it. When the archbishopric of Milan fell vacant in 1075, Henry made an appointment to it. Hildebrand replied with a letter of stern and severe warning which the emperor not only chose to ignore, but to which he chose to reply by holding a council at Worms in January, 1076. There German nobles and bishops made charges against the pope and declared him deposed.

Then Hildebrand unleashed his thunderbolt. On February 22, 1076, he issued a decree excommunicating the emperor and releasing all of his German and Italian subjects from any necessity of obedience to him. For almost a year Henry tried to withstand the implications of the pope's action, but it was impossible. He waited until the very last minute, however. Hildebrand was on his way to Augsburg to a meeting of the German nobility called to consider the selection of a new emperor when Henry met him at Canossa where he was staying. For three days the pope kept the emperor standing barefoot in the snow before he finally relented and released him from the ban of excommunication. Never again was the papacy to enjoy quite the same kind of triumph over the empire.

Indeed its power declined in Hildebrand's own lifetime, for when a few years later in 1080 he again excommunicated the same emperor, Henry was able not only to withstand the excommunication but to drive the pope from his throne and place someone else on it. The very pope who had humiliated the emperor himself died in exile in 1085.

LIGHT IN THE DARKNESS

These contests of strength between pope and emperor which so fill the pages of the story of the Dark Ages are not the only things to be found there. The monastic movement which had done such great service in the missionary expansion of the church had itself fallen victim to the political intrigue and chicanery of the time. But the original monastic ideal had never been lost and now in the pressures of political and religious disorganization it came to the fore once again.

In the year 910 the Duke of Aquitaine, William the Pious, founded a new monastery in the French village of Cluny. So that it would be free from any political control as well as from the interference of the local bishop its charter called for its complete independence except for the protection of the pope. The same charter also called for a strict observance of all the rule of Benedict.

The example of Cluny soon caught the imagination of other Christians who were weary of the struggle and disgusted by the life of the church. Other monasteries patterned after Cluny soon began until there was a genuine Cluniac movement in the life of the Western church. Cluny soon took responsibility not only for the reform of monasticism but for the reform of the whole clergy as well. By word and example the Cluniacs sought to remove the particular scandals of bribery (simony) and immorality from the life of the priesthood (nicolaitanism). Hildebrand had been greatly influenced by them and they were among his strongest supporters in his contest with Henry.

While this revival of stringent monastic discipline undoubtedly had its effect on the life of the church, moving in ever widening circles of influence until it had even captured the papacy, it produced one completely unexpected result which was to change the whole face of Europe. These centuries of political collapse and religious struggle had also been years of great economic distress. Between 970 and 1040 there had been no fewer than forty famines. The lot of the common man, especially if his place happened to be in the territory of one of the greedy barons, was a wretched one. The mood of the times was a somber one. If there was nothing to be looked for in this life, what could be done to insure blessedness in the life of the world to come?

That question which must have been in the minds of many, monks and laymen alike, was soon to receive a very practical answer. Toward the end of the eleventh century the forces of Islam were on the march again and the holy city of Jerusalem, which had always been open to Christians who wished to make pilgrimages to it, was closed. Although other Eastern emperors had appealed for help in recapturing it, their appeals had come at times when other more pressing affairs occupied both the pope and the Western emperor.

But when in the closing years of the century the emperor Alexius Comnenus made an urgent appeal to Pope Urban II, his appeal found a ready response. Himself a product of Cluniac influence, Urban had devoted most of his reign to healing the various breaches that had resulted from the quarrels between Hildebrand and Henry. Now that those ranks had been closed and the life of the church had been reformed, what better act of expiation could be made than a crusade to recapture the holy city of Jerusalem from the heathen Turk?

Alexius had probably thought only in terms of assistance for his hard-pressed empire. But Urban thought in much grander terms of a genuine holy war in which all who would share would receive the promise of forgiveness of sins and life everlasting. It was in this way that he presented the matter to the synod which met in the French city of Clermont in 1095 and it was in this way that it was enthusiastically received. So great indeed was the popular response that before the movement could be properly organized a straggling army of peasants set out under the leadership of some wildly enthusiastic monks. The fact that their expedition met with disaster should not blind us to the deeper reality—the eager desire of the common man to share in this adventure.

It was no straggling army of peasants, however, but a carefully recruited one of nobles and trained soldiery that made its way across Europe beginning in the summer of 1096. Alexius may well have wondered about the wisdom of his appeal when so large a force arrived in his capital city of Constantinople and made so many demands upon him. But it seemed that nothing could stop the enthusiastic army from the West. One after another the Turkish strongholds fell, though sometimes not without long and difficult sieges. Finally in the summer of 1099 the goal was reached and the holy city of Jerusalem itself passed into Christian hands for the first time since 637. A little Latin kingdom was set up with Jerusalem as its capital and Baldwin, a French nobleman, as its king.

The first crusade was not the last. The little Latin kingdom fell back into Turkish hands in 1187 and resisted all efforts to reconquer it. Indeed each one of the four crusades showed a lessening of zeal and enthusiasm; the fourth was a very sad affair indeed, resulting not in the conquest of Islam but in the plundering of the Christian East by the Christian West.

Even though the crusades failed in their objective, they were the principal reason for the end of the Dark Ages in Western Christendom. By bringing Europeans out of their isolation they stimulated the political, economic, and intellectual, as well as the religious life of the West. Jerusalem might remain in Turkish hands, but because men of all sorts and conditions had left home and kindred to fight for it, the long night in which Europe had been blacked out had begun to lift.

11

Men of Light

"Heresy" was a word which had not been heard in Western Christendom for hundreds of years. To be sure, there had been disputes and differences of opinion over questions like predestination or the presence of Christ in the Holy Supper. From time to time individuals had been condemned and their opinions declared out of bounds. But there had been no wholesale defections from the church as there had been with the Marcionites or the Arians. For almost seven hundred years Western Christendom had proved a remarkably cohesive body.

But in the twelfth century "heretics" in the sense of separate groups began to reappear. While a variety of reasons, social and economic, could be cited to account for this development, there can be no doubt that one of the principal reasons was the decaying morale and the cheap politics of the church at its highest levels. Although the New Testament was not generally known or read (remember that there were no printing presses and illiteracy was high), enough of it remained in the understanding of many people to make them aware that the gospel of Jesus Christ had little in common with the grabbing for power and the shameless greed that so strongly characterized the life of the church.

THE CATHARI

Sometimes these protests took an extreme form. Most extreme were a group of people generally known as the "Cathari" (which means "pure ones"). Their origins are difficult to trace, although it seems that they spread into Western Europe from the East. Their ideas were strangely like those of the Gnostics from whom, indeed, they may have been remotely descended. They believed in the evil nature of all material things, a dualistic struggle between a Good Spirit and an Evil One, and the need of the soul to free itself from the evils of bodily existence.

There is little need to rehearse the peculiar ideas of the Cathari (sometimes they are called the Albigenses) since they do so closely resemble the Gnostics. What is important is the fact that these ideas must be seen as a protest against the materialism and corruption of the church. No one would ever have taken these ancient Gnostic teachings seriously had not the situation in the church given a religion which had its foundation in anti-materialism an attractiveness it would not otherwise have possessed. If greed for gain is the obvious faith of the only religion you know, you will easily be attracted, if you have any religious sincerity, by one which flatly declares that all material things are evil.

Not all the protests took such extreme forms as those of the Cathari. Although the full story is surrounded with a great deal of obscurity, we can say with certainty that about the year 1176 Peter Waldo, a wealthy merchant in the French city of Lyons, was moved by his understanding of the gospel to give away all of his possessions to the poor. In itself that would not have seemed strange. If Peter Waldo had done that and then entered a monastery, he would have been no different from many other men of his time.

But apparently that was not his aim. Having voluntarily adopted poverty, Waldo wanted to become a preacher of the gospel. In fact he seems to have gathered a small company of people about him who with him became wandering preachers, proclaiming the message of the gospel in marketplaces, on street corners, or wherever they could get a hearing.

This activity incurred the opposition of the official church, for preaching was something which was not to be undertaken except under proper supervision. On several occasions Waldo and his followers were told to desist from their preaching activities. They refused, believing that they were called by a higher authority than the papacy. In 1184 he was therefore excommunicated for his refusal to obey.

THE WALDENSES

That was not to be the end of his story. Forced out of the Western church, a situation which Peter Waldo had never desired, he saw no alternative but to continue his own church. It was a very simple structure, organized as nearly as possible after the pattern of the New Testament. To make this charter of his faith available to all of his followers, Waldo translated it into Provençal, one of the dialects of that part of France in which he lived.

An indication of the dissatisfaction which men felt with the life of the church can be found in the fact that within twenty years Waldo had followers on both the French and Italian sides of the Alps as well as in parts of Germany and Spain. In fact, by the year 1209 they had grown to such size that an official crusade against them was instituted by the pope. Despite repeated persecution during the thirteenth century, the Waldensians survived, especially in northern Italy. Though their history has been a somewhat complicated one, we should say that they continue as a church to this very day. They have been called the oldest Protestant church in Italy.

Such large defections from the church as the Cathari and the Waldensians indicated a much larger dissatisfaction with the life of the church which had to be met in some way. Unfortunately the typical reaction of the official church was to persecute. This was the beginning of a systematic Inquisition. In 1211 eighty Waldensians were burned at Strasbourg; in 1237 another fifteen lost their lives similarly in Spain. But persecution seldom succeeds; in fact, as the church should have known from its own past experience, the more bitter the persecution the faster the persecuted movement grows. It was somewhat ironic that the Christian church in the early thirteenth century had to learn again the lesson which the Roman Empire had learned a thousand years earlier. "The blood of the martyrs is the seed of the Church."

At least two Christian leaders of the time had different ways of approaching the problem. Their solutions were sufficiently different to warrant our giving them separate study. Remember as we look at the career of each that he was trying to stop the inroads that these separatist groups were making in the strength of the official church.

DOMINIC

In the year 1203 a young Spanish priest named Dominic (he was 33 at the time) went with a group of his companions on a preaching tour among the Cathari. They had been commissioned for the task by Pope Innocent III. It should be stated that the preaching mission was merely an adjunct to a military campaign. If the Cathari refused to listen to the preachers, they were then to be put down by force of arms. In fact, this crusade, which lasted from about 1208 to 1215, turned into a bloody civil war in southern France as the Cathari were put to the sword by the hundreds.

But even in such circumstances Dominic saw the challenge. He realized that one of the great reasons why heresies and separatist groups had grown to such size was the way in which the church had abandoned its responsibility to preach the gospel. The absence of the Word of God from the worship of the church, together with its corrupt life, made it easy for well-intentioned men to fall prey to the teachings of the Cathari. They had never been properly taught by their own church.

Traveling through the Cathari country in extreme simplicity, Dominic preached the gospel wherever he had the chance. Sometimes it was in the open air; at other times he got the use of the castle of a friendly nobleman. Wherever possible he tried to meet with the Cathari leaders and reason with them. Some of these formal debates lasted for days. While we have no statistics, the report is that many were converted by the preaching of Dominic and his associates and returned to the church.

Apparently the results were not all that Dominic had hoped for. His last sermon in Languedoc, a Cathari stronghold, contained the following passage.

> For many years I have exhorted you in vain, with gentleness, preaching, praying and weeping. But according to the proverb of my country, 'where blessing can accomplish nothing, blows may avail.' We shall rouse against you princes and prelates, who, alas, will arm nations and kingdoms against this land . . . and thus blows will avail where blessings and gentleness have been powerless.[1]

The real contribution that Dominic made to the life of the church, was not his preaching mission to the Cathari, however we may estimate its success. It was rather the result of the conviction which grew in Dominic's mind during the ten years he spent working with the heretics. He and his companions in the mission became more and more certain that the existence of the Cathari and the Waldenses indicated a vacuum in the life of the church which needed to be filled. There ought to be an order of priests devoted to nothing but study and preaching, a group which could be available to move in anywhere to conduct preaching missions. At least if in the future this lack in the life of the church was remedied, there might be no need for crusades against the Cathari and persecutions of the Waldensians.

In 1216, therefore, Dominic appealed to the pope to grant him the

This is the charge which Dominic is said to have given his followers as he sent them out as Preachers:

"You are still a small flock . . . but already I have formed in my heart the purpose of dispersing you abroad. . . . The world henceforth is your home, and the work God has created for you is teaching and preaching. Go you, therefore, into the whole world and teach all nations. Preach to them the glad tidings of their redemption. Have confidence in God, for the field of your labours will one day widen to the uttermost ends of the earth."[2]

right to establish such an order. Having obtained preliminary approval, he spent the next few years traveling through Italy, Spain, and France, collecting recruits and organizing chapters. By 1220 his work had met with sufficient success and the Order of Preachers held its first general chapter in the Italian city of Bologna. Dominic did not live long after the realization of his dream. Taken ill while on a preaching mission in Hungary, he returned to Bologna where he died in 1221.

The vision which Dominic had did not die with him. His new movement grew and prospered. Despite his desire to have it called the "Order of Preachers," it became popularly known as the Dominicans. Within a few years of his death Dominican brothers were preaching the gospel all across Europe and even into Asia. And it should be added that intensive and careful theological study formed an essential part of Dominic's plan for the preparation of preachers. (He was almost Presbyterian in his insistence that only those who had been thoroughly trained should be commissioned to preach the gospel!) Small wonder that in later years, as we shall see, it was Dominic's order which produced the greatest thinker in medieval history!

The pope during Dominic's early career was a man named Innocent III, one of the most politically capable men ever to occupy the papal throne. A French bishop who visited Rome during Innocent's reign left this record of his impressions.

> In the time that I spent at the Curia [the papal court], I saw much that I was entirely dissatisfied with; everybody was so taken up with worldly and temporal affairs of politics and law, that it was hardly possible to speak or to hear a single word on spiritual matters.[3]

If that was the impression left on churchmen by the heart of the church itself, should we wonder that there were those who felt that Dominic's solution to the problem, noble as it was, was not nearly radical enough?

FRANCIS OF ASSISI

There is an old story, possibly legendary, which tells how Pope Innocent once dreamed that he saw the great Lateran Church in Rome cracking in two. No one was able to help until a little man whom nobody knew appeared on the scene and, putting his loving arms around the building, made the crack disappear.

That little man was named Francis and he was born in the Italian town of Assisi in 1181. The son of a wealthy merchant, Francis was a playboy, ready for any gay adventure, without a care in the world. Only when his desire for thrills resulted in his being taken prisoner in a border dispute between Assisi and Perugia and his returning home severely ill did Francis begin to think seriously about the meaning of his life.

One wonders whether Francis had in some way heard of Peter Waldo, for his first reactions were much like those of Waldo. Giving away everything he owned (and some things his wealthy father owned as well), Francis began to live as one of the poor. His refusal to abandon what his father thought was an insane way of life led to a family rupture in 1207, after which Francis was on his own.

As a gay young man-about-town Francis had never done things cautiously. Now in his new career he preserved the same characteristics. His enthusiasm won him a handful of associates who joined him in his vow of absolute poverty. Their only dress a simple robe of undyed wool bound at the waist with a rope, their only food whatever they were given, they went two by two joyfully telling about the love of God in Jesus Christ, making the little and unwanted people of the world their special mission.

By 1209 Francis' movement called the Order of Brothers Minor, had grown to the point that he felt it should have simple organization and papal blessing. Drawing up a very simple rule, he went with his brethren to Innocent III to secure his approval. Tradition has it that he appeared before the pope the very morning after the pope had

Although the original Rule which Francis submitted to Innocent III for his approval has been lost, it is thought to have been a simple one. The first statement probably went like this:

The Rule and life of the brothers is this: namely, to live in obedience, in chastity and without property, and to follow the teaching and in the footsteps of our Lord Jesus Christ Who says: "If thou wilt be perfect, go, sell what thou hast and give to the poor and thou shalt have treasure in heaven; and come follow Me"; also: "If any man will come after Me, let him deny himself and take up his cross and follow Me"; again: "If any man come to Me and hate not his father and mother and wife and children and brethren and sisters, yea and his own life also, he cannot be My disciple; and everyone that hath left father or mother, brethren or sisters, wife or children, houses or lands, for My sake shall receive a hundred-fold and shall possess life everlasting."[4]

dreamed of the little man who had held the church together, and that when Innocent saw Francis he recognized him as the man. Whether that is true or not, Innocent did not commit the blunder of his predecessor who had excommunicated Peter Waldo when he had come with a similar request. Francis went away with Innocent's blessing, and what we know today as the Franciscan order was organized.

To Francis the papal blessing was a charter to make the world his parish. Caring little about organization or rules, he was interested only in carrying on his work with brothers who shared his dedication. We should add with sisters too, for in the year 1212 Clara Sciffi, a girl of eighteen, was acknowledged by Francis as the leader of a similar group of women. In cheerful simplicity, using Assisi as an informal base of operations, Francis and his brothers went on their informal preaching tours wherever they felt led, sometimes in their own towns and villages in Italy, sometimes as far away as Egypt and Palestine.

It was, of course, the radiance of Francis' personality that made the success of his mission. With trust as simple as that of a child, he thought of all creatures as his brethren. He had only one purpose in life and that is summarized in the beginning of the prayer which is attributed to him, "Lord, make me an instrument of Thy peace. Where there is hatred, let me sow love . . ." Probably no one in all the history of the church has left such an impression of Christlikeness. Toward the end of his life there appeared on his body five marks, called the "stigmata," in the places where our Lord was wounded on the cross. Whether these were the psychological result of his deep meditation on the passion of Christ or whether, as the Roman Church affirms, a miracle, the fact of their existence is well attested and bears witness to the way in which he identified himself totally with Jesus Christ. When he died in 1226, as one of his early biographers puts it, "He entered eternity, singing."

We do have to notice, however, that during the last years of Francis' life the movement which he had begun was increasingly taken out of his control. Partly because he had no liking for organization and partly because the Roman Curia had no liking for such a freewheeling movement, more and more rules and restrictions were developed and their control and administration were placed in other hands. Though Francis must have felt disappointed by this attempt to regularize what he had conceived as a movement of the spirit, he never rebelled. His bitterness can be gathered, however, from what he said to Cardinal Ugolino in 1218 when the possibility of stricter regulations was under discussion.

> I want you to talk of no Rule to me . . . nor any way or form of life except that which God has mercifully pointed out and granted to me. . . . By your science and syllogisms God will confound you, and I trust in God's warders, the Devils, that through them God shall punish you, and you will yet come back to your proper station with shame, whether you will or no.[5]

But his protests were unavailing and as his movement changed more and more from his original ideal, Francis became more and more of a lonely hermit, never rejecting the decision of the church, but simply withdrawing to do his own work in his own way.

We could wish that an earlier pope had had the grace and the vision to include Peter Waldo in the company of those who were devoted to the renewal of the church. For in the opinion of an outstanding American Protestant church historian, men like Dominic and Francis were able to save a bad situation. Writes Williston Walker,

> It [the Franciscan order] and the Dominican body largely won back the popular support which had seemed to be slipping away from the church. They presented a type of piety that appealed to the best men of the age. They took up into the service of the church that which had most attracted men in the Cathari and Waldenses, and by so doing overcame the opposition which had given to those "heretical" movements their chief support. They profoundly deepened and quickened the popular religious life.[6]

In an age like ours when the church must also face the loss of popular support in many places, we should do well to notice the need for the approach of both Dominic and Francis. Dominic's was intellectual while that of Francis was practical. There are those in our day who try to play off one against the other. But the need for careful study and sound preaching is just as great as the need for a sincere Christian style of life in the world. They are not opposites, but complement each other. Dominic without Francis becomes academic and sterile; Francis without Dominic can become sentimental and vague. To win the world the church needs men who know what they are doing and are not afraid to do it.

12

The Age of the Builders

If you were asked to name the greatest century in human history, how would you vote? Such poll-taking would result in all kinds of answers, but we can safely assume that few, if any, of your friends and associates would name the thirteenth century as their answer. In fact, we tend to think of the thirteenth century as belonging to that nondescript stretch of time we call the Dark Ages, an era filled with blood and barbarism.

Yet the fact is that many responsible historians, if they were asked a similar question, would probably name the thirteenth century as the greatest in human history. The evidence is quite impressive. It was during this century that many of the great universities in the world were developed, Oxford and Paris, for example. It was during this century that Christian theology through the work of men like Thomas Aquinas and Duns Scotus became the "queen of the sciences."

All of these facts, however, as well as many others which could be brought into evidence, would merely be signs of the great achievement of the thirteenth century. It was in this century that Western Europe became Christendom, a political and economic unit the entire life of which was deeply penetrated by Christian principles and Christian ideals. Indeed, some historians have argued that the thirteenth century represents the high-water mark of Christian influence upon society. Never before, they would say, and certainly never since had the Christian gospel so deeply and so significantly influenced society.

Take, for example, the very appearance of a thirteenth century town or city. The skyline of one of our American towns or cities is a very mixed-up thing with office buildings, hotels, smokestacks all competing for attention. In many of our larger cities even the tallest church spire is too small to be seen from any distance. Look at New York or Chicago from a distance and try to find a church!

But the thirteenth century city or town was dominated by the church building. Not only did it stand in the center of the town, but it dominated the landscape. The Gothic architecture which the thirteenth century developed was characterized by a relentless upward thrust, almost as though it wanted to take the whole community and lift it toward heaven. This kind of town planning and town building was a symbol of the way thirteenth century man thought. The center of his life was not a bank or a factory but a cathedral.

Or consider the way in which in this century the church dominated the economic life of the community. Interest rates, which today are a fully accepted part of our economic life, were strictly forbidden on what were believed to be Christian principles. Most of the trade and commerce was carried on through guilds, the grocers' guild, the pepperer's guild, the wool-merchants' guild (some of which still survive in England, though largely as social organizations). All of these guilds were religiously organized and religiously oriented. The prices they could charge and the wages that they paid were determined on Christian principles.

Most important of all, the presence in every community of monasteries with their communal ideas meant that private wealth and private aggrandizement was not the accepted standard. The prominence and prestige of monasteries set a pattern in caring for the poor, who were just as numerous in thirteenth century society as in ours. A sense of responsibility for the needy was deeply inserted into society because of the dominance of Christian influence.

It would be possible to go on at some length discussing the social changes and improvements which took place in this century. It was a time which saw the development of hospitals and homes for the aged and poor. It was a time which saw the gradual improvement of the lot of the serf, whose place in life was almost that of slave. It was a time which saw many men of lowly origin rise to high position in the life of the church. It was a time which saw new respect for women, as symbolized in the development of knighthood and chivalry.

THE INTELLECTUAL CHALLENGE

Certainly the most lasting achievement of the thirteenth century was an intellectual one. It was the time in which the Christian faith was presented and accepted as the crown of all knowledge, the premise without which science and learning were empty and useless endeavors. And since this achievement was so largely the work of one man, we had best stop and have a longer look at him.

The thirteenth century was a time of exciting intellectual discovery and renewal. Much of the new science and learning which came to Western Europe at this time came from the Arabs who, it will be remembered, had pushed as far west as Spain. In many ways they had preserved a greater link with the science of the past than had the

Western European Christians. In Western Europe barbarian invasions and political upheavals had pretty well obliterated the intellectual achievements of the ancient world. Even the books of ancient thinkers and philosophers had been destroyed. But Islamic thinkers had preserved them and made them the basis for further research and development, especially in the fields of mathematics and philosophy. (Did you ever think through, for example, the implications of the fact that our system of numbers to this day is *Arabic?*)

The chief ancient thinker whom the Arabs had used was the philosopher Aristotle. Now that Western Europe had reached some stability and order, Christian thinkers began to be interested in Arabic science and to discover Aristotle too. But in many ways he was a disturbing discovery. Certain of Aristotle's positions were in complete contradiction to the Christian faith. Aristotle's God, for example, was in no way like the God of the Bible. He was impersonal, an unmoved Mover, completely detached from the human scene and situation. The new science seemed to be a real threat to the Christian faith, much in the same way as Darwin's writings seemed to threaten that faith a century ago. How could a man be intellectual and scientific and still be a Christian? This was the question which educated people in the thirteenth century began to ask. And certainly it is one with which we are not unfamiliar.

See if you can follow the line of thinking of Thomas Aquinas in these ideas on how God rules the world. They deal with the questions of philosophers, to be sure; but the questions are also those we asked as children when we were always wanting to know why?

Whether the World Is Governed by Anyone?

. . . I answer that, Certain ancient philosophers denied the government of the world, saying that all things happened by chance. But such an opinion can be refuted as impossible in two ways. First, by the observation of things themselves. For we observe that in nature things happen always or nearly always for the best; which would not be the case unless some sort of providence directed nature towards good as an end. . . . Secondly, this is clear from a consideration of the divine goodness, which, as we have said above, is the cause of the production of things in being. . . . Now a thing's ultimate perfection consists in the attainment of its end. Therefore it belongs to the divine goodness, as it brought things into being, so to lead them to their end. And this is to govern. . . .

THOMAS AQUINAS

The apparent conflict between faith and reason disturbed a great many people but none more than an Italian friar named Thomas Aquinas. The story of his life can be told very simply. Born into a noble family in 1225, he felt challenged by the need for an intellectual restatement of the Christian faith when he was only fifteen. He resolved to join the Dominicans, whose point of view was congenial to him. His family was horrified at the thought and for fifteen months kept him a virtual prisoner in the family castle while they tried to change his mind.

But Thomas' mind was not that easily changed. He joined the Dominican order in 1244 and until his death thirty years later he was student, teacher, thinker, and writer. While he lived in various Dominican houses, most of his career was spent in Paris. His two great works were his *Summa Contra Gentiles,* which was intended to be a textbook for Christian missionaries to the Arab world, and his *Summa Theologica,* which took all the findings of the modern science of that day and used them in a carefully reasoned presentation of the Christian faith.

They do not make very exciting reading today. For one thing many of the problems which bothered the thirteenth century no longer bother us. For another thing, Thomas wrote in a very matter-of-fact and analytical way, using the question and answer method. It would not even be possible to give a brief outline of so vast a system as

Whether the World Is Governed by One?

... *I answer that,* We must of necessity say that the world is governed by one. For since the end of the government of the world is that which is essentially good, which is the greatest good, the government of the world must be the best kind of government. Now the best government is government by one. ... This is expressed by the Philosopher [Aristotle]: *Things refuse to be ill governed; and multiplicity of authorities is a bad thing. Therefore there should be one ruler.* ...

Whether All Things Are Immediately Governed by God?

... *I answer that,* In government there are two things to be considered: the nature of government, which is providence itself; and the execution of government. As to the nature of government, God governs all things immediately; whereas in its execution, He governs some things by means of others. ...

Whether Creatures Need to Be Kept in Being by God?

... *I answer that,* Both reason and faith require us to say that creatures are kept in being by God. ... For the being of every creature depends on God, so that not for a moment could it subsist, but would fall into nothingness, were it not kept in being by the operation of the divine power, as Gregory says. ...

Thomas worked out, covering the whole range of Christian doctrine from creation to the end of the world, carefully assigning what things can be known by reason and what things can be known only by revelation. We can say, however, that the chief characteristic of Thomas' presentation is that he maintains that Christianity is a reasonable faith. Though reason cannot discover its final truth, that final truth contains nothing contrary to reason.

Aquinas' presentation of the Christian faith (sometimes known as Thomism) not only met the intellectual needs of his own time, but has been the official theology of the Roman Catholic Church to this day. Through him, in a very real sense, the thirteenth century still speaks to the twentieth century. Like the cathedrals and universities of the same age, Thomism is one of the living monuments to the greatness of the thirteenth century.

To be sure, many criticisms could be made of this century. It was not Utopia. But when due allowance has been made for all the criticisms, we still have to admit that it represents one of the great achievements in the history of the church. Far from being a part of the Dark Ages, the century of Aquinas, cathedrals, and universities was one of the great times of Christian accomplishment. We are still indebted to it. Perhaps as never again in history, all aspects of human life were pulled together and organized around the center of the church. We must agree that the thirteenth was one of the greatest centuries in Christian history.

Whether God Conserves Every Creature Immediately?

. . . God created all things immediately, but in the creation itself He established an order among things, so that some depend on others, by which they are conserved in being; though He remains the principal cause of their conservation. . . .

Whether God Can Do Anything Outside the Established Order of Nature?

. . . If . . . we consider the order of things according as it depends on the first cause, God cannot do anything against this order; for, if He did so, He would act against His foreknowledge, or His will, or His goodness. But if we consider the order of things according as it depends on any secondary cause, thus God can do something outside such order. For He is not subject to the order of secondary causes, but, on the contrary, this order is subject to Him. . . . Therefore since the order of nature is given to things by God, if He does anything outside this order, it is not against nature. Hence Augustine says: *That is natural to each thing which is caused by Him from Whom is all limit, number and order in nature.*

—from "Treatise on the Divine Government" in *Summa Theologica*[1]

FROM CLIMAX TO DECLINE

That very fact poses an interesting problem. Why was everything gained in that century so quickly lost? If, let us say, by the year 1300 the Christian church had reached the high-water mark of prestige and influence in Western Europe, how could it have touched such depths of disorderliness and lack of respect by 1500 that a Luther was necessary? What happened that one of the great Christian centuries was the prelude to one of the worst Christian collapses?

There is no easy or single answer to such a question. We can begin, however, by quoting a legend that is told of Francis of Assisi. He was being shown through the Vatican by the pope, who pointed out the many treasures which belonged to the church. "You see," said the pope, "I can no longer say, as Peter once did, 'silver and gold have I none.'" "No, sire," was the reply. "Nor can you say, as Peter once did, 'Rise up and walk.'"

In other words, one of the first reasons for the failure of the church to maintain what had been won was its deep implication in material success. It is an easy thing to say that the church in the Middle Ages became more concerned with its own institutional prosperity than it did with the Kingdom of God. Yet it is true. Not all at once, perhaps, but nonetheless certainly the church came to measure spiritual significance in terms of popular esteem, material prosperity, and worldly influence. That kind of false measuring rod spelled disaster ahead.

At this point the story of the church in the Middle Ages should pose some embarrassing and significant questions for the chuch in twentieth century America. Although we see their mistake, do we have the courage to examine our own lives in the light of it? Institutional success, large numbers, material prosperity—are these not frequently the standards we use to measure a church? Almost the first question we ask of someone about his church is "How many members do you have?" or "How big is your budget?" Just about the last question we ask is "What is your church doing?" We are impressed, not by Gothic cathedrals, but by pretentious parish houses or educational buildings with modern kitchens and good social facilities.

It is not that there is something wrong with these things in themselves. No one is suggesting that the church should go underground again. But there is a subtle temptation in them. Because the thirteenth century church yielded to that temptation, the twentieth century church needs to watch its own life closely at this very point. The temptation is to assume that great achievement in terms of material success means equal achievement in the realm of the spirit. Such an assumption can mean disaster for us just as surely as it meant it for them.

Of course, there were many men in the thirteenth century of whom that was not true. Thomas himself was one of them. There is a medieval legend which tells that one time when he was praying, Thomas had a vision of God, who said to him, "You have served me well, Thomas. Tell me what you want and I will give it to you." Thomas' simple reply was "I want nothing but You, Lord."

But that kind of spirit became increasingly rare as the prestige and success of the church increased. When you have beautiful cathedrals, a position of influence, the admiration and respect of an entire society, power to accomplish your will and purpose, it is not easy to ask yourself what is lacking, and it is easy to be irritated by those who suggest that something is lacking. Their very restlessness could destroy the beautiful thing that you have built.

Resistance against criticism of the church led to the second reason why the great achievement of the thirteenth century could not last. Put in theological terms, the church identified itself with the Kingdom of God. Whoever questioned the life of the church, the policy of the church, the doctrine of the church was questioning the Kingdom of God itself. That Kingdom could not be questioned for God himself had promised that it shall conquer. Because the church had persuaded itself that it was that Kingdom, it would listen to no criticism, tolerate no questions, but simply accepted itself as it was.

The people of God had got themselves into this situation before. Way back in the time of Jeremiah they had convinced themselves that nothing could ever happen to the city of Jerusalem because it was God's dwelling place; as long as the temple was there the city was safe. They believed that even when the Babylonians were almost knocking at the city gates.

The church in the Middle Ages had a similar psychology. Its success was impressive. We have tried to outline some of the dimensions of its impressiveness. But that very success led churchmen to identify themselves so closely with the Kingdom of God that they were convinced that nothing could happen to them. And even when something did begin to happen to them, they could neither see nor believe it.

There is still a third reason for this paradox of success that was a prelude to failure. In his great novel, *The Brothers Karamazov*, Dostoevsky says that the medieval church had really yielded to Christ's third temptation, the temptation to take possession of all the kingdoms of this world and rule them. The accusation may be harsh, but it contains a hard core of truth. In the midst of its great success, the church forgot that it is essentially a servant people. That failure can lead only to decay and disaster.

We must be careful not to oversimplify the case. But it would not be too far from the truth to say that as the thirteenth century came to a close, man was made for the church and not the church for man. Of course, the church had all kinds of things to offer man. It could offer him eternal salvation or eternal damnation. It could offer him the medicine of grace as it was mediated through the system of the seven sacraments. Its refusal to minister the sacraments to him could place him in eternal peril.

Still this is a far cry from seeking and saving the lost. It is a far cry from following Him who took upon Himself the form of a servant. The very rise of one monastic order after another was nothing but a protest against the way in which the church was seeking to rule rather than to serve. But in a short time the same fate overtook the protests. The monastic movement which had begun as an attempt to be a servant people soon became hardened into another institution which had its little empire to control.

That the church faced a real crisis and did not know it is best evidenced by the fact that after Francis and Dominic there were no more protests, or rather, that the protests were ruthlessly silenced. The church had gained control. It would not and could not tolerate whoever threatened that control. In former years when Francis or Dominic came along, the church found a place for them, realizing that they had something to say. In years to come, no place could be found for new protests. The only answer would be prison or the stake. The church had lost its power of self-correction.

We shall be spending some time studying the various efforts at reform before the Reformation itself. At this point it is important to see that the need for reform was to be found not in some future pattern of decay, but in the very image of success itself. The great achievements of the Christian church in the thirteenth century clearly indicated the need for reformation, though nobody at the time would have recognized it.

If persecution and invasion had been a threat to the life of the church, success and dominance was an even greater one. The amazing thing is that the people of God have been able to survive both.

13

Dark Night and Morning Stars

Lord Acton, a great British historian, once wrote "Power tends to corrupt, and absolute power corrupts absolutely." No better illustration of the truth of his statement could be found than the story of the church in the late Middle Ages. The great position of power and influence which had been won for the church in Western Europe by dedicated and sincere men began to be the plaything of ambitious and selfish men. Sooner or later ambitious and selfish men are bound to collide with each other in their struggles for power. This is exactly what happened in the story of the church with the result that in a few short years it slipped from a place of universal respect to one of almost universal shame.

The trouble came to a head with Boniface VIII, who became pope in 1294. Unable to understand the growing feelings of nationalism which were developing all over Europe, Boniface became embroiled in a series of political struggles, chiefly with Philip IV of France. Unable to match Philip's military might, the pope tried to bolster his case by issuing increasingly strong claims of power. In 1301 he claimed jurisdiction over all kings and princes and, when Philip paid no attention, in 1302 he claimed papal jurisdiction over all creatures. The claim became even more ludicrous when the pope became the king's prisoner. Though his troops rescued him after three days, he never recovered from the shock and died in a short time.

The struggle had convinced the French king, however, that future popes must be under his control. Boniface's successor reigned a very short time and was followed in 1305 by Clement V, a French archbishop. The fact that his coronation took place in the French city of Lyons rather than in Rome and that Philip was sitting in the front pew for the service is a good indication of what had happened. The papacy had become the tool of the French king. What everyone had suspected became obvious in 1309 when Clement moved the papal residence from Rome to Avignon, a city which, though not technically in French territory, was certainly under French influence.

THE BABYLONIAN CAPTIVITY

For the next sixty-eight years Avignon rather than Rome was the papal seat and the occupants of the papal throne were all French.

Though there were occasional bickerings between king and pope, to all intents and purposes the church had become a department of the French kingdom and it was French political and diplomatic interests which controlled papal policy. This period is sometimes called "the Babylonian captivity" because the papacy was taken under French control somewhat like the Hebrews were taken captive to Babylon. Though the popes lived in great luxury and were granted generous powers of taxation, they were servants and not masters.

The worst was yet to come. When the papal throne fell vacant in 1378 there was an insistent demand that the next pope should not be French. Yielding to this pressure, the cardinals, though most of them were French, chose an Italian who took the title of Urban VI. They soon regretted their choice. Urban declared his intention to remain in Rome and to reform what he considered the scandalous luxury of the French church and clergy.

The quarrel lasted only a few months when the French, who controlled the college of cardinals, deposed Urban and elected one of their own number as pope, Clement VII. Urban, of course, refused to recognize the validity of their action, appointed his own cardinals, and denounced Clement as an impostor. The result was that the church presented the unedifying spectacle of two popes, one in Rome and the other in Avignon, each claiming to be the true head of the church.

Each of them found considerable support for his claim. France, of course, was on the side of Clement as were Scotland, Spain, and parts of Germany. But Urban was supported by a large part of Germany as well as Italy, England, Scandinavia, Portugal, the Low Countries and central Europe. The once proud church of the thirteenth century was now split almost exactly in half.

Shocking as this state of affairs was and painful to many devout Christians, it continued for about thirty years. During that time all efforts to heal the division were unsuccessful. Pope succeeded pope in both Rome and Avignon and the lines became more tightly drawn. Promises were made which were never kept and the scandal grew as the years passed with no solution to the problem.

Finally in 1409 a council met in Pisa to try to resolve the issue. Widely attended by serious representatives from both groups, the Council of Pisa decided that the only solution to the problem was the removal of both popes and the election of a new one. Following its instructions, the cardinals did just that. But instead of solving the problem, Pisa only made a bad matter worse. Neither the Roman pope nor the Avignon pope would accept his removal so that instead of two there were now three popes, each claiming to be the true head of the church, each receiving some political support.

THE COUNCIL OF CONSTANCE

Another council was summoned in 1414. Meeting in the city of Constance, it managed to solve the problem, though not without some difficulty. The Roman pope resigned at the request of the council. The Pisan pope was deposed for immorality. The Avignon pope was also deposed but refused to accept the council's decision. But by this time all of Europe was so sick of the controversy that he had small support and in a few years the Avignon line petered out. A new pope, Martin V, of an old Roman family and impeccable character was chosen and the division was officially at an end.

It is impossible to estimate the damage done by this power struggle. The church had lost its image of holiness and purity. Thinking men all over Europe had seen it for what it had become, a political institution in which, without concern for the gospel, greedy men battled to hang on to their positions. What would have been unthinkable in the thirteenth century now became common—cynicism and distrust of the integrity of the church and its ministry. Though the Council of Constance succeeded in putting the broken pieces back together again, it would take much more than a council to restore the inner strength which the church had lost.

That same Council of Constance which reunited the papacy also dealt with a man who had tried to restore the inner strength. There had been earlier unrest but the official church had been too preoccupied with its own divisions to give it real attention. John Wycliffe, an English priest and master at Oxford, had become more and more disturbed as he watched the growing deterioration in the life of the church. From his vicarage in Lutterworth, to which he had gone in 1374, Wycliffe wrote in 1379 a scathing attack on the whole papal concept.

A worldly system offering limitless opportunities to those who were hungry for power, Wycliffe argued, could not have been what Christ intended for his church. Like every Christian, the pope must be judged by his conformity to the gospel. To assist them in making that judgment, Christians should have the Bible available in their own languages. Though he never finished the task, Wycliffe began to carry out his own idea by translating the Scriptures into English.

Wycliffe's ideas found fertile soil in England and groups gathered around him called the Poor Preachers, and later, Lollards. They were men who frankly despaired of revitalizing the official church and gave themselves to the simple ministry of the gospel, denying many of the dogmas which the medieval church had developed. Recognizing the laziness and immorality of the monks with their "red and fat cheeks and great bellies," as Wycliffe described them, they sought to bring a simple and direct gospel to the people.

To be sure, news of Wycliffe's teaching reached official ears and all sorts of anathemas were directed against him. But England was far away and the papacy was itself divided so that though he was not permitted to lecture at Oxford, he kept his pastorate at Lutterworth. Although Wycliffe died peacefully in his bed in 1384, in 1415 the Council of Constance condemned him and ordered his body to be exhumed and his writings burned. But ideas have a way of traveling and it was not in England but in Bohemia that Wycliffe found his true successor in the person of John Hus.

JOHN HUS

A brilliant young priest who became rector of the University of Prague before he was thirty-five, Hus was also the most popular preacher in the city. Having read Wycliffe's writings, he became convinced of their essential truth and devoted his great talents to proclaiming them openly. He even translated some of Wycliffe's works into Czech. At first he received some encouragement from his ecclesiastical superiors. Whether this was because they approved of what he had to say or because they realized that he was the favorite of many powerful families among the Czech nobility is hard to decide.

When in about 1405 he began a series of sermons on the immorality of the clergy, his ecclesiastical support began to fade. But for the next

When we think of John Wycliffe, we usually remember his work in the translation of the Bible into the English of his day. Here in one of his books he gives some reasons for that translating.

It seems first that the knowledge of God's law should be taught in that language which is best known, because this knowledge is God's Word. When Christ says in the Gospel that both heaven and earth shall pass away but his words shall not pass away, he means by his "words" his knowledge. Thus God's knowledge is Holy Scripture that may in no wise be false. Also the Holy Spirit gave to the apostles at Pentecost knowledge to know all manner of lan-

few years the papal situation was so confused and Czech support for Hus was so strong that no move could be made against him.

After much maneuvering, however, the Archbishop of Prague finally formed an alliance with the Pisan Pope (this was the time when there were three popes) and secured his excommunication of John Hus in 1411. While this meant that he could no longer continue his official duties as preacher and rector, he was still not silenced. His noble friends took him under their protection, and Hus still preached in one Czech town after another, generally in the open air. By this time, his reputation and his ideas had gained an almost European-wide hearing.

Unfortunately for him church authorities were less trustworthy than political authorities. No sooner had he reached Constance with the emperor's safe-conduct than he was arrested and thrown into prison. When he appeared before the council it was not as a theologian with a case to present but as a heretic on trial for his life. The council had already condemned the teachings of Wycliffe before it took up Hus's case. It was not difficult, therefore, to predict how it would decide. Accused of being a follower of the condemned Wycliffe, Hus replied that he would be willing to renounce any errors, provided the renunciation did not offend God or his conscience. But he had attacked the whole concept of the papacy and the status of the clergy, an attack which was not to be tolerated. The council condemned him, removed him from the priesthood, and turned him over to the secular government for punishment. He was burned at the stake on July 6, 1415.

But that was not the end of the matter. Not only did Hus become a kind of national martyr in his native Bohemia to the extent that a civil

---

guages to teach the people God's law thereby; and so God willed that the people be taught his law in divers tongues. But what man on God's behalf should reverse God's ordinance and his will? For this reason Saint Jerome labored and translated the Bible from divers tongues into Latin that it might after be translated into other tongues. Thus Christ and his apostles taught the people in that tongue that was best known to them. Why should men not do so now? . . . This is especially so since all Christian men, learned and ignorant, who should be saved might always follow Christ and know his teaching and his life. . . . I well know that there may be faults in unfaithful translating as there might have been many faults in turning from Hebrew into Greek and from Greek into Latin, and from one language into another. But let men live a good life, and let many study God's law, and when errors are found let them who reason well correct them. . . . May God move lords and bishops to stand up for the knowing of his law.[1]
—John Wycliffe, *On the Pastoral Office*, Part II. 2a

war ensued between his followers and his opponents, but his ideas lived on in the minds of other men, though after what had happened they were understandably more cautious in proclaiming them openly. Though there was no open rebellion, there were signs of much ferment and dissatisfaction.

BRETHREN OF THE COMMON LIFE

In the Netherlands, for example, there had for some years been a movement called the "Brethren of the Common Life." A free association of spiritually minded men, it was a monastic order without vows, laying great stress on devotion and education. In their quiet way some of the brethren wrote and taught exactly as Hus had done. John Pupper was one of them. For him only the Bible had final authority; pope, bishop, or council can be mistaken if they disagree with the Scripture. The inner disposition of the soul was the essential thing; outward religious formalism profited nothing.

A more famous representative of this group was Wessel Gansvoort. After a long period of doubt, Gansvoort came to believe that only the Bible could be a final authority. The church was for him a spiritual fellowship, its priests only the ministers of God who had no powers of their own. Men like Pupper and Gansvoort were saying exactly what

A Hymn of the Bohemian Brethren

Congregational singing was an important part of the life of the followers of John Hus, the Bohemian Brethren, as it is of their spiritual descendents, the Moravian Church. This hymn, based on Psalm 48, was written in Czech in the sixteenth century and translated into German. In these stanzas you will recognize the assurance of God's protection and the place of the word and sacraments in the church.

Praise God for ever:
  Boundless is His favor
To His Church and chosen flock,
Founded on Christ, the Rock,
  Jesus, God's own Son,
  On His fair Mount Zion,
By His Spirit, grace and word:
Blest city of the Lord,
Thou in spite of every powerful foe
Shalt unshaken stand, and prospering grow,
  'Midst disgrace, to God's praise,
  Both in love and unity:
  Praise God eternally.

How great the blessing,
All our thought surpassing,
In His word and sacrament,
In His wise government;—
  Our homes surrounded
  With His love unbounded;
And the teachers or His word,
Gifts from the risen Lord;—
'Midst His flock He dwells Himself, our God,
Jacob's Lord, the Lord of Sabaoth;
  O what grace He displays
  Praise, thanksgiving, majesty,
  Be His eternally![2]
      —John Augusta, 1500–72

Wycliffe and Hus had said before them. But perhaps because they said them quietly and in their own circles, they were never brought before ecclesiastical authority.

What is still more striking, of course, is to compare the positions of men like these with that of Martin Luther. The similarities are striking; the differences are small. In fact Luther himself, who had not read John Hus until after his rupture with the Roman Church, acknowledged that in many ways he could have been called a Hussite. Why was it then that the Reformation did not come sooner than it did, since so many men were thinking this way for so long a time?

In a very real sense that is a question that has no answer. Looking back from our vantage point we can see that many events in history could have happened before they did and we do not really know why they did not. But it is possible to suggest some factors which contributed to the defeat of men like Wycliffe and Hus, the ignoring of men like Pupper and Gansvoort, and the success of a man like Luther.

In the time of Wycliffe and Hus learning and education were still the privilege of a very few. The free discussion of ideas was limited to the specialists. Printing had not yet been invented and the dissemination of ideas was a very difficult process. One of the significant things to remember is that between Hus and Luther a man named Gutenberg had invented what today we should call the printing press. By Luther's time, though printing was still difficult and expensive, books could be printed and circulated. For every one person who knew what Hus was saying, therefore, there were a thousand who knew what Luther was saying.

To this must be added the fact that in 1453 the great city of Constantinople which had held out for so many centuries finally fell to the Mohammedans. Refugee scholars scattered all over Europe, much as they did from Germany in the days of the Nazis, bringing new ideas and new insights with them. We cannot, of course, trace out an exact cause and effect relationship. But we can certainly recognize that the intellectual climate in Europe in 1515 was very different from what it had been in 1415.

During the almost hundred years between Hus and Luther the life of the church had deteriorated markedly. What had been visible to only a few in 1415 was an open scandal and shame by 1515. Men whose private morals would have been shocking in any modern American scandal sheet had occupied the papal throne. High ecclesiastical offices had been sold to the highest bidder openly and without shame. The ecclesiastic who was not using his position to line his own pockets was rare indeed. Matters had gone from bad to worse in such a way that by 1515 even the simple man in the street knew that the church was sick unto death.

If he did not know it, there were capable men who were anxious to tell him. One of the most capable was a product of those same Brethren of the Common Life from whose ranks Pupper and Gansvoort had come. Desiderius Erasmus, though ordained a priest, preferred the life of a wandering scholar. But in addition to great scholarship, Erasmus had a merciless pen. His satires on the corruptions of the clergy made the church the laughing stock of all Europe. Published in 1509, his *Praise of Folly* perhaps did more than any other single work to prepare the way for the Reformation. In Hus's time the church was an institution which the common man never dared to criticize because he stood in such awe of it. But after Erasmus, it was a joke.

These were some of the reasons why, though there were morning stars of the Reformation, the new day did not dawn sooner. Some historians would argue that there were other factors such as the rapid increase of national feeling during the century between Hus and Luther or the personality of Luther himself, who was certainly of the stuff of which heroes are made. Doubtless any complete account of the situation would have to pay attention to such considerations as well as the ones that we have mentioned.

The point is, however, that by 1500 the Christian church was confronted with one of the greatest crises in its history. It had become inwardly weak and corrupt; it had lost the respect of almost everyone. Worse still, it was seriously threatened by the new learning which increasingly sought to dismiss the religion of the church as superstition and seek for the solution to human problems in education and reason. All kinds of revolutions were rising, national revolutions, economic revolutions, intellectual revolutions. Though men did not know it at the time, modern Europe was struggling to be born; and that at a time when the Christian church was at one of the lowest points in its entire history.

How could a church which had murdered its own prophets possibly be strong enough to meet the challenge of such a desperately difficult future? Many men in 1500 must have wondered whether in the new Europe that was gradually emerging there would be any Christianity at all.

PART IV
THE CHURCH REFORMS ITSELF

The Major Reformation Cities

WE thank Thee, O God, the Father of our Lord Jesus Christ, that Thou hast revealed Thy Son to us, on Whom we have believed, Whom we have loved, and Whom we worship. O Lord Jesus Christ, we commend our souls to Thee. O heavenly Father, we know that although we shall in Thine own good time be taken away from this life, we shall live for ever with Thee. "God so loved the world, that He gave His only begotten Son, that whosoever believeth in Him, should not perish, but have everlasting life." Father, into Thy hands we commend our spirits; through Jesus Christ our Lord. Amen.[1] —Martin Luther

ALMIGHTY and merciful God, who art the Strength of the weak, the Refreshment of the weary, the Comfort of the sad, the Help of the tempted, the Life of the dying, the God of patience and of all consolation; Thou knowest full well the inner weakness of our nature, how we tremble and quiver before pain, and cannot bear the cross without Thy Divine help and support. Help me, then, O eternal and pitying God, help me to possess my soul in patience, to maintain unshaken hope in Thee, to keep that childlike trust which feels a Father's heart hidden beneath the cross; so shall I be strengthened with power according to Thy glorious might, in all patience and long-suffering; I shall be enabled to endure pain and temptation, and, in the very depth of my suffering, to praise Thee with a joyful heart—Amen.[2]
—Johann Habermann, 1516–1590, whose prayers were used by Anabaptists, Lutherans, and Reformed.

MOST gracious GOD, our heavenly Father! in whom alone dwelleth all fulness of light and wisdom: Illuminate our minds, we beseech thee, by thine Holy Spirit, in the true understanding of thy word. Give us grace that we may receive it with reverence and humility unfeigned. May it lead us to put our whole trust in thee alone; and so to serve and honour thee, that we may glorify thy holy name, and edify our neighbours by a good example. And since it hath pleased thee to number us among thy people: O help us to pay thee the love and homage that we owe, as children to our Father, and as servants to our Lord. We ask this for the sake of our Master and Saviour . . . Amen.[3] —John Calvin

14
Here I Stand

The strangest thing about Martin Luther is that he never intended to reform the church. He was seeking to solve his own deep spiritual problem. To be sure, when he realized that the solution of his own problem brought him into ever increasing conflict with the official life and teachings of the church, he did not shrink from those consequences. But though he may have been as sensitive to the weaknesses and errors of the church as Wycliffe or Hus, Luther did not begin by openly attacking those weaknesses and errors. He began by attacking Martin Luther's own inner need.

Born in 1483 in the German town of Eisleben, Luther came from a sturdy peasant family which was anxious that he have an education. They sent him to the University of Erfurt from which he graduated in 1505 with a master's degree in philosophy. As far as we know, all throughout his student days Luther was a competent scholar as well as a popular and convivial person. Even though the philosophy taught at Erfurt was of an advanced kind, there is no indication that the young Luther was at all disturbed in his traditional religious position. Apparently he fully accepted all of the dogmas and practices of the medieval church. His father's ambition for Martin was the law and immediately after graduation from Erfurt he studied for that profession.

What could well be called the most significant thunderstorm in history suddenly changed his whole career. Caught in a fierce electrical storm in July, 1505, Luther was knocked down by a bolt of lightning. Certain that he would be killed, he called on St. Anne for help, promising to become a monk if his life were spared. That impulsive vow indicates the degree to which the young student was still the prisoner of the superstitions of his age. As good as his word, Luther entered the Augustinian monastery in Erfurt less than a month later, much to the disgust of his father. On so slender a thread as a thunderstorm history hangs! Luther the lawyer might never have been heard of; Luther the monk changed the whole story of the Western world.

THE UNHAPPY MONK

The experience of the thunderstorm must have given shape to many of the secret fears that were hidden in the mind and heart of an apparently gay young student. For from the day of his entrance into the monastery, Luther was melancholy and depressed. He was certain that he was a sinner doomed to hell. Nothing he could do gave him any hope, any assurance of salvation. With characteristic abandon, he threw himself energetically into fasting, prayer, and religious exercises of every kind, but none of them brought peace to his tormented spirit.

Ordained as a priest in 1507, he was terrified to say his first mass. The more he studied theology, the more distressed and confused he became. In 1508 he went as a lecturer to the almost new University of Wittenberg where he ultimately earned a doctor's degree in theology and became professor of Scripture. He found great help in the advice and counsel of an older monk, Staupitz, who tried to bring his young friend through this dark night of the soul. A brilliant student, a gifted lecturer, a promising young professor in a university faculty, Martin Luther was still a miserable man who sometimes, as he later confessed, almost hated God because he could not feel at peace with Him.

From the years 1513 to 1515 he was lecturing on the Psalms and on Paul's Letter to the Romans. Sometime during this period he began to find what he had been looking for. It came to him in a single phrase from Romans (which is itself a quotation from Habakkuk), "The just shall live by faith" (Rom. 1:17 K.J.V.). It was his meditation on that phrase that set him free from the long struggle in which he had been engaged. The uselessness of the vigils and fastings, the exercises and disciplines in which he had tried to find peace was now apparent. The one thing necessary was a wholehearted confidence in the mercy of God as shown in the cross of Jesus Christ. Surrender to that God brought the assurance and hope which Luther had struggled to find for almost ten years.

Naturally Luther's personal experience of "justification by faith" became the center of his preaching and teaching. Because his had been a very deep experience, he became a forceful preacher and teacher. He was not talking about a theological proposition; he was describing his own deliverance from darkness into light. It may have crossed his mind that the implications of his preaching could have disastrous effects on many of the official dogmas of the church. But about that he was not concerned. The positive preaching of the gospel of free grace and forgiveness in Jesus Christ was his chief concern and task.

TETZEL'S CHALLENGE

It is even conceivable that the church might never have disturbed him in this preaching and teaching had not an episode in a neighboring town brought the situation to a head. The pope was trying to raise money to complete the new St. Peter's in Rome and had shamelessly sold the archbishopric of Mainz to the highest bidder, Prince Albert of Brandenburg. Needless to say, the new archbishop was anxious to get back what he had had to put out for the purchase of his office. To help raise the money, he had secured the services of a Dominican monk named Tetzel, who had a great reputation as a money-raiser through the sale of indulgences.

In granting an indulgence the church claimed the power to release a person, living or dead, from temporal punishment due to sin. This was done through the application of some of the extra merits of the saints (their prayers and good works) to the person needing indulgence. While purchasing indulgences for the living had some appeal, gaining indulgences for the dead had tremendous emotional appeal. By purchasing these slips of paper, a man could free his loved ones from the torment of purgatory. As Tetzel said, "As soon as the money falls into the coffer, the soul springs up from purgatory." Who could be so hardhearted as to resist that kind of appeal, especially for some departed loved one?

But Tetzel's sale of indulgences collided with Luther's deep personal experience. If trust in the redeeming mercy of God is the one thing necessary, then not only are indulgences unnecessary, they are fraudulent. That was Luther's logic and he could not avoid it. He summarized his position in ninety-five propositions which on the evening of October 31, 1517, he posted on the bulletin board on the door of the Castle Church. This was no act of defiance; it was a common way of inviting discussion and debate in an academic community like Wittenberg. No one dreamed, least of all Luther himself, that it was the match that would touch off the explosion known as the Protestant Reformation.

The debate which Luther had hoped would take place in Wittenberg soon had most of Germany involved. Luther's ninety-five theses spoke to the restlessness of many men in the church. The controversy spread so that in a short time word of it came to the ears of the pope. He did not take it very seriously, however, dismissing it as a brawl between German monks and ordering the Augustinian friars to discipline their brother.

The Augustinians did no such thing. Probably they were just a little proud of their man Luther, especially since he had so neatly embarrassed a member of the rival Dominican order. Argument followed argument, meeting followed meeting during which all sorts of compromises were tried and failed. The papal forces realized that they could not deal as summarily with Luther as they had with other rebels in times past because he had powerful supporters in German political circles whom the pope could not afford to alienate. The papal forces were even willing to disown Tetzel, but the debate which Luther had started had by this time gone far beyond that point.

THE BREACH WIDENS

By 1520 indulgences were no longer the question at issue. Forced by frequent defenses before various ecclesiastical authorities to solidify his position, Luther had questioned the infallibility of popes and councils, the preeminence of the clergy over the laity, and the doctrine of the mass as a sacrifice. Positively he had insisted that the whole life and doctrine of the church must be submitted to the scrutiny of the Scriptures and that whatever did not conform must be removed. Justification by faith, Luther's own central experience, was to him the key by which the Scriptures were to be interpreted and understood.

The pope might ignore a quarrel over the sale of indulgences. But this kind of wholesale challenge to some of the basic presuppositions of medieval Catholicism could not be ignored. In June, 1520, the pope issued a bull (a written mandate) condemning forty-one of Luther's teachings. "Arise, O Lord, and judge thy cause. A wild boar has invaded thy vineyard" were the words with which it began. All of Luther's writings were ordered destroyed, and the Wittenberg professor was given sixty days to recant or be excommunicated.

Luther's reply was to burn the papal bull in public. On January 3, 1521, the pope excommunicated Martin Luther and put him under the ban. A century ago, as in the case of John Hus, such action would have meant that in a short time the emperor would have had him burned at the stake. But the new emperor, Charles V, though pressured by the papal forces to rid the empire of this pest, was also aware of the difficulty of his position. Luther's cause had too many friends among the powerful German princes, whose support Charles badly needed as emperor, to warrant any hasty action. He therefore summoned Luther to appear before him and the German Diet (Parliament) at Worms in the spring of 1521. We wonder if Luther remembered the story of John Hus.

Although he realized that he stood alone against an empire, Luther refused to budge unless he could be convinced from Holy Scripture that he was in error. "God help me. Here I stand. I cannot do otherwise." This was the moment at which the break in Western Christendom became final. For the emperor, confronted with such an immovable position, could do nothing but reinforce the decision of the pope and declare Luther an outlaw.

But before that decision had been reached one of Luther's powerful friends, the Elector Frederick, had spirited Luther out of Worms and hidden him in his castle in Wartburg. There Luther lived under an assumed name for eight months. It was not an easy time. Completely isolated from the events in the world around him, Luther's old melancholy returned. Partly to rid himself of these fits of depression, partly because he realized its great importance, he devoted most of his time to translating the New Testament into German. In later years he completed the work by translating the Old Testament as well. He did such an outstanding piece of work that Luther's translation of the Bible is still the classic German version.

THE LATER LUTHER

In the spring of 1522 Luther returned to Wittenberg, disturbed by the excess of some of the reforms which were being carried out in his name. From that time on, the story becomes not so much Luther's story as the story of the Protestant movement. Step by step he began to discard the traditional practices. Private masses, confession, and fasting went first. The wearing of a distinctive religious garb soon followed. In 1525 he married a former nun, Katherine von Bora, and became the devoted father of a family.

By this time, however, the Protestant movement had other leaders, with many of whom Luther found himself in disagreement. With the radicals who represented the peasants he had no sympathy whatever, and when the peasants broke out in open rebellion Luther sided with the princes. But even with as moderate a reformer as Ulrich Zwingli, the Swiss Protestant leader, Luther could not agree. At heart Luther

The Trumpet of the Reformation

It is impossible to separate the Reformation from Martin Luther, or Martin Luther from Paul's Epistle to the Galatians. Luther had such an affection for the epistle that he called it "my wife, my Katherine von Bora." A commentator has said of it that "Martin Luther put it to his lips as a trumpet to blow the reveillé of the Reformation."[1] *Luther himself says this about the importance of the epistle's central message in the Introduction to his famous commentary:*

was a conservative. He wished to make the breach with Rome as small as possible. Where there were great issues, he did not compromise. But on what he considered minor matters, especially in the realm of liturgy, vestments, candles, and incense, he resented those who tried to make them matters of major importance.

In 1526 the Diet of Speyer recognized the right of the German princes, Roman Catholic or Lutheran, to organize national churches. Wherever the prince was Lutheran or Roman Catholic in sympathy, the church in his territory was organized accordingly. In 1529 the second Diet of Speyer retracted the position of the first and ruled that in Roman Catholic districts liberty of worship should not be granted to Lutherans, but in Lutheran districts toleration should be exerted toward Roman Catholics. The Lutherans entered a strong *protest*.

A word needs to be said about the name *Protestant*. Luther would have preferred the term *Evangelical* to describe his movement. (Incidentally, he would have detested the word *Lutheran* because of its exaltation of him.) The protest was not a negative matter, as we so commonly interpret it, but a positive one, a public witness before God "that they could consent to nothing contrary to his Word." It is unfortunate that the name *Protestant* is so often interpreted negatively (we are against the pope, rosary beads, and fish on Friday), when it originally had such great positive meaning. As Protestants today we need to state positively the things in which we believe and spend less time with the things which we reject.

The Magna Charta of the Protestant movement was presented to the Diet which met at Augsburg in 1530. Drawn up by Luther's scholarly young disciple, Philip Melanchthon, it was a confession of the evangelical faith. Melanchthon deliberately wrote it in as conciliatory a way as possible, but it was, of course, too late to placate the papal authorities. But it did become the recognized basis for the new Protestant movement and to this day the Augsburg Confession is the theological basis of all Lutheran churches.

Luther died in 1546. The last years of his life were not happy ones.

We have taken it upon ourselves in the Lord's name to lecture on this Epistle of Paul to the Galatians once more. This is not because we want to teach something new or unknown, for by the grace of God Paul is now very well known to you. But it is because, as I often warn you, there is a clear and present danger that the devil may take away from us the pure doctrine of faith and may substitute for it the doctrines of works and of human traditions. It is very necessary, therefore, that this doctrine of faith be continually read and heard in public. No matter how well known it may be or how carefully learned, the devil, our adversary, who prowls around and seeks to devour us (1 Peter 5:8), is not dead. Our flesh also

For one thing, differences of opinion began to appear among the Protestant leaders, especially those of the newer generation. Luther's old tendency toward pessimism darkened his later years as he watched the movement which he had so personally begun harden into patterns and parties. He had less and less appetite for the organizational life of the church, leaving such matters more and more to the secular authorities while his own piety became more and more inward.

There is evidence that the depression of these later years was also caused by the fact that the Protestant Reformation unleashed radical forces which Luther himself neither understood nor was able to control. We shall be discussing them in more detail in our next chapter. It will be enough to notice here that their radicalism was not only religious and theological but economic and political as well. Since Luther had leaned so heavily for support and protection on the German princes and nobility, he felt compelled to repudiate those who were attacking their control. But he could never quite forget the charge (which his Roman Catholic opponents did not hesitate to make) that it was Martin Luther who had opened this Pandora's box of revolutions which swept over Europe. If only he had remained a dutiful son of the church, things like these would never have happened! What had begun as a moment of deep personal religious insight had moved to a badly fragmented church within a single lifetime.

Of course, the Roman Catholic charge was untrue. As one of our leading church historians writes,

> ... he set off a chain reaction which issued in an explosion that tore away much of Western Europe from the Roman Catholic Church. He was not alone responsible. The ingredients for the explosion were already there. Had he not given the decisive impulse someone else would soon have done so.[2]

Yet the necessary compromises and adjustments involved in organizing a spiritual movement into a church were distasteful to Luther and accounted for much of the unhappiness of his later years.

---

goes on living. Besides, temptations of every sort attack and oppress us on every side. Therefore this doctrine can never be discussed and taught enough. If it is lost and perishes, the whole knowledge of truth, life, and salvation is lost and perishes at the same time. But if it flourishes, everything good flourishes—religion, true worship, the glory of God, and the right knowledge of all things and of all social conditions. To keep from doing nothing, we shall begin again where we broke off, according to the saying (Ecclus. 18:7): "When a man has finished, he is just beginning."[3]

—Martin Luther, *Lectures on Galatians 1535*

Fortunately for the Protestant cause younger leaders were arriving on the scene who had both the talent and zeal for organization and the patience and understanding to deal with the more radical side of the Reformation constructively. Their contribution was a necessary one if the Protestant cause was not to dissolve in impotence. Still all of them honored and respected Martin Luther as the pioneer whose personal courage had made the breakthrough possible.

Indeed, the German philosopher Nietzsche (no admirer of the Christian cause) once said that it was Luther who saved Christianity for the modern world. The revival of learning, the new science, the growing freedom of thought, all of which marked the opening years of the sixteenth century, were beginning to alienate the intellectual from a debased, corrupt, almost fossilized church. By breaking through into new possibilities, Luther made it possible for such persons to remain Christian. Even though many of them, like Erasmus, did not follow Luther out of the Roman Catholic faith, the Roman Church was forced to rethink many of its customs and positions because of the violence of the Lutheran explosion.

We cannot assess the Reformation movement until we have seen it in all of its aspects. Martin Luther was but the first chapter. Other chapters were soon to be written before the Reformation story was completed, but without a first chapter there could be no story. For that reason the entire Protestant world must acknowledge Martin Luther as its pioneer hero.

15

The Radical Reformation

Once the debate inaugurated by Luther's posting of his ninety-five theses had begun, there was no stopping it. Luther himself might see his position as nothing but a challenge to the papal theory of indulgences and allow himself to be drawn away from the teaching of the church one step at a time. But there were others who, when they heard that the break had come, did not wait for Luther's rather cautious leadership, if indeed they knew anything about him. They simply took the news as a signal to say openly what they had been thinking secretly.

Who these others were it is impossible to say with any certainty. History knows them as the *Anabaptists* (meaning *those who rebaptize*), a very broad movement including a great variety of people. As the movement progressed, names emerged, but the beginning of the movement is virtually anonymous. We turn to the story of the Reformation, and the Anabaptists, like Luther, are there from the very beginning.

Indeed there is a good chance that they were there before the beginning. As the decay of the church in the late fifteenth century grew worse, groups of people throughout the church, often very simple people, began to feel that nothing short of a radical solution could save it. While this radical solution took different forms, it usually involved a literal reading of the New Testament. The Christian community, as they understood it, was made up only of those who had been born again. This group of saved Christians had nothing to do with the state, and rejected all worldly possessions and pleasures. Most believed that Christ was to return soon.

As to the extent of such groups in the late Middle Ages we can only guess. But as the Protestant Reformation gained headway, they began to appear openly, believing that Protestantism was of the same spirit as they. When it became apparent that neither Luther nor any of the reformers was willing to go as far as they, the Anabaptists then presented themselves as complete Protestants, taking the principles of the Reformation all the way, freeing them from any compromise with medieval tradition. Such a position brought them the ardent opposition not only of the Roman Catholic authorities but the more conservative Protestants as well.

ANABAPTIST LEADERS

Because the Anabaptist movement was a varied one, we shall look at three of its leaders, each of whom represented a different phase of the radical reformation. The first, and one of the earliest Anabaptists to appear, was a young Swiss nobleman named Conrad Grebel. A native of Zurich, a city which had early espoused the Protestant cause under the leadership of Ulrich Zwingli, Grebel came back to his native city after a brilliant university career in Basel, Vienna, and Paris.

At first he was an ardent champion of Zwingli's. But by 1523 he had begun to disagree with the reformer. Like Luther, Zwingli worked through the government; it was the state which legislated the reform of the church. Grebel had become convinced from his New Testament studies that the church should be completely independent of the state and completely free to control its own life. It was over this issue that Grebel and his adherents, who called themselves the Swiss Brethren, broke with the official Protestant Church in Zurich.

That issue in itself was not sufficient to make the break a serious one. But the Swiss Brethren had a more serious question to raise. Again from their study of the New Testament they became convinced that the practice of baptizing infants was an erroneous one. Baptism, they believed, was for adult believers only, the sign of their conversion and acceptance of Christ as Savior. Though they rejected the control of the state, the Swiss Brethren in 1524 petitioned the city council of Zurich to abolish infant baptism.

The city council took their question seriously and did not reach a decision until 1525. But since that decision favored the continuance of the practice of infant baptism, Grebel and his brethren were commanded to dissolve their movement. Instead of complying, they began to rebaptize those who would join them and began celebrating the Lord's Supper as a group. It should also be noted that at this time Grebel began to travel about in other Swiss cities, preaching his gospel and organizing new groups of brethren. In short, a rival Protestant church was being set up in many Swiss and German communities.

Faced with this situation, the authorities felt it necessary to move. Grebel and his colleagues were arrested and sentenced to life imprisonment for their civil disobedience. Grebel himself died shortly after his sentencing. But one of his colleagues, Felix Manz, escaped, was recaptured and executed by drowning, the first Anabaptist martyr.

Manz's execution was the beginning of a large-scale attempt by the Protestant authorities to stamp out the Anabaptist movement. In various Swiss and German communities hundreds of people were put to death for their religious views which represented not only religious deviation but civil disobedience, since the reformers were just as insistent on the relationship between church and state as the Roman Catholics. But ideas cannot be killed so easily, and the Anabaptist movement steadily gained ground, under a more militant and less educated leadership than that which had been given by men like Grebel.

THE RADICAL RADICALS

One such restless spirit was Thomas Münzer, a former German monk who had gone from town to town attacking Luther for his refusal to surrender what Münzer considered vestiges of medieval superstition. Not only did he attack the practice of infant baptism and the subservience of church to state, but Münzer claimed direct inspiration from the Holy Spirit which, he said, freed him from any dependence upon the Bible. Unable to collect much of a following in any place, he would probably have been lost to history as a harmless crackpot were it not for the fact that he saw the chance to identify himself with the Peasants' Revolt.

Placed in a situation little better than that of slaves, the German serfs had drawn up grievances in 1525 for which they sought relief from their lords. At first Luther had had some sympathy with their cause and tried to act as mediator in their behalf. But the serfs were impatient and could not wait. Their discontent erupted in outbreaks of pillaging, looting, and burning which in turn brought violent reprisals from the German nobility, reprisals, incidentally, which Luther heartily endorsed. The rebellion lasted for about two years before it was finally wiped out.

Realizing the spiritual vacuum created by Luther's withdrawal from the peasant cause, Münzer moved in and was readily accepted as their leader. He was soon captured and executed in 1525 but not before he had given the Anabaptist movement two new characteristics. In origin it had been scholarly and intellectual. But now it became the religion of the landless and oppressed class. Feeling keenly the identification of the Reformation with the ruling class, the serf turned to the Anabaptists for his religious needs.

What was perhaps even more important was the growing conviction on the part of Protestant authorities that Anabaptism represented not only religious heresy but political subversion. Grebel's civil disobedience had been serious enough, but Münzer had actually led a rebellion against the established order. In the minds of the authorities Anabaptism represented almost what Communism does today, a dangerous enemy that threatened to overthrow not only the church but the whole social order.

Unfortunately events in the German city of Münster in the year 1533 made the accusation a plausible one. Originally Lutheran in its sympathies, Münster had become Anabaptist under the leadership of its popular young preacher, Bernhard Rothmann, who, though a Lutheran himself, came more and more under the influence of Anabaptist ideas. Rothmann himself was a highly educated person and his Anabaptism was of the same kind as Grebel's.

The news that Münster was sympathetic to Anabaptist ideas brought radical Dutch Anabaptists flocking into the city. One of them, Jan Matthys, a Dutch baker, was persuaded that Münster was to be the site of the New Jerusalem to which Christ would return and reign with his saints. When the Anabaptists gained political control of the city, Matthys began to reorganize its life into what he believed to be the pattern of a Christian society. After his death in 1534, he was succeeded by a Dutch tailor, Jan Beukelssen, commonly known as Jan of Leiden.

In the meantime both Roman Catholic and Lutheran forces (united for one of the few times in history!) had combined to lay siege to the city and recapture it. They were successful and Münster fell to them in 1535. But during the long siege under the leadership of Matthys and Beukelssen the situation inside the city became extreme. The two Jans were ignorant men who became more and more power-crazed as their situation worsened during the siege. After Matthys' death, Beukelssen became an impossible tyrant.

Convinced that as the divinely chosen representative of the Most High he could do no wrong, the new David, as he called himself, made himself a king in his Zion. He legalized polygamy, taking many wives himself, one of whom he beheaded with his own hand in the public square. Private property was abolished and life in the new Jerusalem proved to be a reign of terror. While historians dispute the extent to which the profligate practices of Jan of Leiden were followed by the Anabaptists in the city generally, there can be no doubt that the example of the leader was an open invitation to many to follow him. When the city fell to the bishop and his Lutheran allies in 1535, many of the citizens were relieved.

After the debacle of Münster, the Anabaptist cause became opposed universally. The conviction that it was nothing but a religious veneer for political revolution had powerful evidence in what had happened in that tragic German city. No one in his right senses would have dared to identify himself as an Anabaptist. Indeed, it seemed likely that the movement would disappear from history or be driven underground and never heard from again.

MENNO SIMONS

That it did not was largely the result of the quiet Dutch priest named Menno Simons. Born about 1496 and ordained to the priesthood in his native Netherlands in 1524, he served first in the little town of Pingjum and later in Witmarsum. Though a priest in the Roman Church (the Reformation movement had not yet reached the Netherlands), he began to read the writings of Luther as well as study the New Testament. But he was bothered by the question of infant baptism, and his reading of Luther's writings and those of some of the other reformers gave him no satisfactory answer.

His first acquaintance with Anabaptism apparently came through the execution of a simple tailor, Sicke Freerks. This event which took place in 1531 disturbed him deeply. Yet what he could find out about the Anabaptists, especially their excesses and their violence, repelled him. The movement came still closer to him, however, when his own brother became a follower of Jan Matthys and was killed in 1535. It was the death of his brother that brought him to his decision. In 1536, at the very time when no sensible person would declare his Anabaptist sympathies, Menno Simons gave up his Roman Catholic faith and position and submitted to rebaptism at the hands of a peaceful and quiet group of Dutch Anabaptists called Obbenites.

Someone had to salvage what was valuable and true in the Anabaptist position. This was the calling which Menno Simons saw and accepted. Soon he was ordained as an elder or bishop. From 1536 to his death in 1561 he was a kind of itinerant Anabaptist missionary in the Netherlands, Germany, and Denmark, organizing congregations, preaching, and writing.

In many ways his position resembled that of Grebel. Because of his understanding of the New Testament, Menno Simons rejected violence completely. He insisted that his followers be complete pacifists, rejecting military service. Theologically he rejected the practice of infant baptism and any idea of the real presence in the Lord's Supper. In his teaching the church was a simple society of believers, totally divorced from the state and completely without regional organization. Each congregation was independent and free to control its own destiny. Simplicity and purity of life were the outward signs of a loyal member of the group; doctrine and theology were strictly biblical. The Bible, especially the New Testament, was the only real authority, although various confessions of faith were drawn up from time to time in an attempt to unite the various societies on a common basis.

The great impression which Menno Simons left can best be gathered from the fact that in many places the Anabaptist movement soon became known as the Mennonite. Although it gained its greatest popularity among the simple people, in the Netherlands it found considerable support among the educated as well. Until Simon's death it was the largest Protestant group in the Netherlands. Never officially recognized, the Mennonites were severely persecuted until about 1600.

We have really carried the story of the radical reformation beyond the point at which it was of critical importance in the story of the Reformation. After the collapse of Münster and the rebuilding by Menno Simons, it was distinctly a minority group. But in its earlier phase, it threatened to be a majority. It threatened to split the Protestant cause into a left and a right, into a conservative wing led by Luther and a radical wing represented by the Anabaptists. Such a division could well have proved fatal to the Reformation.

THE ANABAPTIST CONTRIBUTION

In many ways, before it developed such a violent wing, the Anabaptist cause was an attractive one to thoughtful people. It seemed to deal more honestly with the New Testament, to be less compromising with old traditions, and to offer greater freedom for the church. Unfortunately, partly because it contained such extreme elements, partly because it was so quickly identified with the restless element in the population, and partly because the first reformers saw it as a threat to their own position, there was little or no attempt to meet its challenge. What was needed was a Protestant leader of sufficient vision to in-

It was characteristic of the various groups of Anabaptists, whom we are beginning to call the Radical Reformation, that they were not greatly interested in creeds or formal church organization. Nevertheless, their understanding of the church is one of the marks which distinguishes them from other Reformation movements. Compare this declaration in the Dordrecht Confession, adopted by Mennonites in 1632, with other ideas of the church.

We believe in and confess a visible Church of God, consisting of those, who ... have truly repented, and rightly believed; who are rightly baptized, united with

clude at least part of the Anabaptists in his point of view. But such a leader was not on the scene nor would he be for some years to come.

We may lament the fact that from the very beginning Protestantism has been pluralistic. The fact is not, as we often assume, that there was one original Protestant movement which in later years broke up into separate groups. From the very beginning the Protestant Reformation had at least three versions, one of which (*Calvinism*) we still have to examine. In the structured church of *Lutherans* and the free church of *Anabaptists* we have examples of the variety which has been characteristic of the Protestant heritage from the very beginning.

The question can be raised whether this fact is entirely a cause for lament. Certainly the scandal of denominationalism from which we suffer in the United States of America is a cause for shame. But it can also be asked whether the fact that the Lutheran Reformation was born with a free church critic was not in some ways a healthy thing. Even though the Anabaptist cause became a minority movement, it was always there as a question which the more conservative Protestants had to bear in mind.

Thus, for example, classic Protestantism had to do some careful thinking about the sacrament of baptism because of the Anabaptist question. The vitality of the local congregation was something to which classic Protestantism had to give continued attention because of the Anabaptist idea of a congregation. Above all, the relationship of the church to the state and the independence of the church in its own sphere was a question which the Reformation had to face because of the Anabaptist challenge.

In most instances, the full significance of the Anabaptist movement was not felt in the classic Protestant churches for several centuries. In many instances it was not fully realized until the churches of the

---

God in heaven, and incorporated into the communion of the saints on earth. I Cor. 12:13.

And these, we confess, are a "chosen generation, a royal priesthood, an holy nation," who have the testimony that they are the "bride" of Christ; yea, that they are children and heirs of eternal life—a "habitation of God through the Spirit," built on the foundation of the apostles and prophets, of which "Christ Himself is the chief cornerstone"—the foundation on which His church is built. John 3:29; Matt. 16:18; Eph. 2:19-21; Tit. 3:7; I Pet. 1:18, 19; 2:9.

This church of the living God, which He has purchased and redeemed through His own precious blood . . . may be known by her evangelical faith, doctrine, love, and godly conversation; also by her pure walk and practice, and her observance of the true ordinances of Christ, which He has strictly enjoined on His followers. Matt. 7:25; 16:18; 28:20; II Cor. 6:16.[1]

Reformation and the churches of the Anabaptist heritage came face-to-face with each other on an equal footing in this country. Even though we cannot accept the position of the Radical Reformation, we have to ask ourselves whether we have not benefited from it. Without it Protestantism could have decayed into as helpless a political instrument as the medieval church from which it broke away.

An Anabaptist Hymn

The hymns of the Anabaptists gathered in their collection called the Ausbund *are the hymns of a martyr people. Note how this spirit is reflected in the following stanzas from a hymn ascribed to Michael Sattler. He was pastor to several Anabaptist congregations and helped to prepare an Anabaptist statement of faith. Banished from Zurich by Reformed authorities, he was arrested by Roman Catholic authorities in Austria, condemned to death, tortured and burned in 1527. His wife was drowned a few days later.*

If one ill treat you for my sake,
And daily you to shame awake,
  Be joyful, your reward is nigh,
  Prepared for you in Heaven on high.

Of such a man fear not the will,
The body only he can kill;
  A faithful God the rather fear,
  Who can condemn to darkness drear.

O Christ, help thou thy little flock,
Who faithful follow thee, their Rock;
  By thine own death redeem each one,
  And crown the work that thou hast done.[2]

16
That Frenchman

In the year 1536 the little city of Geneva was a hotbed of excitement. Scarcely a year before, the people of Geneva had gained their political independence from the Duke of Savoy and with it their religious independence as well. For in driving out the duke, they had driven out the bishop, monks, and nuns as well. Their leader in this struggle for independence had been a fiery reformer named William Farel who, though French himself, had made French-speaking Switzerland his particular field of operations.

The fact is that the Reformation had begun in German-speaking Switzerland almost as early as the time of Luther and quite independently of him. As early as 1519 Ulrich Zwingli had come to be preacher at the cathedral in Zurich with many ideas for reform which he soon began to put into practice. Step by step he persuaded the town council to endorse his views until by 1525 his program for reformation, which had been a gradual one, was complete.

Zwingli was killed in battle in 1531. But before his death the Reformation had already spread to some of the other German-speaking cantons (divisions), including Bern, the most powerful. There was, then, a sizable Swiss Reformation which grew up alongside that of Martin Luther. In all essentials the two movements were the same. But because Zwingli and Luther were of a very different background and temperament, there were some differences. For one thing Zwingli had never been confronted with the same personal religious crisis that Luther had experienced. For another, his education had been in a much broader humanist tradition.

The German political authorities, especially Prince Philip of Hesse, saw the necessity of trying to unite these two reformations into a single movement. He brought Luther and Zwingli together at Marburg in 1529 in the hope that they could reconcile their differences and present a united front to the Roman Catholics on the right and the Anabaptists on the left. But though the discussions, which lasted for days, produced many significant areas of agreement, Luther regarded Zwingli as a radical, especially in his views on the Lord's Supper and the conference broke up in disunity.

It was as Zwingli's disciple that Farel campaigned through the French-speaking sections of Switzerland, especially since they were under the political control of the strong canton of Bern. But when Geneva, which had never been part of Switzerland but had belonged to the territory of Savoy, became independent, there was a kind of religious pandemonium. Lutherans, Zwinglians, Anabaptists, pure secularists, and probably some secret sympathizers with the old medieval church were all competing to gain control of the religious life of the newly independent city. Farel, who had so valiantly aided them in the struggle for independence, did not know how to deal with the situation. A fiery and persuasive orator, he was almost completely lacking in any talent for organization and he knew it.

THE VISITOR WHO STAYED

Just at this point a young tourist came to Geneva from Basel where he was making his home. Though he was only twenty-seven, he already enjoyed a considerable reputation in Protestant circles. He was born and raised in the northern part of France, and his family had destined him to an ecclesiastical career almost from his birth. But in 1528, whether from private doubts of his vocation to the priesthood or from disgust with the laxity of the church, he left the University of Paris where he had been studying theology and began the study of the law at the University of Orleans.

Sometime later he returned to Paris where he became part of a group of serious young scholars who were dedicated to reform. Under their influence he became acquainted with the writings of both Luther and Erasmus. Apparently his association with this group brought him a new religious experience which inclined him to cast his lot with the Lutheran cause. He may even have been in prison for a short time. But whatever these facts may have been, in 1534 he left Paris for good and moved to the city of Basel.

What had given him such a great reputation at so young an age

What is the sum of the Christian's life?

Now the great thing is this: we are consecrated and dedicated to God in order that we may thereafter think, speak, meditate, and do, nothing except to his glory. . . .

If we, then, are not our own . . . but the Lord's, it is clear what error we must flee, and whither we must direct all the acts of our life.

We are not our own: let not our reason nor our will, therefore, sway our plans and deeds. We are not our own: let us therefore not set it as our goal

was the fact that while in Basel he had written in Latin and had published a small book which he had entitled *Christianae religionis institutio.* (In English it is commonly known as *Institutes of the Christian Religion.*) It was a simple, systematic presentation of the Christian faith from the new evangelical point of view. Though it had only been published in the spring of 1536, its fame spread rapidly for it filled a badly felt need in the Protestant world. While men like Luther and Zwingli had written pamphlets in response to certain questions and published sermons, here was the systematic presentation of what the evangelical cause represented.

This was the young Frenchman who came on a visit to Geneva from Basel in the summer of that same year. His name was John Calvin. When Farel heard that he was in town, a sudden inspiration seized him. This was the very man whose talents were needed to bring order to the religious chaos of the newly independent city. Impulsive as always, Farel found the inn where Calvin was staying and put the case for Geneva before him passionately. At first Calvin was extremely reluctant; it was the life of quiet scholarship and not the turmoil of ecclesiastical leadership which appealed to him. But Farel was a hard man to refuse and before he left the inn, Calvin had consented to remain in Geneva. This began the association of a man with a city which, with the exception of three years, lasted until his death in 1564, an association that became so close that it is almost impossible to mention one name without thinking of the other.

It is true that Calvin's organization of Geneva was a strict one. At first it was too strict for the inhabitants and he and Farel were banished in 1538. But in three years he was recalled from Strasbourg where he had spent his exile ministering to the little French congregation there. The Geneva that developed from 1541 to 1564 showed the clear mark of Calvin's influence. Moral codes were strictly enforced;

---

to seek what is expedient for us according to the flesh. We are not our own: in so far as we can, let us therefore forget ourselves and all that is ours.

Conversely, we are God's: let us therefore live for him and die for him. We are God's: let his wisdom and will therefore rule all our actions. We are God's: let all the parts of our life accordingly strive toward him as our only lawful goal....

Let this therefore be the first step, that a man depart from himself in order that he may apply the whole force of his ability in the service of the Lord.... the Christian philosophy bids reason give way to, submit and subject itself to, the Holy Spirit so that the man himself may no longer live but hear Christ living and reigning within him.[1]

—from the *Institutes*

the life of the church was carefully organized and supervised with the assistance of lay elders; the commercial life of the city was developed into a flourishing state; education was carefully fostered and the foundations laid for the development of a university. The little city at the head of Lake Leman became a haven for Protestant refugees from all over Europe who, when they were able to return home, carried Calvin's fame with them.

Such a program met with considerable resistance, of course. There were those who resented the strict moral code and the discipline of the church in what they considered their private lives. Calvin's chief controversy was with a Spanish physician named Michael Servetus, who was arrested in Geneva in 1553. Servetus was a radical reformer who denied the doctrine of the Trinity, and the validity of infant baptism. He attacked Calvin as a false teacher. He was tried for heresy in Geneva, convicted, and burned at the stake, though Calvin pled for a more humane form of execution. It is not a happy page in Calvin's story, but this was the sixteenth century and Calvin was a child of his time.

CALVIN'S CONTRIBUTION

If Calvin had merely been the organizer of the Genevan church, we should probably have little interest in him today. It was not what he did in that little city but what he did in the larger field of European life and thought that makes him a figure of such significance. We may look at these accomplishments under three aspects.

1. Calvin was the great systematic theologian and thinker of the Reformation and one of the greatest in all Christian history. The little volume which he first published in 1536 underwent many successive revisions and enlargements until the final edition, published in 1559, was a complete and comprehensive view of the Christian faith from the evangelical point of view.

How is the church to be governed?

Now we must speak of the order by which the Lord willed his church to be governed. He alone should rule and reign in the church as well as have authority or pre-eminence in it, and this authority should be exercised and administered by his Word alone. Nevertheless . . . we have said that he uses the ministry of men to declare openly his will to us . . . Paul shows . . . that this human ministry which God uses to govern the church is the chief sinew by which believers are held together in one body. . . . For neither the light and heat of the sun, nor food and drink, are so necessary to nourish and sustain the present life as the apostolic and pastoral office is necessary to preserve the church on earth. . . .

Here it must now be noted that to this point we have considered only those

Theologians and thinkers do not strike us as very exciting people. But in the sixteenth century Calvin was a very necessary person. Without him the Reformation could easily have fallen apart. To survive, the movement needed an intellectual structure and Calvin was the man to provide it. His book, divided into four sections, presents the whole scope of the Christian gospel beginning with creation and ending with the life of the church in the world.

It would, of course, be impossible to summarize such a huge work in a few paragraphs. But we should emphasize one or two of the characteristic stresses in Calvin's work which, in later developments, gave rise to the system called *Calvinism*.

a. *The sovereignty of God.* While Luther centered his preaching and teaching on his own inner experience of justification and salvation, Calvin made the center of his system the will of God which directs and overrules all events for his glory. From the logical consequences of such a faith in terms of election and predestination Calvin did not shrink. God is responsible for all things; man is responsible for nothing save his wickedness.

We must be careful to point out that careful a thinker as Calvin was, he never presented this faith as a piece of logical abstraction, but always as the ground for unshakable confidence and hope. If God is sovereign and trustworthy, then the believing man has nothing to fear. He can obey and not worry about the consequences. He can believe and not be concerned about the ultimate outcome of things.

b. *The importance of the law.* So great had been Luther's experience of justification and forgiveness, that he inclined to see that experience as the end of the Christian life. For Calvin, on the other hand, it was only the beginning. The experience of God's grace must result in moral character. The law, the Ten Commandments, are means by which the redeemed man shows his gratitude. Calvin's thought car-

offices which are engaged in the ministry of the Word . . . But two [others] . . . are permanent: governing and caring for the poor.

Governors were, I believe, elders chosen from the people, who were charged with the censure of morals and the exercise of discipline along with the bishops. . . . Now experience itself makes clear that this sort of order was not confined to one age. . . . The care of the poor was entrusted to the deacons. However, two kinds are mentioned in the letter to the Romans: . . . one to serve the church in administering the affairs of the poor; the other, in caring for the poor themselves. . . . Here, then, is the kind of deacons the apostolic church had, and which we, after their example, should have.[2]

—from the *Institutes*

ried within it a strong ethical emphasis which made it unique at the time of the Reformation. The inner experience is not enough; it must come to expression in outward acts of obedience.

This ethical emphasis meant that Calvin had a much larger social consciousness than the other reformers. They tended to leave such matters to the state, as in the case of Luther, or simply to withdraw from social problems altogether, as did Menno Simons. But Calvin could not accept that kind of resignation. While he realized the impossibility of ever reaching the ideal, he did not accept that as an excuse for not seeking to make the social order conform to standards of righteousness. Calvin simply could not have understood our common slogan which asserts that the church should stay out of politics. In Geneva he put the church in politics up to its neck. What else could he do? Where else is the Christian to render his obedience to God except in the society in which he lives? And how can he be obedient without seeking to bring the righteousness of his God to bear upon that society?

2. Calvin was the designer and organizer of a pattern of church life. Once again, this was a matter which concerned Luther very little. It made little difference to him whether a church was congregational or episcopal. In fact, as he came to depend more and more upon the power of the princes, he was quite content to let them organize the church any way they found convenient.

Calvin could not share this lack of concern because he believed that the church was a divine society, not a department of the state. That divine society must have its own life and structure. Quite apart from the real dangers of formlessness in so young a movement, the church cannot allow itself to be organized by the state; it must be organized by Holy Scripture.

From his study of the Scriptures Calvin became convinced that the

What are the marks of the true church?

How we are to judge the church visible, which falls within our knowledge, is, I believe, already evident. . . . For we have said that Holy Scripture speaks of the church in two ways. Sometimes by the term "church" it means that which is actually in God's presence, into which no persons are received but those who are children of God by grace of adoption and true members of Christ by sanctification of the Holy Spirit. Then, indeed, the church includes not only the saints presently living on earth, but all the elect from the beginning of the world. Often, however, the name "church" designates the whole multitude of men spread over the earth who profess to worship one God and Christ. By baptism we are initiated into faith in him; by partaking in the Lord's Supper we attest our unity in true doctrine and love; in the Word of the Lord we have agreement, and for the preaching of the Word the ministry instituted by Christ is preserved. . . .

structure of the church should be presbyterian. Although the system underwent many developments after his time, he laid the foundations for it. Ministers were to be assisted in the care and discipline of the congregation by chosen laymen known as elders. Other laymen were to be set apart as deacons for the care of the poor. No minister should be chosen without the consent of the people whom he was to serve. Individual congregations were not independent societies but under the discipline of a college of ministers and elders in a given area. The origin of the presbyterian idea is evident in the order which Calvin proposed.

But the significant contribution was not presbyterianism as such. It was the responsible place which Calvin made for laymen in the life of the church. Although their function was different from that of the minister, elders and deacons were no less important and essential. Calvin's church order was no clerical monopoly.

Such a plan was the logical extension of Calvin's idea of vocation. The Middle Ages had sharply divided the world into religious and secular. The religious were those who gave their full time to God as priests or monks or nuns. The rest of the world was secular. To Calvin this was a completely false division. Every calling was a sacred calling in which it was possible to give glory to God. There was nothing more inherently sacred about being a minister than about being a doctor or a merchant. Every vocation represented a call of God and the opportunity to do Him service. Again Calvin would have had no patience with our slogan "full time Christian service" referring to the ministry or to the missionary field. Whoever did not see whatever he was called to do as "full time Christian service" had not really seen the full meaning of the gospel.

Since this was Calvin's conviction, it followed logically that those who had vocations other than the ministry should share with the min-

> From this the face of the church comes forth and becomes visible to our eyes. Wherever we see the Word of God purely preached and heard, and the sacraments administered according to Christ's institution, there, it is not to be doubted, a church of God exists. . . .
> But that we may clearly grasp the sum of this matter, we must proceed by the following steps: the church universal is a multitude gathered from all nations; it is divided and dispersed in separate places, but agrees on the one truth of divine doctrine, and is bound by the bond of the same religion. . . . In this way we preserve for the universal church its unity, which devilish spirits have always tried to sunder; and we do not defraud of their authority those lawful assemblies which have been set up in accordance with local needs.[3]
> —from the *Institutes*

istry in the official life of the church. A man might be a butcher or baker or lawyer, but he could still be an elder or a deacon, a minister in the church of Christ. Calvin laid the foundation for a whole new concept of the laity in the life of the church.

3. Calvin's greatest contribution was one which we tend to forget. He once wrote Cranmer, Archbishop of Canterbury, "to be ranked among the chief evils of our time . . . [is] that the Churches are so divided . . . the members of the Church being severed, the body lies bleeding. So much does this concern me, that, could I be of any service, I would not grudge to cross even ten seas, if need were, on account of it."[4]

He saw his first great task as one of mediation between the Lutheran and the Zwinglian wings of the Reformation. Although his own sympathies were more with the Lutheran side, he did his best to find formulas and statements of faith which would unite all but the most intractable in both camps. In this effort he was ably assisted by Luther's favorite disciple, Philip Melanchthon, who was equally disturbed by the dangerous division among the evangelical forces. Since the Lord's Supper had seemed to be the principal area of conflict, Calvin gave special attention to it, seeking to find a formula which would safeguard the Lutheran insistence upon the reality of Christ's presence while respecting the Zwinglian refusal to identify that presence with the bread and wine on the Table. His pamphlet on the Lord's Supper won the approval of the aging Luther and Calvin used it as a basis for working out new statements of faith in his attempt to unite the evangelical cause.

A similar observation could be made about the Anabaptists. While Calvin certainly had no sympathy with their more extreme positions, he could feel the force of some of their objections to the dependence of the church on the state, to the lack of moral seriousness which had marked certain elements in the Reformation as well as their insistence upon the purity of the life of the church. It was his intention to recapture as many of the more thoughtful members of that group as he could for the evangelical cause.

At first he was amazingly successful. Ready to make concessions in matters which seemed nonessential, Calvin was able to develop a central Protestant tradition to which most of the European world was responsive. Naturally, there were extremists in all camps who resented his activity, but the mainstream of European Protestantism even as far away as England was willing to accept his leadership. He was certainly the first great ecumenical statesman in the Protestant world.

Unfortunately the unity for which he labored so hard and so successfully did not last. The Lutheran moderates whom he had been able to attract were shortly after his death forced out of Lutheran circles by the more extreme party. The Swiss tended to move back to their old position. The result was that the Protestant division, so clearly foreshadowed at Marburg when Luther and Zwingli had failed to agree, a division which Calvin had devoted his life to overcoming, became a reality. While it is impossible to give the division an exact date, soon after Calvin's death the Protestant Reformation became two distinct denominations, Lutheran and Reformed.

Most of Germany and all of the Scandinavian countries went with the Lutheran side. The Protestant forces in Switzerland, France, Hungary, Holland, and parts of Germany became Reformed. In the British Isles, Scotland became Reformed while England pursued an independent course, borrowing something from both groups. We shall soon be considering how the Reformed movement spread to some of these countries.

It is interesting to note that while the one party took the name *Lutheran*, the other party never allowed itself to be called *Calvinist*, though their opponents often tried to saddle them with that name. Conscious as they were of their identity with the historic church of Jesus Christ, they preferred simply to state that they were the historic church of Jesus Christ, reformed according to the Word of God. While they acknowledged John Calvin as their teacher and theologian, he was not their master. Great as was his contribution to their life, their only master was the Word of God. They lived in the faith that God had "more truth and light yet to break forth out of His Holy Word."[5]

17

They Went to School in Geneva

If we had time, it would be a fascinating story to tell how the Lutheran Reformation was carried from its native Germany into Scandinavia, or to recount the travels of the Reformed faith from Switzerland into other parts of Western Europe. Each story would have its own dramatic moments and its own heroes. Each story is worth telling.

We shall select only two of these stories, one to show to what extent a single man can influence the religious life of a nation, the other to illustrate how political events can alter religious patterns.

THE SCOTTISH REFORMATION

In 1546 a brilliant young preacher named George Wishart was burned at the stake in the public square in the Scottish university town of St. Andrews. Having become acquainted with the writings of Martin Luther while a student in England, Wishart had returned to his native Scotland determined to reform the life of the church. The Scottish Church under the leadership of Cardinal Beaton of St. Andrews had bitterly resisted any attempts at reformation. As early as 1528 another young man, Patrick Hamilton, had been burned at the stake for Lutheran views. The authorities had no intention of allowing Scotland to become another Germany.

Their religious interests were to a degree political ones. The little country of Scotland was in many ways a pawn between two larger powers, England to the south and France across the channel. The ruling faction in Scotland at the time was French in its sympathies and its support. Any encouragement of the Protestant cause would, of course, alienate the French power and bring Scotland into the English orbit. It would mean that Cardinal Beaton would lose not only his religious leadership, but his political status as well.

JOHN KNOX

Wishart's chief disciple was a young priest, much less well educated, but of a rough and ready nature. Indeed, he had been so closely associated with Wishart and so enthusiastic in his cause that it seems strange that the cardinal did not send John Knox to the same stake. But Knox was spared and so the whole story of Scotland was changed.

Events moved rapidly after Wishart's martyrdom. A party of his friends invaded the castle in St. Andrews within a few weeks and murdered the cardinal. Taking possession of the castle, they held it as a fortress until help should come from England. While living in the castle, they formed a Protestant congregation and invited John Knox to be their minister.

But the ships which came sailing into the bay of St. Andrews were not English but French. With Cardinal Beaton's supporters besieging them by land and the French navy cutting off their escape by sea, the Protestant party had no choice but surrender. The castle fell in September 1547 and all its occupants were sent to the French galleys as slaves. That ended the first attempt to make Scotland a Protestant country. Yet even though he was a galley slave for almost two years, John Knox never gave up his confidence that Scotland would still be won for the evangelical cause.

At first the hope seemed very faint indeed. Released from the galleys in 1549 through an exchange of prisoners, Knox did not dare return to Scotland, but made his way to England where he served as minister in Newcastle and as a chaplain to Edward VI. But Scotland was still on his heart—so much so that when he was offered the chance to become bishop of Rochester he refused since he knew that by the acceptance of such a post he would be remaining in England for the rest of his life.

Another setback came in 1553, however, when the English royal throne came into Roman Catholic control and the Protestant leaders had to flee for their lives. The refuge which Knox sought was in Calvin's city of Geneva, which was his home for the next two years, save for a few months spent as pastor of a refugee congregation in Frankfurt. Knox became Calvin's friend and ardent disciple. He left Geneva in the fall of 1555 for a visit to Scotland. Deciding that the time was not yet ripe, he returned to Calvin's city and remained there till 1559.

In the meantime the Protestant party in Scotland had been gathering strength, especially among the nobility. A new Protestant queen, Elizabeth, had come to the English throne. With strong support from that quarter, a strong Protestant nobility, and an absentee Scottish queen (Mary was living in France), John Knox invaded his native country in the spring of 1559. A slight flurry followed, but with English support the Protestants carried the day and in 1560 Scotland became a Protestant country. The change was not accomplished without some violence. Pent-up frustrations from the long history of ecclesiastical tyranny and corruption vented themselves in the sacking of monasteries and the destruction of images in the churches. But John Knox soon took control through the Scottish Parliament in which his friends had a clear majority. Not only were all the customs and usages of the Roman Church abolished, but a new church organization, closely modeled after what he had known in Geneva, was set up.

The doctrine of this church was set forth in the Scottish Confession of Faith, a work which, though written by Knox and five of his associates, was clearly a reflection of the thinking of John Calvin. The structure of the church was contained in a second work called *The First Book of Discipline*. It too represented the form which Calvin had introduced in Geneva, though with some modifications.

Knox's battle was not yet over, however. The young queen returned to Scotland in 1561 and the next six years of Scottish history were in a real sense a struggle between the queen and John Knox. She was determined to win Scotland back to the old faith; he was equally determined to keep it Reformed. Though he was often coarse and rude in his dealings with the queen, Knox knew that he was fighting not only for his own life but for the welfare of what had become Scotland's Protestant majority. His battle was won in 1567 when the nobility deposed Mary and put her infant son James on the throne under a Protestant regency. When Knox died in 1572, he knew that Protestantism was firmly established in his native land. His friend George Wishart had not died in vain. But how much of the story depended on the courage of this single man who, in the words of one of his friends, "in his life never feared the face of man"![1]

AFTER KNOX

We cannot trace here the later history of the Reformed Church in Scotland. It was not really until 1690 that it became stabilized into the

The Scottish Confession of Faith

After a long salutation "to their natural countrymen, and to all other Realms and Nations, professing the same Jesus Christ with them," the Preface to the Confession declares:

Long have we thirsted, dear Brethren, to have notified unto the world the sum of that doctrine which we profess, and for the which we have sustained infamy and danger. But such has been the rage of Sathan against us, and against Jesus Christ his eternal verity, lately born amongst us, that to this day no time has been granted unto us to clear our consciences, as most gladly we would have done; for how we have been tossed a whole year past, the most part of Europe (as we suppose) does understand. But seeing that of the infinite goodness of our God (who never suffers his afflicted to be utterly

pattern which we know today. In the century between Knox's death and that time, the fortunes of the Scottish Church were closely tied to the events of the church in England. Knox himself had laid the foundations for such a development in his close alliance with English interests. But it became even more inevitable when in 1603 Mary's son, James VI, was invited to occupy the English throne as James I of England and the two kingdoms were united under a single monarch.

The union of the two thrones meant that the next century saw repeated attempts to unite the two churches. The English Church had undergone a reformation all its own. Through influences by Luther, Calvin, and other continental reformers, it had retained much of its medieval form, including the bishops. The Scottish Church, on the other hand, had been organized after the Genevan pattern and while Knox's *First Book of Discipline* did make some provision for superintendents whose office was somewhat like that of a bishop, it was an office that soon fell into disuse and disappeared.

James was determined to make the Scottish Church over into the English pattern. Both James and his son, Charles I, insisted upon an episcopal structure for the Scottish Church, though the system was bitterly resented by many Scotsmen. When Charles was defeated by the forces of Parliament, the shoe was on the other foot. The Scottish Church, together with its sympathizers in England, sought to impose a presbyterian order on the English Church. The great assembly which met in Westminster beginning in 1643 was called into being to work out a system of doctrine and government which should unite the churches in the two kingdoms.

This long struggle left two results in Scottish Church life. For one thing, because so much of the struggle centered about the question of

confounded) above expectation we have obtained some rest and liberty, we could not but set forth this brief and plain Confession of such doctrine as is proponed unto us, and as we believe and profess, partly for satisfaction of our Brethren . . . and partly for stopping of the mouths of impudent blasphemers . . . But we have chief respect to our weak and infirm brethren, to whom we would communicate the bottom of our hearts, lest that they be troubled or carried away by the diversities of rumours, which Sathan sparsis [spreads] contrary us, to the defecting of this our most godly enterprise; Protesting, that if any man will note in this our Confession any article or sentence repugning to God's holy word, that it would please him of his gentleness, and for Christian charity's sake, to admonish us of the same in writ; and We of our honour and fidelity do promise unto him satisfaction from the mouth of God (that is, from his holy Scriptures), or else reformation of that which he shall prove to be amiss. For God we take to record in our consciences, . . . that with all humility we embrace the purity of Christ's Evangel, which is the only food of our souls; and therefore so precious unto us, that we are determined to suffer the extremity of worldly danger, rather than that we will suffer ourselves to be defrauded of the same. . . .[2]

church government, the name *presbyterian* became more and more associated with the Reformed Church in Scotland until it finally took over as the accepted title. This accounts for the fact that the movement which stems from the Swiss Reformation has two names in this country. Those churches which trace their origin to the continent of Europe are called *Reformed* while those churches which look to Scotland and the British Isles are called *Presbyterian*. But they are the same in origin and heritage.

A more lasting result of the struggle is the Westminster standards. In an attempt to unite the religious life of the two kingdoms, the Scottish Church gave up its own Confession and Church Order and adopted the Confession, Catechisms, Directory of Worship, and Church Order drafted by the Westminster Assembly. In a short time these documents were repudiated by the English Church which returned to its episcopal heritage. But they were maintained by the Scottish Church and form the doctrinal and ecclesiastical basis for the life of every Presbyterian Church in the world today.

THE DUTCH REFORMATION

Though the Roman Church in Scotland was one of the most backward and corrupt in all of Europe, in the Netherlands it was enlightened and humane. The sixteenth century found the Netherlands the most prosperous land in Europe with a flourishing commerce and industry. Moreover, the long tradition of the Brethren of the Common Life, a tradition which had found its full flower in the career of a man like Erasmus, had given the country an educational level second to none as well as a gentle and tolerant religious point of view. Such Protestantism as existed in the land was largely made up of the followers of Menno Simons and they were a small minority. The vast majority of the citizens of the Netherlands saw no need for religious change.

There was only one possibility of trouble. The Netherlands was not an independent country but under Spanish control. In 1555 the Emperor Charles V, who had been popular in the country, abdicated and was succeeded on the Spanish throne by his son Philip II. The new king was almost fanatical in his loyalty to the papacy and was equally fanatical in his determination to bring the Netherlands firmly under Spanish control. In fact he was convinced that his success as a monarch depended upon the zeal with which he stamped out the hated Protestant heresy everywhere in his dominions.

The southern part of the Netherlands was French speaking and through contacts with Geneva contained a number of Calvin's followers. They began to feel the full force of Philip's persecution, but at first their martyrdom did not make a great impression on the population. It was only when the Dutch nobility began to feel the pinch of the king's determination to limit their power that the situation began to grow tense. In 1566 the three leading nobles, the counts of Egmont, Horn, and Orange-Nassau, issued a protest against the growing Spanish tyranny, demanding the removal of Spanish troops and the ending of religious persecutions.

The king was furious, but concealing his anger, he invited the three counts to discuss the matter. The count of Orange-Nassau was wise enough to suspect treachery and warned his two friends, but they accepted the royal invitation and went straight to their death. This became the signal for a struggle for independence which was not completed till 1609.

WILLIAM THE SILENT

The leader in the struggle was William of Orange-Nassau, more familiarly known as William the Silent. At the time he was a Roman Catholic. But as the struggle intensified, William realized that identification with Rome meant identification with Spain. He also realized that the sturdiest fighters that he had in his army were the Calvinists. But it was not merely such logic but deep religious conviction which brought him to join the Reformed Church in 1573.

Many others had made a similar decision as they felt the cruelty of the Spanish forces led by the Duke of Alva. The church which they joined was for the most part an underground movement. In fact, the only places it could worship openly were outside the country where

The Defense of William of Orange

The revolt of the Netherlands against Spain, led by William, Prince of Orange, had been dragging on for over a decade. In 1580, King Philip II of Spain issued a proclamation against William, naming him a "public plague" and offering a reward for his death. William replied in a long defense to the Dutch States-General, a reply which was followed in the next year by the Provinces of the Netherlands declaring their independence. This is part of William's concluding statement:

The principal thing they have set out to accomplish is *the extirpation of the reformed religion.* I do not intend, my Lords, to enter here into the question as to which is the true religion by which God is best served and worshipped according to His Word. I

Dutch refugees had fled to escape the Spanish fury. But one of the early martyrs of the church, a minister named Guido de Brès, had written a confession of faith which formed a basis for gathering this underground and refugee church.

Unlike most other confessions of faith, this one was De Brès' personal work. One of the field preachers of the Reformed cause in the Netherlands, he believed that if only King Philip really knew what the Reformed Church represented, he would cease his relentless persecution of it. Accordingly he wrote this confession of faith in 1561 and seeing no other way of getting it to the king, threw it over the wall of the Spanish governor's palace with a request that it be delivered to his majesty.

Of course, the king never saw it. It would have made no difference had he done so. The persecution continued as savagely as before. De Brès himself lost his life in a few years. But when finally in 1568 the Reformed Church began to organize (though the first meetings had to be held outside the Netherlands), it was De Brès' confession, now known as the *Belgic Confession,* which became the theological basis for the church.

Bit by bit the forces of William the Silent began to turn back the Spaniards. By 1581 they had been entirely driven out of the northern provinces, which declared themselves an independent republic and chose William as their leader. They did not enjoy his leadership long for he was struck down by an assassin's bullet in 1584. But he had lived long enough to give the new nation which he had led to independence his own loyalty to his church together with a broad tolerance for the religious rights of others. Holland became the first country in Europe to offer freedom to religions other than the prevalent one

---

would rather leave that to be decided by those who are better versed in the matter than I. Yet I wish everyone to know by my profession what I believe about the matter. But this I must let you know, that such is the state of your country that it cannot continue to exist without the exercise and free use of the said reformed religion. You can see for yourselves how greatly the number of those who profess it has increased. . . .

Who, therefore, can say he loves his country if he would help to drive out such great numbers of its people and thus leave the country waste and desolate? . . .

Wherefore take pity on yourselves; and if that which concerns you does not move you, take pity, I say, upon the many poor people who have already been ruined, and on those who may suffer likewise; upon the many poor widows and fatherless children; upon the many churches destroyed, and the many pastors wandering up and down the country with their poor flocks. . . .

And as to that which particularly concerns myself: you can easily see, my Lords, that it is my life that they seek, upon which they have set a great price.

and in years to come became an asylum for refugees from everywhere.

The Netherlands became Reformed largely because the Calvinist party led the struggle for independence. It is easy to understand why the Anabaptists could not assume such leadership; their historic position usually called for nonviolence and nonresistance. It is not so easy to understand why Lutheranism, which was at first as strong as Calvinism, did not take such an active part. Though there are doubtless other factors of historical and economic aspect, it is possible that one of the great factors was the Calvinist emphasis on making a witness in society. Calvin himself had upheld the right of revolution when the state opposes the true faith. It takes little imagination to see how Calvinists in the Netherlands applied that principle to their own situation.

THE DEVELOPMENT OF THE DUTCH CHURCH

Once able to organize itself on its own soil, the Reformed Church in the Netherlands soon began to make its own adaptation of the Genevan pattern. The same presbyterian form of organization which we have already seen in Geneva and in Scotland was set up for the Netherlands. To Guido de Brès' confession was added the catechism which had been written in 1563 for use in the Rhenish Palatinate, commonly known as the *Heidelberg Catechism* from the name of the capital city. Many of the Dutch refugees had become acquainted with it during the years of their exile and felt that they could produce nothing finer. A liturgy was also adopted to which additions were made from time to time.

The Reformed Church in the Netherlands was not very old before it was convulsed by a fierce civil war over the exact implications of the doctrine of predestination. The controversy had begun over the writ-

---

They have vowed and appointed me to death, and say that as long as I shall be among you they shall not cease to war against you. . . .

If you therefore, my Lords, should judge that either my absence or my death would serve you, then I am ready to obey whatever you command me. . . . If you are convinced that I have a love for your country and that I have sufficient experience to offer advice, then be assured that this is the only means to bring us deliverance from our enemies.

This being the case, let us with one heart and one will come together, and let us stand side by side in defense of the good people of this country who desire nothing else but our sincere counsel, and who are ready to carry out all we say. And in doing this, if you continue to show me the same favor which you have shown to me heretofore, I can assure you that, with God's help, what you shall decide will be for the preservation of yourselves, your wives and your children, and all things sacred and holy.

JE LE MAINTIENDRAI—"*I Will Carry On*"[3]

ings of a theological professor named Jacob Arminius, though he died before the discussion had reached its fullest extent. The more liberal party, sometimes called Arminians, sometimes Remonstrants, were opposed by a conservative group who insisted upon a strict interpretation of the doctrine. To settle the question, a synod was summoned in 1618 in the city of Dort. Delegates came from Reformed Churches all over Europe and from Great Britain as well. After almost a year of study and discussion, the decision was made in favor of the conservative position. The findings of the synod were carefully spelled out in a series of propositions known as the Canons of the Synod of Dort, and these too became part of the doctrinal standards of the Reformed Church.

So rapid has been the expansion of the Netherlands after its independence, however, that even before the Synod of Dort met, the first pioneer settlers from the Netherlands were building their log cabins in the new world of North America. The Reformed Church was beginning to plant outposts in New Netherland along the Hudson valley even before it had completed its organization in the mother country.

Though in many ways the story in Scotland differs from that in Holland, there are basic similarities. For one thing, each movement had its hero. What makes the story in Holland of particular interest is that its hero was a layman. William the Silent provides an excellent illustration of Calvin's insistence that the life of the church does not depend entirely upon its ministers.

What is even more striking is the way in which the story of the Reformation in each country is closely allied with the story of politics. There may be those who find this distressing, believing that only religious reasons should influence the history of the church. They forget that the church is the body of Christ in the world and that her Lord is the Master of all history, not merely church history. If the Scottish Reformation was the result of an English alliance, the Dutch Reformation of the struggle for independence from Spain, these facts are not cause for shame. They simply reinforce our faith in the God who uses history for the achievement of his purposes.

PART V
THE WORLD CHALLENGES THE CHURCH

•

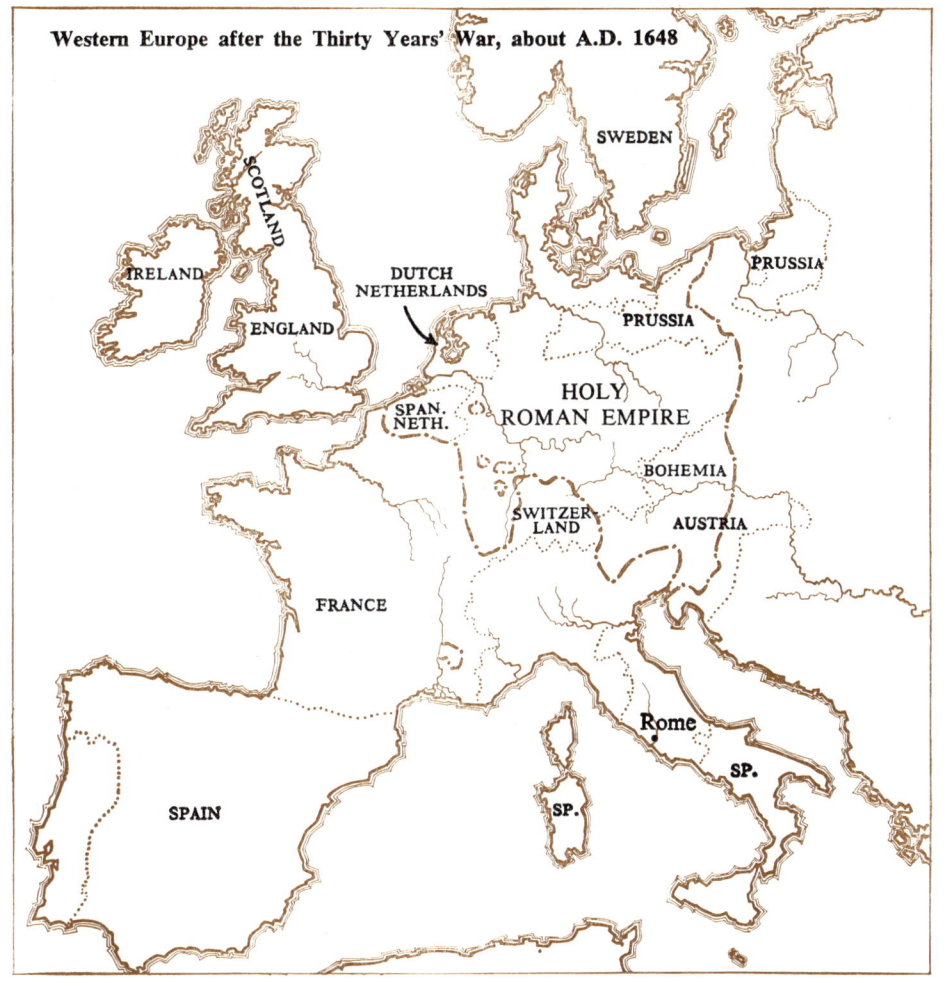

Western Europe after the Thirty Years' War, about A.D. 1648

•

TEACH us, good Lord, to serve thee as thou deservest; to give and not to count the cost; to fight and not to heed the wounds; to toil, and not to seek for rest; to labour, and to ask for no reward, save that of knowing that we do thy will; through Jesus Christ our Lord. —Ignatius Loyola (1491–1556)

LORD, give us hearts never to forget Thy love; but to dwell therein whatever we do, whether we sleep or wake, live or die, or rise again to the life that is to come. For Thy love is eternal life and everlasting rest; for this is life eternal to know Thee and Thy infinite goodness. Therefore, O Thou, whose name and essence is Love, enkindle our hearts, enlighten our understandings, sanctify our wills, and fill all the thoughts of our hearts, for Jesus Christ's sake— Amen.[1] —Johann Arndt, a Pietist (1555-1621)

KEEP me, O Lord, while I tarry on this earth, in a daily serious seeking after thee, and in a believing affectionate walking with thee; that, when thou comest, I may be found not hiding my talent, nor serving my flesh, nor yet asleep with my lamp unfurnished; but waiting and longing for my Lord, my glorious God, for ever and ever.[2]
—Richard Baxter, a Puritan (1615–91)

LET thy mighty power enable us to do our duty toward thee and toward all men with care, diligence, zeal, and perseverance. Help us to be meek and gentle in our conversation, prudent and discreet in ordering our affairs, observant of thy fatherly providence in everything that befalls us, thankful for thy benefits, patient under thy chastisements, and readily disposed for every good word and work. Amen.[3]
—John Wesley (1703–91)

18

Thrust and Counterthrust

At first it was difficult for the Roman Church to believe that the Reformation had really happened or that it would last. After all, the papacy had faced rebellions before in its long history and had always been able, with the help of the state, to put them down. It was a shattering experience to realize, therefore, that this time large parts of Western Europe had been permanently lost to papal control. It was even more shattering to discover that the help of the state could no longer be counted upon. A new spirit of nationalism was moving in Europe to which the demands of the papacy were of no interest.

Once it was realized that the Protestant Reformation was to be a permanent division, there were two distinct reactions on the part of those who wished to see the Roman Catholic faith restored to its former position. The first was so largely the inspiration of one man, a man who influenced the life of the Roman Church in the sixteenth century almost as deeply as Luther and Calvin influenced the Protestant Reformation, that he deserves our special attention.

THE COUNTER-REFORMATION

Ignatius Loyola was born into the Spanish nobility somewhere between 1491 and 1495. He chose the army as his career but in 1521 he was seriously wounded in the siege of Pampeluna. During a lengthy convalescence, he did extensive devotional reading which convinced him that he must become a soldier for Christ. A long retreat followed, after which Ignatius began his studies, first in his native Spain and then from 1528–1535 at the University of Paris. Incidentally, John Calvin was a student at the same university during some of these years and it is interesting to speculate whether he and Loyola ever met.

It was while he was a student in Paris that Ignatius gathered together a small group of followers who were to become the core of the movement which he proposed to start. The movement gradually gathered strength until it was formally launched in 1540 by the pope. Known as the *Society of Jesus* (or more popularly as the Jesuits), it was another religious order, with the traditional monastic vows. What made the Jesuit order different, however, was a fourth vow, to go, without question or hesitation, wherever the pope might command.

Another distinction of the order was the rigid military nature of its organization. Ignatius had not been a soldier for nothing. The order was governed by a general who had absolute authority over every member and whose decisions were subject to no review, except by the pope himself. Furthermore, to keep them free from all ecclesiastical entanglements, no Jesuit was allowed to hold any ecclesiastical office, unless, of course, ordered to do so by the pope.

While the purpose of the new order did include missionary work among the heathen (in which field, incidentally, it had a splendid record, traveling as far away as China), there can be no doubt that its principal purpose was a counterattack against Protestantism. For such a purpose the Jesuits were ideally suited. Their military organization made them splendid shock troops for the papacy; the fact that they were a new organization freed them from any of the stigmas attached to some of the older orders in the popular mind. Their freedom from all ecclesiastical authority except that of the pope enabled them to move freely wherever they would. Often the Jesuits were more unpopular with the local Roman Catholic authorities than with the Protestants because of their freedom of movement.

Although Loyola died in 1556, his order was already not only firmly established but hard at work. Its freshness and its high purpose captured the loyalty of many young Roman Catholics who were seeking for a more creative way to express their faith. Study the best leadership of the Roman Church in those days and you will find that for the most part they were members of the Society of Jesus. As educators, they were among the most progressive in Europe; indeed, education was a large part of the Jesuit program for recapturing Europe for the papacy. Largely as the result of their efforts, Bohemia, Moravia, and Poland, all of which had been Protestant countries, reverted to Roman Catholicism. And when you add to this the story of Jesuit missions among the Indians in North America and the natives of South America, the record is a very impressive one indeed.

There can be no doubt that the Jesuits lifted the hopes of the Roman Church after the shock of the Reformation. But it became apparent to many that another approach was necessary—some internal reform of the Church itself. While no one would concede any essential point to the Reformation, it was obvious that there was corruption and weakness which needed correction.

THE COUNCIL OF TRENT

It was in 1545 that Pope Paul III summoned an ecumenical council to meet in Trent. It was the longest council on record since it did not finally adjourn until 1563, although during the ten years from 1552 to 1562 it did not meet at all. One reason for the length of the council was the great debate which it saw as to the extent of the concessions which might be made to the Protestants. Many of the German bishops, for example, wanted to allow the use of German hymns in public worship and the marriage of priests. Some of the liberal Italians felt that much of the Lutheran emphasis on justification by faith was right.

But more conservative points of view finally prevailed. The importance of the Council of Trent was not in the reforms which it brought about in the Roman Church, though there were some. The importance of the Council of Trent was the way in which it defined the Roman Catholic position, making any reconciliation with Protestantism impossible. The Roman Church as we knew it down to the Ecumenical Council of 1962 was largely the product of Trent. Protestant positions such as justification by faith alone and the sole authority of Scripture were put under the ban. The machinery of ecclesiastical government was tightened. It could be argued that it was Trent which made the old church of Western Europe into Roman Catholicism.

PROTESTANT SCHOLASTICISM

The hardening of Roman Catholicism produced a similar effect in Protestantism, though in a different way. For Protestantism, of course, no such general council as Trent was possible. Already divided into Lutheran and Reformed camps, these divisions were still further divided by national boundaries. But within the broad divisions of the Protestant world, there came a similar hardening of positions in the movement known as Protestant *scholasticism*.

It seems to have come first in Lutheranism. After Luther's death, as we have noticed, there was a strong movement, led by Melanchthon, to find a middle ground of union with the Reformed. A party within Lutheranism had always resented and resisted this movement, and after Melanchthon's death that group came into control. Threatened by a renewed Rome on the one side and, as they believed, by the Calvinists on the other, they felt it necessary to spell out in exact detail what Lutherans believed. This would allow for no misunderstanding or possibility of compromise.

The result of this tendency was an extensive theological document called the Formula of Concord. Drawn up by a number of Lutheran theologians in Germany in 1577 and finally ratified in 1580, it sought to answer both Trent and Geneva point by point.

Since Trent had already issued its decrees by this time, it is obvious that the Lutherans saw their Formula as a counterattack. Every theological topic was treated in great detail and with great precision. Lutheranism had now become a definite formal system of theology as rigid and inflexible in its own way as the theology of Trent.

A similar movement was longer in coming in the Reformed churches. Indeed, it would be difficult to point to any single document which would typify Reformed scholasticism quite as adequately as the Formula of Concord represents the Lutheran development in this direction. The first evidence of it was probably the Synod of Dort, assembled in the Netherlands in 1618, but representing a much wider group of Reformed churches. Its Canons have the same theological explicitness as the Formula, but they do not pretend to be a complete theological system, dealing only with the single question of election and predestination.

The greatest single example of scholasticism in Reformed circles would probably be the Westminster standards. One has only to compare them with any of the confessions of faith from the era of the Reformation itself to see how much more detailed and theologically exact they are. Such questions as the inspiration of Scripture, which in earlier times had never been discussed but simply assumed, were gone

The Creed of the Council of Trent (1564)

This creed, a summary of the doctrines of the Council of Trent, was made officially binding on all Roman Catholics. Here are excerpts from its concluding paragraphs:

I acknowledge the holy, Catholic, and apostolic Roman Church as the mother and teacher of all churches; and I promise and swear true obedience to the Roman Pontiff, vicar of Christ and successor of Blessed Peter, Prince of the Apostles.

I unhesitatingly accept and profess all the doctrines . . . handed down, defined, and explained by the sacred canons and ecumenical councils and especially those of this most holy Council of Trent . . . And at the same time I condemn, reject, and anathematize everything that is contrary to those propositions, and all heresies without exception that have been condemned, rejected, and anathematized by the Church. I . . . promise, vow, and swear that, with God's help, I shall most constantly hold and profess this true Catholic faith, outside which no one can be saved and which I now freely profess and truly hold. . . . So help me God and his holy Gospel.[1]

into in great detail. Or such questions as the fallen angels, in which the earlier confessions had had no interest at all, now became points for discussion. But the Westminster standards, though enormously influential in the history of the British Reformed churches, never enjoyed usage in the Reformed churches on the continent.

The high-water mark of Reformed scholasticism was reached in a document called the Helvetic Consensus Formula, drafted in Switzerland in 1675. Though it never enjoyed wide approval outside the land of its origin, it did not hesitate to affirm the doctrine of predestination in its starkest form and the inspiration of the Bible in its most extreme statement. Since Hebrew, the language of the Old Testament, had no vowels, a system of vowels was added to the text by a group of Hebrew scholars between the sixth and eighth centuries A.D. The Helvetic Consensus Formula maintained that a Christian must believe in the literal inspiration not only of the original consonants, but of the vowels added centuries later as well!

The scholastic movement within Protestantism suffered from two major weaknesses. The first, the effects of which are still with us, is that the meaning of faith was subtly changed from the Reformation concept of personal trust and total commitment to intellectual assent to a

Form of Agreement of the Helvetic Reformed Churches (1675)

Here are the first two propositions of a creed known as the Helvetic Consensus Formula, adopted by the Reformed Churches of Switzerland. Although the formula was abandoned in fifty years, it still represents the point of view of some Protestant Christians.

I. God, the Supreme Judge, not only took care to have His word, which is the "power of God unto salvation to every one that believeth" (Rom. i. 16), committed to writing by Moses, the Prophets, and the Apostles, but has also watched and cherished it with paternal care ever since it was written up to the present time, so that it could not be corrupted by craft of Satan or fraud of man. Therefore the Church justly ascribes it to His singular grace and goodness that she has, and will have to the end of the world, a "sure word of prophecy" and "Holy Scriptures" (2 Tim. iii. 15), from which, though heaven and earth perish, "one jot or one tittle shall in no wise pass" (Matt. v. 18).

II. But, in particular, the Hebrew Original of the Old Testament, which we have received and to this day do retain as handed down by the Jewish Church, unto whom formerly "were committed the oracles of God" (Rom. iii. 2), is, not only in its consonents, but in its vowels—either the vowel points themselves, or at least the power of the points—not only in this matter, but in its words, inspired of God, thus forming, together with the Original of the New Testament, the sole and complete rule of our faith and life; and to its standard, as to a Lydian stone, all extant versions, oriental and occidental, ought to be applied, and wherever they differ, be conformed.[2]

doctrinal system. The test of genuine Christianity was not in the personal experience of God's redeeming grace in Jesus Christ but in an ability to subscribe to the orthodox position.

No one will deny that the Christian faith needs statements of doctrine and confessions of faith exactly as the human body needs a skeleton. But a skeleton alone is not a living being. In an ever increasing way these systems of doctrines did not represent a living faith but a dead orthodoxy. The reaction was bound to come sooner or later, as we shall be seeing in the near future. Scholasticism made the Protestant cause, at a critical time, a dead one by substituting scholastic discussion of abstractions for the living experience of faith.

The second weakness lies in the fact that scholasticism is by its very nature defensive. At the very time that the Roman Church (which had its own scholastic side, as Trent showed) was under the impulse of the Jesuit movement going out to conquer the world, a scholastic Protestantism was withdrawing behind its theological formularies like a besieged city. We must admit to our shame that Protestantism compares very unfavorably with Roman Catholicism in missionary effort in the seventeenth century. It seems to have lost its nerve.

A dramatic symbol of this defensive attitude took place in Geneva in 1597. Francis of Sales, one of the leaders of the Roman Catholic counterattack, paid several visits to Geneva where he tried to convert Theodore Beza, Calvin's successor, to the Roman Catholic faith. Of course, he was not successful, but his very presence in Geneva symbolizes the aggressiveness of the Roman Church and the defensiveness of the Reformed. Half a century earlier it would have been the other way around. It would have been the Protestant who would have invaded Roman Catholic territory in the name of his evangelical faith. But by 1597 apparently Protestants were glad to be able to hold the territory which was theirs, and dug themselves in behind their theological defenses.

THE THIRTY YEARS' WAR

It would have been a fine thing if the warfare could have been confined to this kind of theological combat. That, however, was not to be the case. In 1619 Frederick V, a Protestant, was chosen king of Bohemia. His father-in-law was King James I of England; his mother, the daughter of William the Silent. The Roman Catholics were not inclined to accept Frederick's election and declared war on Bohemia. Because Frederick was Reformed, he got no help from the Lutheran princes and even his father-in-law stood fairly much to one side. The result was that by 1623 Frederick had lost not only Bohemia but his own Rhenish Palatinate as well, and Protestantism had been ruthlessly suppressed in both places.

But that was only the beginning. Encouraged by the ease with which they had won Bohemia and the Palatinate, the Roman Catholic forces turned their attention to the Lutherans in northern Germany. That brought both Denmark and Norway into the fray and what had started as a local action in Bohemia became the Thirty Years' War which eventually involved all of Europe in a holocaust of destruction.

It was a war which seesawed back and forth all throughout its complicated course. By 1629 the Roman Catholics, who had two remarkable generals in the persons of Tilly and Wallenstein, thought they had conquered most of Protestant northern Germany. But they had not reckoned on the intervention of Gustavus Adolphus, the King of Sweden, himself a general of no mean ability. Nor had they reckoned on the fact that France, though a Roman Catholic country, would ally itself with the Protestant cause rather than see an imperial victory.

Everything taken by Wallenstein and Tilly was now reconquered by the triumphant Protestants, who might have swept all Europe before them, had not Gustavus Adolphus been killed at the battle of Lützen in 1632. For the next sixteen years the war dragged on in a kind of stalemate, though large areas were devastated and the costs in human misery were incalculable. When peace finally came with the Treaty of Westphalia in 1648, it was not because either side had won but because both sides were exhausted.

The irony was that the religious settlement reached at Westphalia was not very different from what the situation had been before the war began. It merely legalized what had been a kind of unofficial boundary between the faiths. It also recognized the Reformed along with the Lutheran as an official form of Protestantism. Certain concessions were made for minorities in Protestant or Roman Catholic territories.

It is easy to relate the settlement effected by the Peace of Westphalia. It is much more difficult to evaluate the condition of Protestant Europe after the war was over. To be sure, Reformed Europe had not been as badly destroyed by the war as Lutheran Europe. The strongholds of the Reformed faith in Holland, Switzerland, and Britain had not been directly involved in the conflict. Only in Germany had it suffered badly.

But even in countries which had not been directly involved, the aftermath of the Thirty Years' War was a state of exhaustion bordering on despair. On all sides religious enthusiasm was at an all-time low. People were willing to accept the settlement and to seek to maintain the *status quo* which it established. The creative time of both Roman Catholic and Protestant Europe had come to an end.

Obviously there is a definite relationship between this condition and the fascination with scholastic orthodoxy which so strongly marked the postwar era. The elaboration of theological systems was a safe occupation. It kept one within one's own limits, free from any temptation to encroach upon someone else's territory. While Lutheran still battled with Reformed and both with Roman Catholic, it was an abstract theological warfare that injured no one.

We need not be surprised that this same postwar era saw the beginning of a sceptical attitude toward all religion. After all, it was religion that had drenched Europe in blood for a period of thirty years, at least religion in an organized form. Did not that fact argue that human happiness was not to be found in organized religion but in some other place, philosophy, education, or free religion of the spirit? Such may have been the secret thoughts of many persons and they began to be the open statement of some of the more daring thinkers in Europe.

In fact, it would be difficult to find a more critical era in Christian history than that which can be seen in about the year 1650. The great upsurge of spiritual enthusiasm brought about by the Protestant Reformation had spent itself. The succeeding upsurge of the Roman Catholic Counter-Reformation was almost entirely played out. European Christianity had settled back into a fossilized orthodoxy, a petrified institutionalism, each equally lifeless. Men went through the form, but the form was increasingly dead.

But even while European Christianity had been battling itself into exhaustion, there had been religious developments in Protestant England which were to change not only the course of British history but the course of European Christianity as well. What seemed to be dying was once again to be resurrected into new life—and that from a direction which no one was expecting.

19

Puritan and Pietist

The English Reformation was a movement which had left many people dissatisfied. When King Henry VIII had broken with the papacy, it had been with as little change in the structure of the English Church as possible. Anxious to obtain a divorce from Catherine of Aragon so that he might be free to marry Anne Boleyn, Henry had removed the English Church from papal control when Rome would not comply with his wishes. Theologically Henry had no quarrel with medieval Catholicism; in fact he had won papal approval for his attack on Luther. His effort, therefore, was directed toward making himself head of the Church of England with very little internal change.

During his lifetime, matters went little further. The monasteries were suppressed and their income diverted to the crown, which used part of its wealth to form six new dioceses. Toward the end of his life, Henry showed some small Protestant sympathy by ordering the use of the English Bible and the use of the English language in minor parts of the service. But at the time of Henry's death in 1547, the Church of England remained what he had wanted it to be, a church which differed from medieval Catholicism in no way save that it was under royal rather than papal control.

His successor was his ten-year-old son Edward VI. Edward's youth meant that England was really controlled by a regency, the most important of which was Thomas Cranmer, the man whom Henry had appointed Archbishop of Canterbury in 1532. Ably assisted by the Duke of Somerset, the uncle of the young King Edward, Cranmer began a skillful policy of moving the English Church steadily in a Protestant direction while in no way disturbing its outward medieval structure. A first English Prayer Book in 1549 was soon followed by the second in 1552, clearly revealing the effects of his friendship with such leading Reformed theologians as Peter Martyr and Martin Bucer, both of whom he invited to teaching positions in England. It should also be added that Cranmer had great liturgical skill and much of the incomparable prose of the Book of Common Prayer remains as his lasting monument.

Edward's death and the accession in 1553 of his half-sister, Mary Tudor, a devout Roman Catholic, brought Cranmer's experiment to an abrupt end and indeed finally cost him his life. Mary was succeeded by her half-sister, Elizabeth, in 1558, who was anxious to steer a middle course between both extremes. The daughter of Henry and Anne Boleyn, she bore no love to the papacy because of its attitude toward her mother. But at the same time she also distrusted the continental Reformers because of what she considered their radical attitude toward the power of the state.

The resulting Elizabethan settlement, as it was called, was an attempt to satisfy everybody. While the Protestant and even Calvinistic stance of the English Church theologically was assured, the ancient episcopal structure was also guaranteed in an attempt to satisfy the Roman Catholic attitude. And the complete control of the state over the church was also maintained to satisfy the queen.

THE PURITANS

Like most compromises, it proved unsatisfactory to several groups of people. The one which concerns us was a group who became known to history as the Puritans. Though remaining in the church, they felt and said that the Elizabethan settlement had not gone far enough; much remained in the English Church to be *purified* so that the English Church might conform to the pattern of the continental Reformation. While there were many things that they objected to in form and liturgy, their chief objection centered in the direct control of the state. One of their principal points of contention was for the independence of the church in its own sphere.

We do not have the time to trace out here the varying manifestations or fortunes of Puritanism during the century following Elizabeth's accession. The fact is that it was as much a frame of mind as it was an organized movement. While some people were willing to accept the structure of the English Church, others sought to modify it in a Presbyterian direction, while still others, influenced by the Anabaptists, felt that separation and organization into independent churches was the only solution.

A minority movement for a long time, the various Puritan groups gathered strength during the reign of Charles I (1625-1649). They proved to be the winning side in the civil war which broke out in 1642, but it was the more radical wing which took control, executed the king, and established the Commonwealth which lasted under the leadership of Oliver Cromwell till 1660. Thereafter Puritanism became a minority movement once again, though definitely outside the bounds of the Church of England.

The significant side of Puritanism, whatever form it took, was its emphasis upon inwardness. We must remember that at this time all Protestant churches were state churches, churches in which, in theory, every citizen was a member of the church by virtue of his citizenship. This situation seemed to the Puritan mind to be a terrible travesty. While they had no objection to insisting that every citizen attend church, it seemed wrong to them that any should be members of the church except those who were conscious and definite believers. Personal experience and not mere citizenship should be the test of church membership.

Of course, the Anabaptist position was essentially the same. But the Puritans were not a withdrawn minority like the Anabaptists. The idea of a state church did not upset them; they only insisted that within the larger body of that church, membership should be limited strictly to those who had made a credible profession of their faith. It was almost a church within a church, a society of confessing Christians within the parish or congregation, which the Puritans advocated.

Persecuted as they were during the reigns of Mary, Elizabeth, James, and Charles, many of the Puritans took refuge in Europe, especially in Holland, which had the most open door of any European nation. Here they met many people who were ready to listen because of the widespread following which Menno Simons and the Anabaptists had already gained. The growing scholasticism of the Dutch Reformed Church proved to be a fertile soil for the Puritan theory of a church within a church. It was in the Dutch town of Middleburg that Jean de Labadie, one of the ministers (a French Roman Catholic convert), began a similar movement within the Reformed Church soon after 1660.

Many of the innovations which Labadie introduced would be accepted as matter-of-fact routines today, house to house visitation and prayer meetings, for example. His preaching had a warmly personal character, free of the expositions of dogmatic orthodoxy to which

What Were the Puritans Like?

The Puritans have often had what we may call a very bad press. In our accounts of them we may not go as far as the historian Macaulay, who remarked sourly that the Puritans hated the sport of bear-baiting, "not because it gave pain to the bear, but because it gave pleasure to the spectators"; nevertheless, we may picture them as very gloomy and grim. Here is a kindlier description of "an old English Puritane," written by a Puritan in 1646.

Dutch congregations had long been accustomed. But what brought down the wrath of the authorities and led to his expulsion in 1670 was his refusal to baptize the children of any but converted Christians and to admit to the Lord's Table any but those who could testify to their faith. Plainly it was the Puritan pattern of a church within a church which Labadie was seeking to establish and the Dutch would have no part of it.

THE PIETISTS

It was to Germany that Labadie went after his expulsion from Holland and it was in Germany that the movement which he had begun reached its full development, though on Lutheran rather than Reformed soil. In Europe the movement was called *Pietism* rather than *Puritanism,* but it was essentially the same religious point of view.

In many ways Labadie was an eccentric who was unable to build or to hold a following. The real father of German Pietism was Philip Jacob Spener. As a young minister he had come under the influence of the Labadists whose practices confirmed his own personal attitudes. When he became a pastor in Frankfurt in 1666, he began to put some of his theories into practice. He began by gathering a group of interested persons in his own home for Bible study, prayer, and a discussion of the sermon. Spener's emphasis was not upon Lutheran orthodoxy, but upon sincerity of faith and purity of life. He stressed moderation in food and drink, abstinence from the theater, card playing, and dancing, as well as personal devotion. His aim was to develop a group of regenerate Christians within the congregation.

In 1675 Spener published a book *Pia Desideria* describing his aims and his methods. Although it was bitterly attacked by the representatives of Lutheran orthodoxy, the author continued his Frankfurt ministry until he was called to be court preacher in Dresden in 1686. Here,

> The Old English Puritane was such an one that honoured God above all, and under God gave every one his due. His first care was to serve God, and therein he did not what was good in his own, but in God's sight, making the word of God the rule of his worship. He highly esteemed order in the House of God: but would not under colour of that submit to superstitious rites, which are superfluous and perish in their use . . . He made conscience of all God's ordinances, though some he esteemed of more consequence. He was much in praier; with it he began and closed the day. In it he was exercised in his closet, family and publike assembly. He esteemed that manner of praier best, where by the gift of God, expressions were varied according to present wants and occasions; Yet he did not account set forms unlawful. . . . He esteemed reading of the word an ordinance of God both in private and publike . . . The Lord's day he esteemed a divine ordinance, and rest on it necessary so far as it induced to holinesse. He was very consciencious in the observance of that day as the Mart day of the Soul . . . He accounted religion an en-

however, his religious zeal soon encountered opposition from both the university and the prince and he accepted a call to Berlin where the court was sympathetic with his program. He retired in 1698 and died in 1705.

Spener was the saintly pioneer. The organizer of the movement was his younger colleague, August Hermann Francke. As a young professor at the University of Leipzig, Francke had come under Spener's spell and been forced out of his position as a result. Through the influence of his older friend he obtained a position in 1692 in the new University of Halle. Under his leadership the school rapidly became the center of Pietism. Connected with the university was a preparatory school and an orphanage. Young persons trained in Halle went as missionaries to India, almost the first in Protestant history. Because of his close association with the Prussian king, Francke had a significant part in organizing the whole educational system of that country.

Though Pietism generally remained within the Lutheran Church, one group was distinctive. In 1722 Hussite refugees from Bohemia and Moravia settled near the estate of Nicholas, Count von Zinzendorf. A graduate of Halle himself, the Count was greatly impressed by the devotion of these refugees. He identified himself with them and became their bishop. Under the inspiration of Zinzendorf's leadership and his worldwide vision, the Moravian Church, as it came to be called, became the pioneer missionary church in Protestant history, the only church which even today has a larger membership in its missionary fields than it has in its homeland.

Pietism was a less influential movement in the Reformed Churches because the scholastic movement against which it was a protest had never gained dominance in them. But in the Dutch Church by the mid-eighteenth century Pietism had become the strongest party.

gagement to duty, that the best Christians should be the best husbands, best wives, best parents, best children, best Masters, best servants, best Magistrates, best subjects, that the doctrine of God might be adorned not blasphemed. His family he endeavoured to make a Church, both in regard of persons and exercises, admitting none into it but such as feared God; and labouring that those that were born in it, might be born again to God . . . He was a man of tender heart, not only in regard of his own sin, but others' misery, not counting mercy arbitrary, but a necessary duty: wherein as he prayed for wisdom to direct him, so he studied for cheerfulnesse and a bounty to act . . . In his habit he avoided costlinesse and vanity, neither exceeding his degree in civility nor declining what suited with Christianity, desiring in all things to express gravity. His whole life he accounted a warfare, wherein Christ was his captain, his arms, praiers and tears. The Crosse his Banner and his word *Vincit qui patitur*.[1]

Of greater importance to us is the hold which the Puritan and Pietist movement gained on American Christianity. For one thing, New England, the strongest of the settlements in the new world, was almost entirely a Puritan settlement. But though this fact of history is well known, we tend to forget the influence which Pietism had on other American churches. Count Zinzendorf came to this country with a large part of his Moravian movement, for example. And many, though not all, of the men who volunteered for service in the Dutch and German churches in North America were of the Pietist persuasion, the calling to serve in the wilderness answering their sense of mission. Two examples will suffice. Henry Muhlenberg, the great pioneer of American Lutheranism, was a graduate of the University of Halle. Theodore Frelinghuysen, the great preacher of revival in the Dutch Reformed Church in New Jersey, was a strong Pietist. Perhaps nowhere in the world did Puritanism and Pietism gain such strength as in the American church. We still feel the effect of it today.

Many present-day writers are quite critical of the Pietist movement but, put in its own time and setting, we can see its true values. It was responsible for the revival of religious seriousness at a time when religion tended to become outward formality. What is more important, Pietism restored one side of the Reformation emphasis which had fallen into great neglect. The necessity of personal experience which had been so strongly present in a man like Luther and which had almost entirely been replaced by theological orthodoxy became a central Pietist emphasis. Nor should we forget that it was Pietism which stirred the church into good works. Missions, hospitals, orphanages, systematic care of the poor—wherever Pietism prevailed, these were its signs.

Great as its accomplishments were and necessary as Pietism was as a reaction against the dead formalism of orthodoxy, we do have to point out its weaknesses, especially since it has proved to be such an influential movement in our own tradition. Perhaps the most significant weakness was its theological carelessness. To be sure, Pietism was in reaction against a theology that was a lifeless scholastic orthodoxy, the only concern of which was in dotting doctrinal *i*'s and crossing dogmatic *t*'s. We cannot blame men like Spener and Francke for thinking that this kind of thing had little to do with the gospel. But just because the theology which they knew was so irrelevant, they tended to dismiss theological concern without a second thought. It was the heart and not the head that mattered.

Surely we all can recognize that that kind of thinking is still with us, that there is a straight line that runs from the early Pietists to the crudest kind of contemporary evangelism. But what is less readily recognized is the way in which this withdrawal from intellectual effort has seriously damaged Protestantism. It has reduced the Protestant experience to an individual and private religious experience with no connection to the events of the world around it. And the consequences have been disastrous.

The early Reformers were men who knew the value of individual experience. But they were also men who knew the necessity of building that experience into a total philosophy. A man like John Calvin, for example, not only stressed individual experience, but he had a theology that involved an interpretation of the meaning of history and the life of society as well. Reformation theology was no withdrawal into the shell of private religion but rather the enabling of private religion to meet the world with a faith that was large enough to endure and conquer.

It is to the Pietist that we largely owe the unhappy division of life into religious and secular. The refusal of religion to speak to the social, economic, and political situations of history, a refusal which many people still consider to be very religious, can be traced back to the Pietist reluctance to develop an adequate theology.

A second unhappy consequence of Pietism has been the identification of religion with moralism. We have already noticed the Pietist insistence upon purity of life as an evidence of Christian seriousness. With that insistence surely no one can quarrel. But the Pietist went on to list certain social evils of his century in which the pure could not participate, such as the theater, dancing, drinking, and card playing. We cannot even quarrel with his list since we are not in a position to know exactly what these things involved in his society. (This was one of the places that Count Zinzendorf and the Moravians separated themselves from classical Pietism.)

The Pietist moral standard was an expression of the Pietist religious fervor. As that religious fervor waned, it became easy to substitute the tests of outward morality for it. The end result was the identification of the Christian gospel in the minds of many (even to this very day) with what could be called negative virtue. "A Christian is one who does not drink, smoke, dance, or play cards."

Admittedly such an identification would have horrified the Pietist as much as anyone since it left out the religious conversion which he knew was so essential. Yet by putting such great stress on the moral evidences of conversion and in such particulars, he made the result inevitable. The result in Christian ethics was sad indeed. Scores of persons still believe that the Christian ethic consists largely in the observance of these "thou shalt nots" which, after all, are relatively easy to observe.

In the meantime the real Christian ethic, "Love thy neighbor as thyself," goes virtually unnoticed. Again without intending it, Pietism produced the new Pharisee. The very kind of negative legalism against which our Lord had protested so strongly became in large degree the Protestant standard, replacing the ethical marks of discipleship which He had stressed. "By this all men will know that you are my disciples, if you have love for one another" (John 13:35).

Someone has said that the contemporary American Protestant is much more the child of Pietism than he is of the Reformation. That may be an exaggeration. But it is interesting to observe how much of of our twentieth century theological thinking has been an attempt to go back to the Reformation, a tacit admission, it would seem, that we were deriving our heritage from another source.

Still Pietism had not yet made its greatest contribution to the life of the church. Born in Britain, developed in Germany, it was to return to Britain and there become responsible for one of the greatest movements in Protestant history.

A Hymn on the Love of Christ

Feeling, the inner feeling of the individual Christian, was the characteristic emphasis of the hymns of Pietism. This hymn, written by Adam Drese, who was associated with the Pietist leader Spener, is a good example. This was one of the hymns of the German Pietists brought to America by the Moravians in the eighteenth century. On Christmas Eve, 1741, the new Moravian settlement in Pennsylvania founded by Count von Zinzendorf took its name Bethlehem from the words of this hymn.

Jesus, call Thou me,
From the world to Thee;
Speed me ever, stay me never;
   Jesus, call Thou me.

Not Jerusalem—
Lowly Bethlehem
'Twas that gave us Christ to save us;
   Not Jerusalem.

Favored Bethlehem!
Honored is that name;
Thence came Jesus to release us;
   Favored Bethlehem!

Wondrous Child divine!
Warm this heart of mine;
Keep it burning, for Thee yearning,
   Wondrous Child divine!

Do not me reject;
Let Thy light reflect
From me ever, blessed Saviour;
   Do not me reject.

O that look of love!
May I here, above,
Give Thee blessing never ceasing,
   For that look of love.[2]
       —Adam Drese (1620–1701)

20

The World Is My Parish

Fire! fire! rang the cry in the little English village of Epworth on a cold February night in 1709. The vicarage, home of the Reverend and Mrs. Samuel Wesley and their large family, was ablaze, and no one could save it. Their little six-year-old son, John, was trapped in the upper story beneath the burning thatch. Just before the roof came crashing in he was rescued. For all the years of his long life he would think of himself as "a brand plucked from the burning."

Deciding to follow in his father's footsteps, John Wesley went to Oxford to prepare himself for the priesthood of the Church of England. In 1726 he was elected a fellow of Lincoln College, Oxford (a fellowship which involved his ordination as a deacon). Later, while John was away assisting his father, his younger brother Charles came to Oxford. Charles attracted a very small group of serious-minded students including a charity scholar named George Whitefield. Distressed by the state of the English Church, they formed a group which by prayer, fasting, Bible study, and frequent participation in Holy Communion proposed to do something about it. John joined them upon his return and became their leader. The jeers of their fellow-students who called them a "Holy Club," "Bible Moths," "Enthusiasts," or "Methodists" in no way deterred them.

There was much reason to be distressed about the English Church. Not only was it still a department of the state, closely reflecting political trends and changes, but it had in many ways become lazy and indifferent. Worn out by the theological battles of the previous century, the dominant school of thought had become *latitudinarian;* that is to say, the center of interest was in morality and virtue, preached in an uninspired fashion, rather than in doctrine, ecclesiastical organization, and liturgy. Enthusiasm of any sort was considered fanatical. It was a church which, though it still retained the loyalty of the gentry, had lost the common man.

In 1735 John Wesley accepted an assignment from the Society for the Propagation of the Gospel and came to the new world with his brother Charles. Savannah, Georgia, was the scene of his ministry, but it was not a happy experience. Even while a leader in the Oxford Holy Club, John Wesley was disturbed about his own lack of inner peace and confidence. He had accepted the call to Georgia because he hoped that in so strenuous an assignment he might lose himself and his spiritual worries. Before he went he wrote, "My chief motive is the hope of saving my own soul.... I cannot hope to attain the same degree of holiness here which I may there."[1]

By 1737 he was ready to return to England. His forthright preaching had brought him into conflict with the authorities. His rigid discipline had alienated many of the members of his flock. But his real reason for returning was the fact that he had not found what he was looking for in Georgia. The same spiritual unrest which had plagued him in Oxford had followed him to the new world. "I went to America to convert the Indians, but O! who shall convert me?"[2]

THE INNER AWAKENING

While in Georgia, however, he had met the Moravians and had been much impressed with the strength of their spiritual life. After his return to London, he spent a good deal of time with the little Moravian group there and was especially influenced by their leader, Peter Böhler. Late in the afternoon of May 24, 1738, after he had attended evensong in St. Paul's Cathedral, this unhappy priest of the English Church decided to visit a Bible study and prayer group he knew would be meeting that night. What happened is worth recording in Wesley's own words.

> In the evening I went very unwillingly to a society in Aldersgate-street, where one was reading Luther's preface to the Epistle to the Romans. About a quarter before nine, while he was describing the change which God works in the heart through faith in Christ, I felt my heart strangely warmed. I felt I did trust in Christ, Christ alone, for salvation; and an assurance was given me that He had taken away my sins, even mine, and saved me from the law of sin and death.[3]

Charles Wesley Sings of His Conversion

The story of John Wesley's conversion is well known. It is remarkable that his brother Charles had a similar experience just three days earlier, on May 21, 1738, Pentecost Sunday, when he found peace for his soul in reading Luther's Commentary on Galatians. He expressed his joy in the event by writing a hymn, four stanzas of which follow. On Wednesday of that week Charles wrote in his journal: "Towards ten, my brother was brought in triumph by a troop of our friends, and declared, 'I believe.' We sang the hymn with great joy, and parted with prayer."[4]

We may pause here long enough to notice the striking similarity between Wesley's experience and that of Luther. In each case there was the same hunger for religious confidence and peace. Both men had thrown themselves enthusiastically into the observance of religious formalities without result. Both men found their answer in Paul. Indeed, it was Luther's commentary on Paul's Letter to the Romans that proved to be the turning point in John Wesley's life.

The heart that was strangely warmed in Aldersgate Street that May evening soon began to blaze with religious passion. After his experience, Wesley's first move was to visit Germany and the headquarters of the Moravians who had been so influential in leading him to his new understanding of the faith. On his return to England, he offered himself for every available pulpit he could find, preaching his newfound faith with ardor and devotion. But he was almost never invited back. His kind of preaching was not welcome in the English Church of that day.

In the midst of his discouragement over his inability to get a hearing, he learned that his former associate, George Whitefield, whose enthusiasm had met with a similar reception, had begun preaching in the open air. In many ways it was a practice which shocked Wesley's rather strict churchmanship. But once he saw Whitefield in action, preaching to three thousand people in a field near Bristol, he changed his mind. ". . . all my life (till very lately) [I have been] so tenacious of every point relating to decency and order, that I should have thought the saving of souls almost a sin, if it had not been done in a church."[5] The very next day he preached his first open-air sermon, the beginning of a career which was to last for fifty years and include forty thousand sermons.

The sheer recounting of Wesley's activities in the next half century is astounding. He began preaching every morning at five, "one of the

Where shall my wond'ring Soul begin?
  How shall I All to Heaven aspire?
A Slave redeem'd from Death and Sin,
  A Brand pluck'd from Eternal Fire,
How shall I equal Triumphs raise,
And sing my great Deliverer's Praise!

O how shall I the Goodness tell,
  Father, which Thou to me hast show'd,
That I, a Child of Wrath, and Hell,
  I should be call'd a Child of GOD!
Should know, should feel my Sins forgiven,
Blest with this Antepast of Heaven!

And shall I slight my Father's Love,
  Or basely fear his Gifts to own?
Unmindful of his Favours prove?
  Shall I the hallow'd Cross to shun
Refuse his Righteousness t'impart
By hiding it within my Heart?

No—tho' the Antient Dragon rage
  And call forth all his Hosts to War,
Tho' Earth's self-righteous Sons engage;
  Them, and their God alike I dare:
JESUS the Sinner's Friend proclaim,
JESUS, to Sinners still the same.[6]

most healthy exercises in the world," as he called it. He never traveled less than 4,500 miles in a year (mostly on horseback). Accepting his own average figure would mean that his preaching tours in England, Scotland, and Ireland covered 225,000 miles and must have involved literally millions of hearers!

THE OUTER AWAKENING

Great as Wesley's gifts were as a preacher and an evangelist, his talent for organization was even greater. For Wesley soon saw that the huge crowds who gathered to hear him and Whitefield could just as quickly be lost if something were not done to channel their religious enthusiasm and keep it alive. He was not content with a hit-and-run performance; he was equally concerned with following through. But he realized that the parish church was not the place to which his converts should be sent. Not only did they come, for the most part, from the poor, but their new enthusiasm would be completely dampened by the lackadaisical attitude of the average parish and its clergy.

Wesley began his preaching in 1739 and as early as 1739 he was organizing his followers into societies with chapels, simple buildings in which they could hold their meetings. He made it abundantly clear that they were not churches. Difficult as it was, Wesley wanted to remain a loyal son of the Church of England. To pay for these chapels, the society was divided into groups of twelve, each with a collector. Each member pledged himself to give a penny a week.

But John Wesley's shrewd mind soon saw that what had been organized for financial reasons held very great possibilities for spiritual growth and development. It was the small group in which experiences could be freely shared, doubts and temptations openly confessed, in which the new Christian would have the best chance to grow in grace. The bands of twelve became class meetings, each with its own leader. The class meeting became the foundation stone in the Methodist movement.

Naturally Wesley's success was the occasion for much bitter opposition within the Church of England. More than once he was brought before an irate bishop who admonished him to cease his activities. When one such ecclesiastical dignitary charged him with invading another man's parish without his consent, the famous reply was, "I look upon all the world as my parish." And he did. Social evils such as the slave trade and the horrible conditions in English prisons and hospitals were things which he publicly denounced. Sunday schools and every conceivable kind of charity were things which he publicly favored. Great as was his passion for souls, John Wesley never lost sight of the fact that souls are deeply conditioned by social conditions.

THE BROADENING MOVEMENT

It had been one of his great hopes to keep his Methodist societies in some way, at least, loosely connected with the English Church, even though that church did not seem to want them. As the numbers of his followers increased and the supply of ordained ministers was slim, he made use of lay preachers. But the Methodist movement had been carried across the Atlantic to the new world of America, which was now an independent republic, and by 1784 something had to be done. As early as 1780 he had asked the bishop of London for help and had been refused. After much heart-searching he ordained men for service in America himself without the bishop's permission. Later he did the same for Scotland, and finally for England. That decision meant, of course, that Methodism was now a separate church, even though John Wesley to his dying day professed his loyalty to the Church of England.

Right up to his death in 1791 he continued his activities. At the time of his death, his movement counted 294 preachers and almost 72,000 members in Great Britain, 198 preachers and 43,000 members in America. But statistics of that sort hardly tell the whole story. One of England's greatest historians claimed that it was John Wesley who saved England from a bloody disaster like the French Revolution. While most historians agree that that verdict is probably an exaggeration, it does contain a strong element of truth.

For John Wesley's principal mission was to the poor and outcast, principally the victims of the first phases of the Industrial Revolution. These victims were without money, without steady employment, sweated and abused when they did have work, herded into impossible living conditions in great cities, spending most of their free time in

John Wesley Writes of His Ministry

Throughout much of his long and busy life, John Wesley kept a journal. The day-by-day entries tell a great deal about his times, his early spiritual struggle, and the evangelistic labors which took him up and down Great Britain. A sampling of the journals, from the early years and the late years of his ministry, will give something of the story.

gin shops. Who knows what might have happened if the voice which captured their attention had been one representing another gospel? It was from just such a class that revolution was born in France and later in Russia. While society in England was probably more stable, there were real possibilities for trouble in the situation as it was.

Not that John Wesley thought of himself as a social reformer. He was out to save souls. But it was the gospel which he devoted his life to preaching, and this meant that he was never afraid to denounce social injustice in the name of his Lord. The real product of John Wesley's mission was new people, men and women who had been lifted from their hopelessness to new dignity and freedom as the children of God. What the English situation might have been without them we cannot say. But with them social change came without disaster.

Nor was Wesley's influence confined to his own Methodist movement. George Whitefield, his early associate, broke with him in later years over the question of Calvinism. The Calvinistic Methodists under Whitefield's leadership and under the patronage of a pious noblewoman, Selina, the Countess of Huntingdon, became a separate group, though representing essentially the same evangelical position as the Wesleys.

Even greater was his influence in his own Church of England. For as Wesley continued his work, there was a growing evangelical party which developed in that church. These men did not employ all of his methods and they certainly did not approve of his break with the church when he ordained men for service in America. But they shared his point of view and believed that it was possible to develop that point of view within the English Church.

September 17, 1738 (London).–I began again to declare in my own country the glad tidings of salvation, preaching three times, and afterwards expounding the holy Scripture, to a large company in the Minories. On Monday I rejoiced to meet with our little society, which now consisted of thirty-two persons.

The next day I went to the condemned felons, in Newgate, and offered them free salvation. In the evening I went to a society in Bear Yard, and preached repentance and remission of sins. The next evening I spoke the truth in love at a society in Aldersgate Street: some contradicted at first, but not long; so that nothing but love appeared at our parting.

June 11, 1739.–I look upon all the world as my parish; thus far I mean, that, in whatever part of it I am, I judge it meet, right, and my bounden duty, to declare unto all that are willing to hear, the glad tidings of salvation.

And they were right. While there were always several points of view represented within the Church of England, the dominant party when Wesley began his ministry was, as we have seen, latitudinarian. A century later it was universally acknowledged that the dominant group within the English Church was the evangelical party. As late as 1768, six students were expelled from St. Edmund Hall in Oxford for "too much religion." But the tide was turning. Wesley himself did not live to see it. But the rise to power and prominence of the evangelical party within the Church of England was largely the result of the work of John Wesley, a son whom that church was never able fully to accept.

We have spoken exclusively about John Wesley. A word should also be said about his younger brother Charles, who was his able assistant and whose talent contributed greatly to the successful spread of Methodism. John Wesley had not much more than begun his field preaching when he realized the power of music in the work of evangelism. The Methodists must be a singing people! But the possibilities were limited. The tradition still called almost exclusively for the singing of the psalms in meter, and such a close use of the Old Testament gave little chance for the expression of evangelical fervor. Isaac Watts, a Congregational minister, had tried rewriting the metrical psalms from a New Testament point of view and had been severely criticized for doing so.

No, if the Methodists were to be a singing people they must have their own hymnbook. John Wesley did not hesitate to make use of catchy and popular folk tunes for his music. For the verses he turned to his brother Charles, although he wrote a few himself. Writing for one edition of the Methodist hymnbook after another, Charles Wesley became England's greatest hymn-writer—and its most prolific. More

March 24, 1785.–I was now considering how strangely the grain of mustard-seed, planted about fifty years ago, has grown up. It has spread through all Great Britain and Ireland; the Isle of Wight and the Isle of Man; then to America, from the Leeward Islands, through the whole continent, into Canada and Newfoundland. And the societies, in all these parts, walk by one rule, knowing religion is holy tempers; and striving to worship God, not in form only, but likewise "in spirit and in truth."

October 24, 1790.–I explained, to a numerous congregation in Spitalfields church, "the whole armour of God." St. Paul's, Shadwell, was still more crowded in the afternoon, while I enforced that important truth, "One thing is needful"; and I hope many, even then, resolved to choose the better part.

This is the last entry in the journal. He died March 2, 1791, with the words, "The best of all is, God is with us!"[7]

than 5,500 hymns came from his pen, including such universal favorites as "Jesus, Lover of my soul," "Love Divine, all loves excelling," and "Hark! the herald angels sing." Though Charles was more loyal to the English Church than John and strongly disapproved of his ordinations, they remained close fellow-workers. The three years that John lived after the death of Charles in 1788 were lonely ones indeed.

Great as John Wesley's talent for preaching was, we must not underestimate the great contribution made by Charles Wesley's talent for hymn-writing. That made it possible for the gospel to sing its way into the hearts of the hearers, even as it found its way there through preaching. It would be foolish to claim the importance of one over the other. Together they made a powerful combination.

Of course, the evangelical movement whether expressed in Methodism or within the Church of England was not without its weaknesses. In general they were the same weaknesses which we have already noticed in Pietism, for the evangelical revival was largely Pietist in its origin and inspiration. But we may add one additional weakness which showed itself strongly in English and American evangelicalism and, like so many others, is still influential today.

The evangelical emphasis fell on the individual. It was his personal salvation that was at stake; it was his personal decision that was sought. The entire proclamation of the gospel was in individual terms. In many ways such an emphasis was quite understandable. Men like John Wesley had had an individual experience which they could communicate. In a lazy and indifferent church, it was only individuals who could make changes.

Necessary as such an individual emphasis may have been, it seriously weakened the evangelical doctrine of the church to the point where there almost was none. " 'What God has thus joined, let not man put asunder (Mark x.9): to those to whom he is a Father, the Church must also be a mother,"[8] wrote John Calvin. But that point of view would have meant nothing to an evangelical. The nurture of the church, the corporate character of the Christian gospel, the church as the body of Christ, these were all concepts which he lost.

The result was that while in many ways the evangelical revival greatly strengthened the church, in this way it weakened it. For the logical consequence of an exclusive stress on the individual is that religion becomes a private business. The church and its worship become something which is there for my benefit, to give me strength and renewal; if I do not find what I am looking for, I shall leave and look for it somewhere else.

All of this kind of thing, which has a very modern sound, is the result of making individual salvation the end of the Christian gospel. We can easily understand how a long lack of concern for the individual in orthodox Protestantism led to such a reaction. But we must also understand how the reaction itself was unhealthy. If, as someone has remarked, our age will be known as the age in which Protestants rediscovered the church, the evangelical revival was the age in which we began to lose it.

PART VI
THE CHURCH FACES NEW WORLDS

•

The Territory of the United States in 1789

•

LORD, here is a poor sinner, thy creature redeemed by the blood of thy Son, that has long been a slave to other masters, and withheld from thee thy just and dear-bought property; here, Lord, I would now, freely and without reserve, devote and surrender myself, my soul and body, and my all to thee, to be universally and for ever thine. And let the omnipotent God, let angels and men, be witness to the engagement.[1]
—Samuel Davies (1723–61)

O GOD, we pray for thy Church, which is set today amid the perplexities of a changing order, and face to face with a great new task. We remember with love the nurture she gave to our spiritual life in its infancy, the tasks she set for our growing strength, the influence of the devoted hearts she gathers, the steadfast power for good she has exerted. When we compare her with all other human institutions, we rejoice, for there is none like her. But when we judge her by the mind of her Master, we bow in . . . contrition. Oh, baptize her afresh in the life-giving spirit of Jesus! . . . Put upon her lips the ancient gospel of her Lord. . . . Fill her with the prophets' scorn of tyranny, and with a Christlike tenderness for the heavy-laden and down-trodden. . . . Bid her cease from seeking her own life, lest she lose it. Make her valiant to give up her life to humanity, that like her crucified Lord she may mount by the path of the cross to a higher glory.[2]
—Walter Rauschenbusch (1861–1918)

O LORD, our heavenly Father,
You hear us praying here in Takoradi.
You hear our brothers praying in Africa,
in Asia, in Australia,
in America, and in Europe.
We are all one in prayer.
We praise and honor you,
and we beg you
that we may rightly carry out your commission:
to witness and to love.
In our church and throughout the whole world.
Accept our prayers graciously,
even when they are somewhat strange.
We praise you and pray to you
through Jesus Christ, our Lord.
Amen.[3] —a young contemporary African Christian

21

The New World of America

Mention the settlement of America to almost anyone and the first picture he will probably see is that of the Mayflower in Plymouth Harbor while the pilgrim passengers step off on Plymouth Rock as they begin a new life in a new world. Ask the average American why they came and he will reply without any hesitation that they came to establish a new way of life in which religious freedom could be enjoyed by all.

Since the Pilgrims have become such an important part of our American mythology, it is a good thing for us to ask exactly who they were and why they did come. Actually, they were Separatists, people who believed that no reforming of the Church of England could ever make it right and that the only alternative was to leave it altogether. The chief exponent of this point of view in England had been Robert Browne who had actually formed the first independent congregation in England, in Norwich. Persecuted by the civil and religious authorities alike, he had fled with many of his people to Holland. He returned to England, however, and became reconciled to the English Church in 1586, serving as one of its clergy from 1591 until his death in 1633.

But many of Browne's followers (in England the Pilgrims were called *Brownists*) were opposed to any reconciliation and continued their separatist movement. One such group was the Separatist congregation in Scrooby, which also migrated to Holland and from Holland sailed for the new world of America in 1620.

The religious freedom which they sought was simply the freedom to organize a church as they saw fit without any harrassment from ecclesiastical officials. It is hard to say what their attitude toward other churches might have been since in that small original company there

June, 1607. When I went first to Virginia, I well remember we did hang an awning (which is an old sail) to three or four trees to shadow us from the sun, our walls were rails of wood, our seats unhewed trees till we cut planks, our pulpit a bar of wood nailed to two neighboring trees. . . . This was our church. . . .[1]

—Recollections of Captain John Smith

were no other churches. Their sole aim was to have a church freed from all control by the state, organized on what they considered to be purely spiritual lines. They were sure that the Reformation had not gone far enough. They believed that they were taking it all the way. The words of their leader John Robinson (who did not ever get to America) clearly state their purpose.

> I bewail the condition of the reformed churches who are come to a period in religion . . . The Lutherans cannot be drawn to go beyond what Luther saw. And the Calvinists, as you see [they were in Holland at the time], stick where Calvin left them . . . Luther and Calvin were precious shining lights in their times, yet God did not reveal his whole will to them . . . I am very confident that the Lord hath more truth and light yet to break forth out of His Holy Word.[2]

MASSACHUSETTS BAY

Great as was the heroism of the Pilgrims, Plymouth never became an important colony. In 1630 its population was only three hundred. The more important colony was begun a few years later some fifty miles north of Plymouth and under very different auspices. The Massachusetts Bay colony was one of the most carefully planned religious migrations in all history.

The Puritans, as we have seen, were a party who chose to remain within the Church of England while battling against its formalism and its state domination. But in the England of 1625 they were having a hard time of it. Charles I, a monarch of strong high church convictions, was on the throne and the agent for his ecclesiastical policies was Archbishop Laud who had been merciless in his efforts to rid the church of Puritan influence.

The Bay Company, whose first settlers came to Salem in 1629 and then a year later to the more famous settlement of Boston, was composed of upper middle class Puritans, many of them university graduates, quite different from the simpler folk who had come to Plymouth. The two leaders of the colony were John Winthrop and Thomas Dudley, both laymen. Winthrop, a conservative aristocrat, was governor of Massachusetts Bay twelve times and proved a clever lawyer in protecting the interests of the colony against threats of interference from England.

Dudley was a less attractive person. His rigid insistence upon strict Calvinism and his stern opposition to the toleration of any other religious point of view colored the whole history of New England. His attitude toward tolerance can be seen in a little poem which he wrote.

> Let men of God in courts and churches watch
> O'er such as do a Toleration hatch,
> Lest that ill egg bring forth a cockatrice
> To poison all with heresy and vice.³

Though they had many objections to some of the forms and ceremonies in the English Church, the first settlers in Massachusetts still considered themselves to be loyal sons of that church. As one of them said, "We do not go to New England as Separatists from the Church of England, though we cannot but separate from the corruptions in it; but we go to practice the positive part of church reformation, and propagate the gospel in America."⁴

But developments in Massachusetts made it clear that the purification of the Church of England was almost a total one. It was not an emended version of the church but a total reconstruction that the colonists were seeking. Indeed, when two colonists in Salem, John and Samuel Brown, suggested the use of an expurgated prayer book, they were unceremoniously shipped back to England.

So radical was the purification of the church that the end result was almost the same as the Separatist church in Plymouth. In fact when Samuel Fuller, a Plymouth physician, came to Massachusetts to bring help in a medical crisis, he found such great similarities between the two churches that a federation of the two colonies followed.

The real concern of the Massachusetts Bay Colony, however, was more in the organization of society than of the church. It was their intention to form a theocracy in which state and church would be seen more closely affiliated than they had been in old England. Only the members of the church had the privilege of voting in the community. The church was entirely supported by public taxation. Any dissent from the church or criticism of it was a form of treason against the

> August, 1630. We, of the congregation, kept a fast, and chose Mr. Wilson our teacher, and Mr. Nowell an elder, and Mr. Gager and Mr. Aspinwall, deacons. We used imposition of hands, but with this protestation by all, that it was only as a sign of election and confirmation, not of any intent that Mr. Wilson should renounce his ministry he received in England.⁵
>
> —John Winthrop, *Journal*

state. No other form of religion, therefore, could be permitted. " 'Tis Satan's policy to plead for an indefinite and boundless toleration," said one of the Puritan leaders.

Because they realized that they were setting up a completely self-contained society which could in no way be dependent upon England, the Puritan leaders provided as soon as they could for a total educational system. As early as 1636 they founded their college in Cambridge. Through a bequest from an interested Puritan clergyman in New England, it received the name of Harvard. A complete public school system became law in 1647.

There is not the time here to trace out the later history of New England, the protests against the organization by people like Roger Williams and Anne Hutchinson, the gradual modifications which the theocracy had to undergo, the ways in which the control of the church over society was relaxed. Even though the experiment has to be called a failure, it left a lasting mark upon American religious life far beyond the bounds of New England. The narrow intolerance of the Puritan disappeared. The control of the church disappeared. But the moral view of society, the insistence that all social and economic questions must be seen and solved in the light of their moral significance, an attitude which is peculiarly American, is our lasting New England heritage. Students of American society may disagree as to whether it has been a healthy or a harmful heritage, but no one can disagree as to its existence or its origin.

NEW NETHERLAND

The great place occupied in American history by the various New England settlements often makes us forget that there were other Protestant settlements in the new world equally as early, even if somewhat less dramatic. The young Dutch republic was also interested in the new world and as early as 1609 commissioned the English explorer Henry Hudson to make its claim. That claim was established by him to the land lying on either side of the river which still bears his name.

Small outposts were established in this new Dutch territory as early as 1614, though they involved only a tiny handful of people. They grew slowly, especially since Holland was a prosperous country free from religious persecution and actively practicing that very toleration which was so hateful to the New England mind. But by 1624 there were sufficient people in the colony, even though there were neither religious nor economic pressures to bring them, to require some form of religious ministration.

At first the Dutch Church commissioned two young men, Jan Huyck and Bastian Krol to serve as "Krankenbezoekers" or "Comforters of the Sick." They had the power to perform any ministerial act except the Sacrament of the Lord's Supper. Working out of the two settlements of New Amsterdam and Fort Orange (New York and Albany) they conducted Sunday services, using the liturgy and sermons of distinguished divines in Holland, conducting catechism classes, calling on the sick, and baptizing babies.

Helpful as their ministry was, it was soon realized that it was not enough. In 1628 an ordained minister, Jonas Michaelius, was sent out. In the spring of that same year a congregation was organized in New Amsterdam, the first congregation of what we today know as the Reformed Church in America. A second congregation was organized in Fort Orange in 1642 when Domine Johannes Megapolensis arrived from the Netherlands.

Megapolensis was a man of great gifts. Feeling a concern about the Mohawk Indians who lived all around him in the Hudson and Mohawk valleys, he learned their difficult language so that he could teach them the Christian faith. Many of them were baptized and joined his congregation. Both in Forth Orange and later in New Amsterdam he showed great friendliness to the Jesuit missionaries in New France, including the famous Isaac Jogues, and more than once used his good relationships with the Indians to rescue the missionaries from trouble.

It was Megapolensis who advised the surrender of the colony to the English in 1664, despite the protests of the colorful governor, Pieter Stuyvesant. Though for a brief period in 1674 it returned to Dutch

August, 1628. From the beginning we established the form of a church; and as Brother Bastiaen Crol very seldom comes down from Fort Orange, because the Directorship of that fort and the trade there is committed to him, it has been thought best to choose two elders for my assistance and for the proper consideration of all such ecclesiastical matters as might occur . . . One of those whom we have now chosed is the Honorable Director himself [Peter Minuit], and the other is the storekeeper of the company, Jan Huyghens. . . .

At the first administration of the Lord's Supper which was observed, not without great joy and comfort to many, we had fully fifty communicants— Walloons and Dutch; of whom, a portion made their first confession of faith before us, and others exhibited their church certificates.[6]

—Letter from Rev. Jonas Michaelius

control, New Netherland really came to an end in 1664 when it became the two English colonies of New York and New Jersey.

Although there were only thirteen Reformed congregations in the colony at the time of the surrender, they had a firm foothold in the new world and continued to multiply even in the new situation of English control. For the next century the authorities in Amsterdam continued to administer these American congregations. There were, of course, great difficulties because of distance and lack of communication. The greatest difficulty was the fact that the Dutch authorities insisted that theological education and ordination could take place only in Holland. Despite these difficulties and the tensions which they later created, the Reformed Church soon took its place as one of the significant denominations in the two provinces in which it had begun.

The Dutch story was quite different, then, from the New England story. The Puritan settlement was for deeply religious motives of which their church was the central expression. The Dutch settlement, on the other hand, was simply a colonial expansion into which the Reformed Church tried to follow its own people. It is a sad commentary on both settlements that with few exceptions like Megapolensis in Albany or John Eliot in Massachusetts, neither church felt an urgency about bringing the gospel to the native Indian population which they found on these shores. Such an attitude was in marked contrast to that of the Roman Catholic Church in New France which, while it ministered to its own people, also had large-scale missionary activity among the Indians.

THE DISSENTERS

In the English colonies, apart from the Puritan colonies of New England, it was the Church of England which tried to follow its own people. In all of the southern colonies it was the established form of religion; in others like New York it enjoyed a highly preferred position. But there was good reason to suppose that in spite of its dominant position the English Church was by no means the preference of many English-speaking persons in the new world. A family census taken in New York in 1695, for example, revealed the following:

Dutch Reformed	1,754
French Reformed	260
Dutch Lutheran	45
Church of England	90
English Dissenters	1,365

On the basis of such figures it is obvious that the needs of the majority of English-speaking persons in New York were not being met by the English Church. That need was apparent also to Francis Makemie, a Presbyterian minister. Born in Ireland in 1658, Makemie had come to America in 1683 because he had been moved by the desperate need of Presbyterian settlers on the eastern shore of Maryland. Once he had arrived there, he soon made the whole eastern seaboard from New York to the Carolinas his parish. For these colonies contained large numbers of Scottish and particularly Scotch-Irish immigrants. While in some places in South Carolina they had been able to organize themselves into congregations, for the most part they were left entirely unprovided for.

Francis Makemie can well be called the father of Presbyterianism in this country. For he went up and down the eastern seaboard preaching to Presbyterians and organizing them into congregations wherever possible. Twice he crossed the Atlantic seeking funds from well-to-do Irish Presbyterians for his work. Sometimes that work was not easy. When he preached in New York in 1706, for example, he was clapped into jail by the governor for being a disturber of the peace. Asked by the governor, Lord Cornbury, to promise to give up preaching, Makemie replied, "If your Lordship require it, we will give security for our behaviour; but to give bond not to preach . . . if invited by the people, we neither can nor dare do it."[7]

In this same year of 1706 Makemie was able to organize the first American presbytery. Though it contained only seven ministers and stretched from Long Island to Virginia, it meant that the Presbyterian cause had at last been firmly established in the new world. In the next century growth was extremely rapid. Within ten years of its formation the original presbytery had become a synod with four presbyteries,

Philadelphia, March 28, 1707. . . . We are so far, upon our return home; tho' I must return for a finall Tryall which will be very troublesome and expensive. And we only had liberty, to attend a Meeting of Ministers we had formerly appointed here [the second meeting of the first organized presbytery]; and were only Seven in number, at first, but expect a growing number: Our design is to meet yearly, and oftener, if necessary, to consult the most proper measures, for advancing religion, and propagating Christianity in our Various Stations, and to mentain Such a Correspondence as may conduce to the improvement of our Ministeriall ability . . .[8]

—Letter from Rev. Francis Makemie

and others soon followed. Much of the growth was due to the great numbers of Scotch-Irish immigrants who came pouring into the country. By 1740, it has been estimated, more than 500,000 Irish Presbyterians had moved to the new world. It was fortunate that Francis Makemie had done his pioneer work so well that there was an organized Presbyterian Church here to meet them when they came.

The great variety of American denominations had always been the occasion for a good deal of comment, much of it unfavorable. It is true that some sects, like the Christian Scientists, Seventh Day Adventists, Mormons, Jehovah's Witnesses, were purely American developments of a later period. It is also true that many of the splits within American churches were over local issues, though some were brought to this country.

But for the most part the pluralism of American Protestantism can be very simply explained by the great variety of religious backgrounds from which the first settlers came. The Puritans in New England, the English in Virginia, the Germans and the Swedes in Pennsylvania, the Dutch in New York and New Jersey, the Scotch-Irish in the middle colonies and in the south, to mention only the most prominent groups, all brought their churches with them to the new world. The Congregational, Episcopal, Lutheran, Reformed, Moravian, and Presbyterian churches were the result.

The existence of this large number of denominations was not the result of any desire for competition or rivalry. That may have been true

Pennsylvania, 1741. *April 2.* The purchase of the tract of 500 acres, which had been offered by Nathaniel Irish, was concluded at Philadelphia between William Allen and Henry Antes, for the Brethren. . . .

June 27. . . . The Brethren had by this time removed from Nazareth, and were living together as a family in a small house they had built hurriedly in the spring. It was now time to proceed to the erection of a more commodious dwelling. . . .

December. On the 2d of the month Count Zinzendorf landed at New York. Having remained several days with our friends in that city, he set out for Philadelphia on the 6th and arrived there on the 10th inst. David Nitschmann, *Episc.*, arrived there from the Forks on the same day. . . .

December 24. (Sunday.) We celebrated the Lord's Supper and held the Festival of Christmas-eve. The Brethren's settlement in the Forks received the name of Bethlehem on this day.[9]

—Annals of Early Moravian Settlement in Georgia and Pennsylvania

later as the country opened to expansion. But originally it was simply the result of a desire to minister to the needs of a group of people for whom a church had a special responsibility. In fact it was a long time in some instances before any need was seen beyond that of the immediate group. The Dutch Reformed Church in New York and New Jersey, for example, continued to hold its services in the Dutch language right down to the American Revolution, even though English had become the language of almost everyone. This was also true of the Moravian Church in America, which made extensive use of the German language and was largely controlled by church authorities in Europe until the middle of the nineteenth century. These were signs that the churches had a very limited scope of their mission in the new world.

Apart from New England, where the ties with the mother country had been severed for obvious reasons, there was in these early days a complete dependence on the mother church. It was well into the eighteenth century, for example, before any American church except New England Congregationalism had any facility in the new world for the education of its ministers. Since all these churches originally conceived of themselves as mere outposts, they naturally looked to the church at home for education and for direction. When the movement for American institutions and American organization finally came, it did not come, as we shall see, without a good deal of tension and struggle.

The movement not only changed the life of all the American churches, it also for the first time made them really aware of each other's existence. Not without reason has it been called "the Great Awakening." Though no one realized it at the time, not the least result of the Awakening was the new awareness of their destiny not as outposts of European and British Christianity but as American churches.

22

The Great Awakening

It is almost impossible to say exactly when it began or by whom it was started. Most historians date the beginning of the Great Awakening from the first visit to America of George Whitefield, the celebrated English evangelist, in 1739. While it is certainly true that Whitefield did much to bring the movement about, it must also be true that other men in America had been thinking along similar lines. The immediate enthusiasm which Whitefield encountered is indicative of that. One man alone could not have been responsible for a movement which in the opinion of more than one scholar altered the whole character of American Protestantism.

The fact is that in 1739 the situation in American churches generally was ripe for change. The development which they had undergone since their colonial formation was not unlike the scholasticism which had developed earlier in the European churches. It was the "high and dry" school of thought which was almost universally in control. In New England, for example, the fervent piety of the early Puritans had all but disappeared in favor of a sterile scholastic orthodoxy. In most Episcopal circles religious zeal was at a low ebb. Presbyterians and Reformed alike contented themselves with the explanation and defense of their respective confessions of faith.

THEY PREPARED THE WAY

It was a state of affairs which was distressing to a number of American ministers of different denominations. In New Jersey two men of very different backgrounds had already begun to kindle the fires of revival. A young German minister named Theodore Frelinghuysen had come to the combined Dutch Reformed churches of Raritan and New Brunswick in 1720. Quite possibly he had been influenced by Pietism during his education in Europe. But he was shocked by the religious conditions which he found in the new world. Church life was wooden and artificial, a formality that was given perfunctory attention. The young domine (minister) soon became a controversial figure by his fiery preaching and his unorthodox methods in seeking to develop religious enthusiasm in his congregations.

He soon discovered an ally in a Presbyterian minister whose responsibilities were in the same neighborhood. Gilbert Tennent, a kind of wandering apostle to Presbyterians in New Jersey and eastern Pennsylvania, was equally disturbed by the formality of his church. In many ways he was his father's son. For his father, William Tennent, had been upset by the Presbyterian insistence upon a ministry trained in either a British or New England university. In his opinion, such limitations kept many good men out of the ministry. He was also suspicious of the religious zeal and sincerity of some of the graduates of these institutions. In spite of bitter Presbyterian opposition, William Tennent had started his own college in 1728. After many relocations, the log college which he began on the Neshaminy became the forerunner of Princeton University.

Frelinghuysen and Gilbert Tennent became fast friends, cooperating closely in bringing revival to New Jersey. Blunt and outspoken, they made many enemies. One does not speak of the dangers of an unconverted ministry, as Tennent did, without stirring up opposition. Nor does one begin to insist upon strict rules of church life and discipline, as Frelinghuysen did, without incurring the anger of those who are intent upon defending the old ways.

Another center of revival was in the western Massachusetts town of Northampton. Here the leader was a man of much greater intellectual power than either Frelinghuysen or Tennent. Jonathan Edwards too had been deeply disturbed by the lack of enthusiasm and commitment in New England Congregationalism. As early as 1735 he had tried to combat it with a new style of preaching which made striking use of vivid imagery instead of the abstract theological propositions which were typical of most sermons. His success was so spectacular that his published report, *A Faithful Narrative of the Surprising Work of God in the Conversion of Many Hundred Souls in Northampton and the Neighboring Towns and Villages*, went through three editions and twenty printings in three years. Here was ample evidence that many churchmen whose names we do not know were ready for something new.

While Theodore Frelinghuysen, Gilbert Tennent, and Jonathan Edwards were all aware of each other's efforts, their work was local in its influence. What was needed was some event that would give these local movements cohesion and colony-wide significance. That event, obviously, was the arrival of George Whitefield, filled with youthful enthusiasm, in 1739.

WHITEFIELD'S MISSION TO AMERICA

An early associate of the Wesleys in England, Whitefield was a preacher of enormous power. A skillful orator, he knew how to play on the emotions. He could laugh or cry, dramatize the biblical characters, use illustrations from the weather or from the daily paper to great effect. From the day he arrived in Philadelphia in the fall of 1739 thousands of people crowded to hear him wherever he went, from Georgia to Massachusetts—fifteen thousand people gathered to hear him on Boston Common, for example. So cool-headed a skeptic as Benjamin Franklin was moved to give all the money he had in his pockets when he heard Whitefield make an appeal for his orphanage.

Interestingly enough, it was an orphanage started by Whitefield that brought the Moravians to Pennsylvania. They had originally gone to Georgia in 1735 to establish missionary work among the Indians. It was while on the voyage to Georgia that John Wesley met the Moravians. The fighting between the English and Spanish colonists made it almost impossible to carry on work along the frontier. When Whitefield visited Savannah in 1740 and offered to bring the Moravians with him to Pennsylvania where he had purchased a large tract of land, they were happy to accept. A group of them agreed to help him erect an orphanage for Negro children in what is now Nazareth, Pennsylvania. When the building was half finished, however, Whitefield was drawn into a theological discussion with Peter Böhler (who had been of great help to John Welsey). Whitefield, a strict predestinarian, could not tolerate Böhler's conviction that Christ died for *all* men. Whitefield ordered him to leave Nazareth and take his Moravians with him. The Moravians then purchased some land nearby and founded what is now the city of Bethlehem.

Although Whitefield was of strong Calvinist convictions and a priest of the Episcopal Church, he had no interest in denominationalism.

> 'Father Abraham, whom have you in Heaven? Any Episcopalians?' 'No.' 'Any Presbyterians?' 'No.' 'Have you any Independents or Seceders?' 'No.' 'Have you any Methodists?' 'No, no, no!!' 'Whom have you there?' 'We don't know those names here. All who are here are Christians . . . men who have overcome by the blood of the Lamb and the word of his testimony.' 'Oh, is this the case? Then God help us, God help us all, to forget party names, and to become Christians in deed and in truth.'[1]

"Although I profess myself a minister of the Church of England," he wrote on another occasion, "I am of catholic spirit, and if I see any man who loves the Lord Jesus in sincerity, I am not very solicitous to what outward communion he belongs."[2]

George Whitefield concluded his tour in 1741. Commenting on the results of his work, a contemporary historian has written,

> ... he had caused streams of revival to flow from Georgia to the borders of Canada. He had unified the Great Awakening, which may well be defined as the first great spiritual movement that overflowed the boundaries of the separate North American colonies. No longer were the provinces entirely self-contained units.[3]

The reading of some of Whitefield's sermons and other evangelistic literature helped to bring about a spontaneous revival among laymen in Hanover County, Virginia. Presbyterian evangelists from the Middle Colonies preached in the area; one of these, Samuel Davies, was persuaded to remain as a pastor. Under the leadership of Davies, himself a product of the Great Awakening, a number of churches were organized. In 1755 Hanover Presbytery was established, to be known as the "mother presbytery" of the South and Southwest.

Before his death in 1770, Whitefield paid no fewer than seven visits to America. He died in Newburyport, Massachusetts, while on his last tour. While none of the succeeding visits was as successful as the first, no man did more to change the face of American Protestant life.

For one thing, as was mentioned in the quotation, he brought the isolated fragments of colonial Protestantism together in their first real ecumenical contacts. Before this time the Congregationalists in New England, the Reformed in New York and New Jersey, the Presbyterians in the middle and southern colonies had all been pretty much confined to their own preserves. Through his complete disregard for denominational labels and his intense dedication to saving souls, Whitefield brought at least those who sympathized with him in these denominations into a sense of common mission. For the first time in their history American Protestants began to think in a national context.

Whitefield also put a stamp on American Protestantism which it

Here is an eyewitness account of Whitefield's visit to Middletown, Connecticut, in 1740:

Now it pleased God to send Mr Whitefield into this land; and my hearing of his preaching at Philadelphia, like one of the Old apostles, and many thousands flocking to hear him preach the Gospel; and great numbers were converted to Christ; I felt the Spirit of God drawing me by conviction; I longed to see and hear him, and wished he would come this way. . . . then on a Sudden, in the morning about

has never entirely lost. His insistence upon a conversion experience even for those who were members of the church, his stern opposition to all forms of worldly amusement and pleasure, even his revival techniques, became part of American church life to the present day. In many ways men like Billy Sunday or Billy Graham stand straight in the tradition begun by George Whitefield, and the revivalism and the moralism still strong in many Reformed and Presbyterian churches are his heritage.

It must be said also that the Great Awakening left behind it a legacy of division as well. Not everyone was enthusiastic about its aims or its methods. There were conservatives in all the churches who viewed with alarm the light way in which the awakeners took historic theological differences and abandoned historic ecclesiastical procedures. The split was less dangerous in New England Congregationalism because of the looseness of its organization, but there were definite parties. In the Reformed and Presbyterian churches, however, the breach widened until it was complete. Presbyterians split into Old Side and New Side and the breach was not healed until 1758. In the Reformed Church it lasted even longer and the two groups were not reunited until 1770.

The Old Side (or Old Light) parties in these denominations tended to represent the scholasticism against which the Great Awakening was a protest. Although they may not fully have realized it, they were defending some things which were important. Sectarianism may have deserved the ridicule which Whitefield gave it. But theological integrity was another matter and the Old Lights saw it being swept away in a flood of religious emotionalism. They wondered (and not without some reason) what would be left when the emotionalism had died. Furthermore they were disturbed by the freedom with which the revivalists treated the historic concern of the church for an educated ministry. Though they were fully aware of the difficulties of insistence

8 or 9 of the Clock there came a messenger and said Mr Whitfield . . . is to preach at Middletown this morning at ten of the Clock, I was in my field at Work, I dropt my tool that I had in my hand and ran home to my wife telling her to make ready quickly to go and hear Mr Whitfield preach at Middletown, then run to my pasture for my horse with all my might; . . . we had twelve miles to ride double in little more than an hour . . . and when we came within about half a mile or a mile of the Road that comes down from Hartford weathersfield and Stepney to Middletown; on high land I saw before me a Cloud or fogg arising; . . . made by the Horses feet; . . . every horse seemed to go with all his might to carry his rider to hear news from heaven for the saving of Souls, it made me tremble to see the Sight, how the world was in a Struggle; . . . it was said to be 3 or 4000 of people

upon it in the new world, they did not relish the prospect of turning their pulpits over to tradesmen turned preachers, even when they had been educated in a log college. Perhaps the splits were not without their benefit, however. For in the reunions which took place the one party gained a new appreciation for theological integrity and education while the other received a new sense of urgency about evangelism.

During this period other Presbyterians came to the colonies, among them Reformed Presbyterian and Associate Presbyterian groups, representing the most conservative Scottish and Irish Presbyterians. The Reformed Presbyterians, descendents of the Covenanters who had defended their Reformed principles in the time of the Stuart kings, still refused to compromise with the established Church of Scotland. The Associate Presbyterians had seceded from the Church of Scotland over differences in church life and doctrine. For the most part, these two groups maintained their distinct identity, keeping in close relationship with their parent bodies in Scotland. In 1782 the two Associate presbyteries and one Reformed presbytery united to form the Associate Reformed Presbyterian Church.

BAPTISTS AND METHODISTS

The Great Awakening had two other unexpected results. For one thing it thrust two denominations which up to this point had had little influence into great prominence. The Baptists had been in the colonies for years but had always been a small minority both in numbers and in prestige. The Great Awakening was the occasion for their rapid growth. Since the revival had none of the opposition in their ranks that it encountered in others and since they had none of the limitations which hindered its progress in the Old Line colonial churches, whole communities, especially in Virginia, Kentucky, and Tennessee became strongholds of the Baptists.

The Methodists, of course, were still a very small group since the

---

Assembled together; we dismounted and shook of our Dust; and the ministers were then Coming to the meeting house; . . . the land and banks over the river looked black with people and horses all along the 12 miles I saw no man at work in his field, but all seemed to be gone—When I saw Mr. Whitfield come upon the Scaffold he lookt almost Angelical; a young, Slim, slender youth before some thousands of people with a bold undaunted Countenance, and my hearing how God was with him every where as he came along it Solemnized my mind; and put me into a trembling fear before he began to preach; for he looked as if he was Cloathed with Authority from the Great God; and a sweet sollome solemnity sat upon his brow And my hearing him preach, gave me a heart wound; By God's blessing: my old Foundation was broken up, and I saw that my righteousness would not save me.[4]

Wesleyan movement in England was still very new. Their great growth, in fact, came in the next century with the opening of the frontier. But the Great Awakening gave them a genuine head start in American church life. In 1773 there were 1,160 Methodists in the thirteen colonies. Just ten years later there were 12,000. It is clear that many of those who were influenced by the Awakening were distressed by the coolness of their reception in their own churches and found a more congenial home in Baptist or Methodist churches which had welcomed it wholeheartedly.

THE LIBERALS

There was an even stranger result of the Great Awakening and that was the rise of theological liberalism. Signs of this development were apparent in Jonathan Edwards' time. His keenest opponent was not an Old Side Calvinist but a Boston minister named Charles Chauncy, who wrote two pamphlets attacking revivalism, *Seasonable Thoughts on the State of Religion in New England* and *Enthusiasm Describ'd and Caution'd Against.* Chauncy's attack was from the point of view of the liberal rationalist who questioned anything but the calm use of reason in religion.

Although he was a man before his time, Chauncy's attitude was to find increasing support as the fires of the revival began to die. Many people, especially young college students, began to rebel against the excessive emotionalism of the revival. It was perhaps an inevitable reaction that they should turn to a rational form of religion. Especially in New England people became tired of the controversy and of its excesses. Some insight into what happened may be gathered from the fact that in Edwards' heyday Yale was a hotbed of the revival while half a century later it was impossible to find more than a handful of professed orthodox Christians in the entire student body.

The chief spokesman for the new liberal attitude which arose after the Great Awakening had lost its power was William Ellery Channing. Brought up in the Old Light tradition of New England Calvinism, Channing gradually abandoned most of its propositions. In the optimistic setting of the new American republic (Channing was ordained in 1803), he was impressed with the dignity of human nature and its inherent possibilities for goodness. Because of his optimism he made reason the rule for religion, although he himself did not reject miracles or the inspiration of Scripture. While Channing himself was capable of great emotional power as a preacher, it was to the intellectual side of his congregation that he always made his appeal.

Because of a dispute over the doctrine of the Trinity, what Channing had hoped would become the liberal party in New England Congregationalism became instead the Unitarian denomination. But the point of view which he represented had effects far beyond the confines of the relatively small denomination with which his name is associated. The full implications of this point of view come later in our story, but its origins belong in the movement which we have been discussing.

Indeed the real losers in this era in American history were the Old School orthodox in every church. Down to the Great Awakening, they had been the dominant party. American Protestantism had been every bit as scholastic as its British and European counterparts. But after the American Revolution they continually lost significance. Even where they continued in some strength (as in the Presbyterian and Reformed churches), they had been considerably influenced by revivalism. Though they might not share its theology, they had adopted many of its methods. In all Protestant churches the anxious bench replaced the catechism class and the free service the historic liturgy.

Leadership in thought as well as in numbers passed to the New Light parties and to the liberals. It was a gradual attrition but the time finally came when Old School orthodoxy and its methods completely disappeared from the scene. Today the conservative or fundamentalist wing in every church is entirely New Light in its approach. Even though the great enthusiasm kindled by the Awakening finally died down, it left a lasting influence on American church life. It might be said that the Great Awakening terminated the Puritan age and inaugurated the Pietist or Methodist age of American church history.

Many questions can be asked about this influence. For example, both revivalist and liberal Protestantism were equally indifferent to theology. This doubtless accounts for the fact that America has produced only one theologian of international reputation, Charles Hodge of Princeton, who came from the Old School side of Presbyterianism. In fact it would be characteristic of many American Protestants that this lack is something in which they would glory. To them, theology is only a hairsplitting kind of discipline which has little religious reality in it.

But the refusal to think seriously and constructively about the Christian gospel (for that is all theology is) is one for which we American Protestants have paid a heavy price. Many of the shocking clashes between religion and science could have been avoided had we been theologically trained and disciplined. Much of the agony experienced by those who felt the challenge of knowledge to religion could have been spared them if religion had been intellectually developed. After all, it was only in America that someone could actually write and publish a *History of the Warfare of Science with Theology in Christendom* (by Andrew D. White).

At the same time we dare not underestimate the positive good accomplished by the revivalist and the liberal. Not only did the Great Awakening bring new life and enthusiasm to a dying church, but its invasion of the moral and social life of the community was a lasting one. The revivalist insistence on personal righteousness was taken up and continued by the liberal insistence on social righteousness. Perhaps in no nation in modern times has there been a greater effort to bring Christian principles to bear on national life. Although we may argue about the degree to which it has been successful, that the relevance of the Christian gospel to every kind of personal and social question has been an American assumption no one can deny.

We may admire it or criticize it. But we have to admit that the Great Awakening was the greatest single influence in the making of American Protestantism.

23

On the Frontiers

To try to compress the story of American Protestantism in the nineteenth century into a few pages might well seem to be a foolish and impossible assignment. But it is neither so foolish nor impossible as it may at first seem when we recall that the America of that era was in the age of the frontier, and that most of the dramatic events of the period were simply the response of the church to the call of the ever expanding horizon.

GEOGRAPHICAL FRONTIERS

The church's movement to the frontier had a very practical beginning. For not long after the American Revolution and the establishment of the new republic, settlers began crossing the Appalachian mountain chain, which for so long had confined the thirteen colonies to the Atlantic seaboard. As they left the old settlements for life on the new frontier, the churches at home became aware of their responsibility for following them.

In a relatively small number of cases, the procedure was not a difficult one. Sometimes whole sections of communities in New England or Dutch New York and New Jersey migrated together to new homesites in Ohio or Illinois. Typical New England or New Jersey communities were reconstructed on the plains, even to as accurate a reproduction of the village meetinghouse as the early settlers could muster. When this kind of orderly transition to the new location took place, the problem was not too difficult a one. The new community simply sent back home for a minister, who was usually supplied and supported by the established church along the coast until the new community could gain its financial independence.

But this kind of orderly migration was the exception rather than the rule. More often the immigrants were those who felt frustrated or dispossessed in the home community and left in search of new possibilities. Most often they left behind them the morals and religion of a community in which they had always felt strange and disinherited. The new settlements which they founded across the mountains were often expressions of the settlers' rebellion against the way of life they had left.

In this kind of frontier life the old established churches along the coast suffered from a double disadvantage. For one thing, their traditional insistence upon a fully educated ministry slowed their ability to supply the demands of the frontier considerably. Churches like the Methodist and Baptist, which could make a layman into a preacher by a single act, had a great advantage over those denominations which required a higher education of at least seven years.

Even more to the point was the inability of a trained ministry to reach the frontier mind. New communities made up almost entirely of the dispossessed and disinherited were hardly able to understand a Yale or Princeton graduate nor he them. Nor was the Presbyterian or Reformed idea of a stable congregation in a stable community effective in the fluid situation of the frontier where men were always on the move, exchanging what they owned for the promise of greener pastures father west.

None of this is intended to excuse the failure of the Old Line churches to keep pace with the growth of the country. We can accuse them of a lack of creative imagination in the face of such a tremendous challenge, while remembering that we have been equally lacking in creative imagination in the face of similar challenges. But it does explain why the new regions of the Middle West and the Southwest were so largely captured by the Methodists and the Baptists.

For one thing, the Methodists and Baptists had far less invested in the older settlements along the Atlantic coast. Having ministered, for the most part, in the older settlements to the lower classes, they found it natural to follow these people as they moved westward. The greater simplicity of their organization and their smaller demands in terms of education gave them a flexibility which the older denominations simply could not equal.

Typical of the frontier Methodist preachers was Peter Cartwright, a contemporary of Abraham Lincoln in Illinois. Following the plan

In the early fall of 1812 two men set out on horseback to make a tour into the new American West for missionary purposes. These two were Samuel Mills, a young Presbyterian minister, and John F. Schermerhorn of the Reformed Church, traveling under the auspices of the Massachusetts and Connecticut Missionary Societies. Schermerhorn reported: "Intemperance prevails greatly . . . also profanity and gambling. The Sabbath is not regarded as the Lord's time." In Pennsylvania they found "whole counties, containing from 5,000 to 10,000 people, without regular preaching; and . . . in Virginia, west

organized by Francis Asbury, the great architect of American Methodism, Cartwright was responsible for a circuit with twenty or thirty preaching places. His only equipment was a Bible together with a Methodist hymnbook and "discipline." Most of his life was spent on horseback riding from point to point on his circuit. Preaching to raw frontiersmen, Cartwright used neither culture nor eloquence in his approach to them. "We murdered the King's English at almost every lick," he wrote. "But there was a divine unction . . ." "A lettuce growing under a peach tree" was the way Cartwright once described the Presbyterian ministry with its insistence upon scholarly sermons composed in the context of intellectual argument and persuasion. The frontier wanted raw emotionalism, hot and strong, and it was the Methodist circuit rider and the Baptist lay preacher who were able to supply it.

This is not to say that Presbyterians sat at home wringing their hands while the country moved west. No more heroic page in the history of the frontier exists than that written by Marcus Whitman, a young Presbyterian physician who had heard of the appeal of some Oregon Indians to have "the white man's Book of Heaven." Ordained to the ministry in 1835, Whitman made his first trip over the difficult Oregon trail soon after. It can be argued that it was Whitman's pioneering of the Pacific Northwest that saved that territory for the United States. At any rate, it was his visit to Washington that had a significant part in the Webster-Ashburton Treaty of 1842 which gave our present states of Oregon and Washington to the United States instead of Canada.

But Marcus Whitman was a missionary of the gospel and not of the United States. Not only did he establish preaching places in the great Northwest, but medical missions as well, stations which could minister to the exhausted white pioneer as well as to the native Indian. It was in one of these medical mission stations that he and his wife were mur-

---

of the Blue Ridge, a district containing 150,000 inhabitants, only three clergymen were settled."[1]

Samuel Mills takes up the account in Ohio: "From Cincinnati Mr. Schermerhorn and myself came down the river Ohio to Laurenceburgh in the Indiana territory. . . . crossed the Ohio into Kentucky . . . and continued our course within 30 miles of the falls of the Ohio, preaching occasionally. We found the inhabitants in a very destitute state; very ignorant of the doctrines of the Gospel; and in many instances without Bibles or other religious books. The Methodist preachers pass through this country in their circuits occasionally . . . There are, in the Indiana territory, according to the last census, 24,520 inhabitants; and there is one Presbyterian minister . . . In the Illinois territory, containing more than 12,000 people, there is no Presbyterian or Congregational minister. There are a number of good

dered by a band of hostile Indians in 1847. But even Whitman's martyrdom had its beneficial results, for it inspired another Presbyterian pioneer, Sheldon Jackson, to a career that took him all through the Northwest and finally into Alaska.

Equally interesting is the story of what happened to Old Line Presbyterianism when it attempted to move to the frontier. At least three denominations represent frontier versions of Presbyterianism. In 1800 a revival broke out in Kentucky and Tennessee, and many pioneers were converted under the evangelistic preaching in gatherings called camp meetings. There were not enough seminary-trained men to meet the spiritual needs of the frontier settlers, but the Synod of Kentucky took stern action to discourage preaching it considered irregular. The Cumberland Presbyterian Church began on February 4, 1810, when three Presbyterian ministers, concerned with meeting the spiritual needs of the settlers, met in the log home of one of them to form a separate presbytery. They felt that this action was necessary to express (1) their reaction to those elements in scholastic Presbyterian theology which they believed inconsistent with an evangelistic message, and (2) their judgment that rigid educational standards for the ordination of ministers should be relaxed to meet the critical needs of people on the frontier.

About the same time, five Presbyterian ministers in Kentucky, known as "New Lights," seceded from the church under the leadership of Barton Stone. At first the secession was called the Springfield Presbytery but as Stone's thinking carried him further and further away from classic Presbyterianism, he called his movement the Christian Church, one part of which was later to merge with the Congregationalists, and is now part of the United Church of Christ. Another part soon united with what was to be known as the Disciples of Christ.

The largest of these Presbyterian adaptations, and the largest Prot-

---

people in the territory who are anxious to have such ministers amongst them. They likewise wish to be remembered by Bible and Religious Tract Societies. . . .

"We left Lexington [Kentucky] on the 14th of December, and proceeded on our way to Nashville, in Tennessee . . . pursuing our course down the river to New Orleans. . . . General Jackson was expecting to go in a few days, with about 1,500 Volunteers to Natchez. Mr. Blackburn introduced us to the General, who, having become acquainted with our design, invited us to take passage on board his boat. We accepted the invitation; . . . making sale of our horses, we embarked . . . we lay by three days on account of the ice. . . .

"Upon our arrival at New Orleans, we were soon made acquainted with a few religious people. The number of those possessing this character, in this place, we are constrained to believe is small. . . . There is no Protestant church in the city.

estant movement developed entirely in America, was the Disciples of Christ. Thomas Campbell and his son Alexander were originally Presbyterians of the most rigid kind. But in their ministry in western Pennsylvania and West Virginia they discovered that the fine distinctions of Scottish Calvinism meant less and less. The rivalry of various denominations also distressed Thomas Campbell. What mattered was not the theological differences but the basic message of the Bible. "Where the Scriptures speak, we speak; where the Scriptures are silent, we are silent" was his watchword.

His son, Alexander, a far more controversial figure, carried his father's ideas into an organized form. Using the Scriptures as his sole authority, Campbell's church rejected infant baptism, insisted upon a weekly celebration of the Lord's Supper, developed a congregational form of organization. Its piety was a simple devotion to Jesus Christ without any elaboration of a theology of his person. One of the largest Protestant denominations in the country today, the Disciples of Christ represents the most successful attempt to meet the religious needs of the American frontier.

MISSIONARY FRONTIERS

The frontiers that fascinated the nineteenth century American church were by no means limited to the North American continent. American ships, after all, were exploring the world, their captains and sailors returning home with strange stories of faraway and romantic places. It was not a coincidence that in the shipping center of Salem, Massachusetts, the first five young men were ordained for Christian service overseas in 1812. Their commissioning was the result of the work of the "American Board of Commissioners for Foreign Missions" which had been formed in 1810, largely under Congregational auspices, though it soon became the missionary instrument for most of the Ameri-

---

Attempts have been made to obtain a subscription for building one, but have failed. . . .

"We find that, in order to have the Bible circulate freely, especially among the Catholics, the consent of those high in office must be obtained. . . . We were referred to Father Antonio, as he is called . . . He said he should be pleased to have the Bible circulate among those of his order . . . The priests acknowledge the nakedness of the land. Father Antonio gave it as his opinion, that we should very rarely find a Bible in any of the French or Spanish Catholic families, in any of the parishes. . . . The present is certainly a new and interesting era in the history of New Orleans. . . .

"We expect to leave this place soon, and proceed on our way to Georgia through the Creek nation."[2]

can denominations including the Presbyterian and Reformed churches.

One of the young men ordained in the Tabernacle Church in Salem in 1812 was Adoniram Judson. India had been his destination, but political conditions there made it necessary for him to transfer his work to Burma. It is also interesting to note that on the long voyage to the East, Judson had become convinced of the truth of the Baptist point of view. This change in theological conviction meant the loss of support by the Congregational commissioners. But it was not without its advantage since another denomination was awakened to its missionary responsibilities as the Baptists undertook Judson's support.

The movement begun in Salem soon captured the imagination of many Americans. In New York in 1819 a prominent physician, a member of the Reformed Church, was reading a pamphlet about the work of the American Board while waiting for one of his patients. What he read there deepened a discomfort which he had had for some time and soon thereafter John Scudder offered his services to the Board.

Sent by them originally to Ceylon, this Reformed doctor was ordained to the Christian ministry there in 1821 by a group of Congregational, Baptist, and Methodist missionaries—an early example of the ecumenical church in action! In 1836 he transferred the scene of his labors to the Indian mainland. Here he labored indefatigably until his death in 1855. On a visit to America he was asked about the discouragements of missionary work. "I do not know the word," replied Scudder. "I long ago erased it from my vocabulary." The great medical institutions at Vellore in southeast India are a testimony to the extent to which he did not know the meaning of the word. Even more impressive is the fact that his seven sons all followed him into the missionary field and that for almost a century and a half some member of the Scudder family has been actively engaged in the world mission of the church.

The missionary impulse given to the American churches by men like Judson and Scudder was one which was followed by countless others as the nineteenth century continued. To be sure, the same concern for the world mission of the church was felt in other parts of the globe, especially in Great Britain. But Americans were in the forefront of the movement. As commerce opened up countries like Japan and China which had long been closed to Western influence, American missionaries were soon there. So extensive did the missionary operations of the major churches become that soon after the middle of the century each one organized its own mission board, feeling that the American Board was no longer an adequate instrument for the work.

It has become fashionable in some quarters to criticize the motives of these missionary pioneers, suggesting that their real purpose was not the spread of the gospel but the spread of American influence and commercial sway. It is, of course, possible that some of those who went did so from unworthy motives. Certainly all who went to India, China, and Japan went as Americans, just as incapable of dissociating themselves from their origin and training as any of us would be. Probably their initial efforts involved many clumsy mistakes. What pioneer does not make them?

Yet one has only to read a little of what these pioneers wrote to realize how far from their minds any desire to spread the *American* gospel was. It was not Americanism but a concern for Asiatics who did not know Jesus Christ that inspired the famous haystack prayer meeting that led to Adoniram Judson's career in Burma. John Scudder did not give up a profitable medical practice in New York to take the American flag to the Far East. He was moved by a very childlike concern about the fate of those people and a deep sense of responsibility for them.

The existence of strong churches in all these countries today, each living its own life and producing its own leadership, and in many instances making a rich contribution to the life of the world church is evidence enough of the validity of their call. Indeed it is the very strength of these churches today which poses one of the chief problems to American missionary effort. We must become fellow workers with them and no longer be their leaders. Though the situation may at first seem hard to accept, it is a tribute to the strength which the first missionaries brought to the situations into which they came. A church which is able to direct its own life in its own setting is a far greater tribute to their work than one which would be unable to exist by itself.

SOCIAL FRONTIERS

The nineteenth century saw the invasion of a third frontier by American Protestants. The invasion of the social frontier was made with bitter opposition on the part of many church members. But there had been good church members who had opposed the missionary frontier too!

Before the nineteenth century, the problem of slavery disturbed only a few Christian consciences. Among the first to speak out against slaveholding, were a number of concerned Quakers. Although many in the Old Line Protestant churches felt uneasy about the institution of slavery, their early proposals were for gradual emancipation and for the plan of colonization, which sought to purchase freedom for Negro slaves and transport them back to Africa.

As the century progressed to its midpoint, the lines began to harden between anti- and pro-slavery forces. Although Quakers and Unitarians were among the early leaders in the abolition movement, abolitionist sentiment spread to other churches as well, particularly in the North. Church leaders in slaveholding sections of the country responded by a defense of slavery from scriptural arguments. Significant landmarks in the slavery controversy are the rupture which took place in both the Baptist and the Methodist Episcopal churches in 1845 over this issue, with the formation of Northern and Southern churches as a result.

In Presbyterianism the story was somewhat different. The denomination had been split in 1837 into Old School and New School churches, largely over matters of doctrine and church government. Each of these two bodies managed to hold together for a longer time across sectional lines. Anti-slavery agitation was much stronger in the New School church with its large Northern membership. Tensions mounted until in 1857 a number of Southern presbyteries withdrew to form (in 1858) the United Synod of the Presbyterian Church in the U.S.A. It had a short life for in 1864 it was welcomed into the Presbyterian Church in the Confederate States of America.

That church had been formed in 1861. Despite many tensions and pressures Old School Presbyterianism remained together until the General Assembly of 1861. Since by that time many Southern states had already seceded from the Union and others were on the point of doing so, there were not many Southern commissioners at the Assembly. Even so, Gardiner Spring's resolutions expressing loyalty to the United States were at first tabled by a vote of 123 to 102. Later on in the session, however, they were adopted by a vote of 156 to 66.

The adoption of these resolutions, however, made the presence of any Southern delegates impossible. On December 4 of the same year, representatives of forty-seven Southern presbyteries gathered in Augusta, Georgia, to form the first General Assembly of the Presbyterian Church in the Confederate States of America. This is the denomination which today we know as the Presbyterian Church in the United States.

After the Civil War, the rapid industrialization of the North led to all kinds of human misery. It was literally an age in which the rich grew richer while the poor became poorer. While the wealthy purchased diamond collars for their dogs or gave elaborate parties costing thousands of dollars, shop girls worked seventy-two hours a week for five dollars. Laborers received two dollars a day when work was available and starved in their tenements when it was not. Thousands of immigrants poured into the cities with nothing to sell but their muscles. Forced to live in slums, completely at the mercy of their employers, the struggle for survival often took them to crime and corruption.

There were many churchmen who believed that conditions like these were none of the church's business; some, in fact, were sure that this was God's will for American society. But that kind of conviction was by no means a universal one. The remedies proposed were not often effective and sometimes those who proposed them were cranks. But there were many sincere Christians who believed that the gospel had a social as well as an individual application and set themselves to do something about it.

Perhaps the best known of these pioneers on the social frontier was Walter Rauschenbusch. A Baptist minister of German descent, he spent the first years of his ministry in Hell's Kitchen, one of the most vicious slums in New York City. It was during these years that he came to realize that sin was not only an individual but also a social reality. It was his contention that the salvation of the individual was not enough; so long as the social order in which he lived and worked was untouched by the gospel, the kingdom of evil would remain in all of its strength.

Becoming a theological professor in later years, Rauschenbusch produced several books which have become classics in social Christianity. His *Prayers of the Social Awakening* reveal his own deep personal religious faith and his great social concern. The later *Theology for the Social Gospel* is still the best illustration of the way in which a theology which minimizes none of the historic Christian doctrines can have a passionate responsibility for the world for which Christ died.

It must be admitted that the Social Gospel encountered the bitter opposition of many in the churches. Sometimes this opposition was deserved since there were many proponents of the Social Gospel who in their zeal for the *social* very well neglected the *gospel*. But the conscientious leaders of the movement knew that in giving the church a prophetic voice in society, they were acting in the best Christian tradition of prophet and reformer.

24

Our Own Time

It is not easy to talk about the church in our own time. We live much too close to the main events to see them in their full perspective. But it is possible, even so, to single out some signs of discouragement and some signs of hope.

DISCOURAGING SIGNS

The years of the First World War (1914-1918) marked the end of an era in the life of the church, just as they did in so many other areas of civilization both West and East. Just as the impact of a vicious international conflict shattered the hopes and ideals of a world that had pretty well convinced itself of the unlimited possibilities of human progress, so it forced the Christian church to rethink some of its own assumptions and to reassess its estimate of its place in the world.

1. *The fall of liberalism.* The discouraging aspects of this experience may be grouped in four categories. The first of them is the fact that the experience of two world wars and an economic collapse spelled the end of the liberal, optimistic view of Christianity which had so largely come to dominate Protestant thinking. William Ellery Channing, whose views we examined briefly in chapter 22, had in fact become an influence in much wider circles than the relatively small Unitarian Church. Directly or indirectly the kind of thought first proclaimed by him became the dominant school in both European and American Protestantism.

In this interpretation of Christianity not only were the classic theologies shelved as relics of a bygone age, but the very assumptions on which they had been based were dismissed as meaningless. Jesus Christ was now interpreted as a master ethical teacher whose message to the world, as one outstanding German church historian summarized it, was the "Fatherhood of God and the Brotherhood of Man." The Kingdom of God, which had formed the center of his preaching, was now thought to be an ideal social order, easily realizable in terms of the history of this world. Sin was dismissed as the product of an unfortunate environment, a lack of education, both of which were capable of correction by human reforms. It was "the growing pains of humanity," as one preacher of the era put it. With the obvious support of most of society, the growing resources of science and technology, the church felt that the prospects for the future of humanity were bright indeed.

This liberal reinterpretation of the gospel, though it had been in the making since the beginning of the nineteenth century, was in large part the result of a nasty collision between the forces of science and religion occasioned by the publication of Charles Darwin's *Origin of Species* in 1859. Though it had not been Darwin's intention to challenge the Christian religion, his account of human origins and his theory of evolution seemed to contradict that set forth in the Bible. While some stubbornly clung to a literal interpretation of the biblical accounts of creation, the majority of Protestant leaders abandoned the field to take refuge in a religion which they felt was beyond the power of science to attack.

However free such a religion may have been from the attacks of science, it was by no means free from the shocks of history. As social idealism was blown to bits by the bombs, as irrational evil displayed itself in the horrors of concentration camps and gas chambers, as the resources of science proved much more effective for human destruction than ever they had for human assistance, the bankruptcy of the liberal myth became more and more evident.

2. *The irrelevance of the church.* A second result of the cataclysms which overtook the world in the twentieth century was the discovery by the church that its support was much more apparent than real. While statisticians have questioned whether the churches ever had the large support they claimed to have had in the nineteenth century, the events of the twentieth century revealed that much of the support had been from custom and not from conviction. In country after country in Europe, which had thought of itself as a Christian society, the numbers who remained revealed that Christianity was a minority movement.

Some left because they were disillusioned with the sentimental liberalism of the church's position. Others left because they felt that the church's powerlessness to prevent the collapse of society indicated its irrelevance. Still others dropped by the wayside because there was no longer any Christian social pressure forcing them to conform. This development was just as true in Roman Catholic countries as in Protestant. France, for example, which had once been declared the "eldest daughter of the Church" was said by a Roman Catholic prelate to be a missionary territory. In England where more than 60 per cent of the population claimed to belong to the Episcopal Church, far less than 10 per cent acknowledged that they were regular attendants at its services of worship.

While the situation in the United States has not as yet revealed the same decline, we must never forget that the most recent figures reveal that something like 80,000,000 Americans acknowledge no connection with any form of organized religion.

3. *The challenge of Communism.* The final result of the social collapse was the rise of Communism, the most determined rival Christianity has known since the rise of Islam. Although Communism was first expounded in the nineteenth century by a German exile living in England, Karl Marx, it remained a paper theory advocated only by a few cranks until the period directly after the First World War, when it became a reality in Russia.

Though its philosophy is basically anti-religious, it has often been pointed out that in many ways Communism is a religion and a hideous parody of the Christian gospel. It has its messiah, its golden age, its New Jerusalem, its apocalyptic future. Because it sees all of these things as capable of realization within history, it proved to be a powerful opponent against a church which had postponed every consideration of justice and freedom to a time beyond history. The Communist taunt has always been that Christianity promises only "pie in the sky by and by" whereas Communism offers at least the possibility of bread and butter next week.

By downtrodden people whose elemental needs had been ignored by the church for centuries this kind of propaganda won immediate and uncritical acceptance. While we have no desire to criticize any particular communion of Christians, we cannot avoid pointing out that Communism won its greatest victories precisely in those countries in which the church had become an introverted institution, so occupied with its own status and preservation that it had never concerned itself with the social situation in which it lived. There is a story that at precisely the same time at which Lenin and his associates were laying final plans for the Russian Revolution, the Synod of the Russian Orthodox Church, meeting in a nearby location, was engaged in a furious debate about the number of buttons which should be on priests' vestments. The story may be legendary but it will illustrate the basic reason why in so many apparently Christian countries Communism swept the field.

4. *The revival of ancient religions.* To this picture of discouragement and defeat must be added one more factor—the revival of missionary zeal on the part of ancient religions. As empires broke up with the resultant formation of new nations in Asia and, more recently, in Africa, Christianity, which had always been a minority movement in

these places, faced new handicaps. As a religion it was identified with the forces of Western colonialism from which freedom had at long last been obtained. As a religion its record in the matter of race relations was by no means spotless; too often it had been the white man's religion. Ancient religions like Buddhism and Islam which had been static for centuries were galvanized into activity by the new political situation. In Africa, for example, the Christian missionary no longer faced the simple problem of primitive tribal religions; he now faced the aggressive missionary endeavor of a determined Mohammedanism as well.

HOPEFUL SIGNS

Comparing the church of the nineteenth century with that of the mid-twentieth century, a casual observer might well conclude that he was seeing the beginning of the decline of the Christian cause. Faced with loss of support and active opposition in its home territories and ancient strongholds, almost defeated in many places by an aggressive and ruthless Communism, struggling against apparently insuperable difficulties in Asia and Africa, the church seems to have entered what many have not hesitated to call the "post-Christian" era. Yet the student of church history has seen enough similar periods in the two thousand-year story of Christ's cause on earth to know that this kind of negative evidence is never conclusive. What then are the signs of hope?

1. *A theological revival.* Out of the collapse of false optimism has come a new theological seriousness in all of the churches. This does not

Judgments such as those expressed in the quotations of several Christian leaders point to some of the discoveries and experiences of the church in recent years which may be regarded as signs of life and hope. Consider whether any of these signs can be found in the church as you know it.

Facing the "Terrible Questions" of Our World

The theology of Barth, criticize it as we may, is the Christian thinking of a great Christian mind, explosive and often unduly emphatic, but none the less of incalculable import for the Church of our time. . . . He is compelling us to face again the problems of life and death. He thrusts upon us those terrible questions which are rampant in the world. He bids us seek the answer to them on our knees before the Lord, to listen that we may obey.[1]

mean that the classic positions of men like Luther and Calvin have simply been restated. Too much has happened in terms of expanding scientific and historical knowledge to permit that as a workable solution. But the classic theologians have been carefully studied to present the gospel to twentieth century man, conditioned as he is by the world view of the century in which he lives. Though recast in a different framework, the Christian doctrines of sin and grace, of forgiveness and redemption are no longer relegated to an age that is past. They are seen as divine realities which must come alive and speak to the desperate need of man in the present.

Although many names are associated with this theological revival, the pioneer in many ways was Karl Barth. While still a young pastor in Switzerland, he realized the bankruptcy of liberalism when he tried to preach it against the background of the artillery duel just over the border. Though many of his conclusions have been criticized, no one can deny that more than anyone else he has been responsible for the revival of theological seriousness in contemporary Protestantism. We still have serious questions to face in presenting the gospel to the modern world, but the basic question is now a very different one. No longer do we ask, "What part of the Christian gospel is still acceptable to modern man?" but "How can we state the gospel to modern man in ways which will be faithful to the gospel but relevant to the human situation?" A church which takes the gospel seriously in this way is one which cannot be defeated by the circumstances of history.

2. *A biblical revival.* It is no accident that when Karl Barth began his reconsideration of the Christian gospel, his first book was a commentary on Paul's Letter to the Romans. In other words, the plight of the modern church has led it to a fresh study of the Scriptures. Frightened by the attacks of modern science and the findings of historical criticism, the older liberalism had put the Bible into a very secondary

Ears "Re-opened to the Word of God"

Thus through the onslaught of anti-Christian propaganda the Church's ears were re-opened to the Word of God. . . . God's Word challenged us, questioned the reality of our own religion, and forced us to recognize God simply and solely in His Word. . . . Jesus Christ, the Word made flesh, was recognized and acclaimed afresh as the sole Word of God. And one of the strongest Bible movements in the history of the Church has taken place during the last few years in the Evangelical Church, through its new understanding of the Old and New Testaments.[2]

place. A few passages, like the Sermon on the Mount, remained central, but for the most part it was considered as nothing but the record of Israel's history, a record that was not always trustworthy. Its earlier stories were classified as part of the common stock of human mythology.

While not ignoring the assured results of biblical criticism, indeed making use of them to enrich its understanding, the church in our day has once again accepted the Bible as the voice of the living God to his people. Even in the Roman Catholic Church, the Word of God has assumed its rightful place as that by which the church must form its life and to which it must always submit its very existence.

This biblical revival is evidenced by things as different as a great renewal of biblical scholarship in every Christian communion and the development of serious Bible study groups in local congregations. It is not the kind of study, however, which is simply interested in learning about the Bible as one would learn about the writings of Shakespeare. It is the kind of study which begins in the faith that the Bible speaks a living Word which we must hear if we are to live and witness as Christians in the world. There is perhaps no more hopeful sign than the way in which groups in congregations which once had been purely social or vaguely religious now have the study of the Bible as their real reason for being.

3. *The ecumenical movement.* Not since the seventeenth century had the Protestant churches attempted to move out of their isolation. In the early years of the twentieth century, especially in missionary fields, the need for conversation and cooperation became more and more apparent. In 1910 an international and interdenominational delegation met in Edinburgh to formulate policy for the world missionary enterprise. The work of that assembly came to fruition in 1948 in Amsterdam when the World Council of Churches was formed, bringing to-

"The Great New Fact of Our Era"

As though in preparation for such a time as this, God has been building up a Christian fellowship which now extends into almost every nation, and binds citizens of them all together in true unity and mutual love. No human agency has planned this. It is the result of the great missionary enterprise of the last hundred and fifty years. . . . Almost incidentally the great world-fellowship has arisen; it is the great new fact of our era. . . . Yes; here is one great ground of hope for the coming days—this world-wide Christian fellowship. . . .[3]   —William Temple

gether almost all the Protestant and Eastern Orthodox churches of the world. Subsequent meetings of the Council have been held in Evanston, Illinois, in 1954, and in New Delhi, India, in 1961.

The ecumenical movement, of which the World Council is the chief symbol, has been a disappointment to those who expected too much from it as well as to those who expected too little. Some have felt that it would lead to the speedy reunion of Christendom and that, of course, has been far from the case. On the other hand, those who felt that it should be nothing but a kind of league for limited objectives have been alarmed by some of the developments. The encouraging thing, however, is the fact that the ecumenical movement's real concern is "unity in mission." Face to face with the staggering task of witnessing to the gospel in today's world, the churches are able to converse together so that while genuine differences are never minimized, common witness can be made.

The most recent aspect of this movement is the new attitude of the Roman Catholic Church. Under the leadership of Pope John XXIII and Pope Paul VI barriers which had separated that church from the rest of Christendom for centuries began to come down. While no one supposes that a reunion of Protestantism with Rome is possible for years to come, if ever, at least the mutual exchange of ideas and concerns is now possible. And in some parts of Western Europe there have been limited attempts at joint witness. The urgency of mission has led to at least a form of unity.

4. *The laymen's movement.* Although it belongs in a little different category than the movements we have been discussing, no one can deny that one of the most significant signs of hope in the church of our

Discovering "the Ministry of the Laity"

The growing emphasis in many parts of the world upon the function of the laity . . . springs from the rediscovery of the true nature of the Church as the People of God. The word "laity" must not be understood in a merely negative way as meaning those church members who are not clergy. . . . The phrase "the ministry of the laity" expresses the privilege of the whole Church to share in Christ's ministry to the world. We must understand anew the implications of the fact that we are all baptized, that, as Christ came to minister, so must all Christians become ministers of His saving purpose according to the particular gift of the Spirit which each has received, as messengers of the hope revealed in Christ.[4]

time is the discovery of the ministry of the laity. Once again, this is a discovery which is as vital in Roman Catholicism and Orthodoxy as it is in the various Protestant churches.

To be sure, the laity had always occupied a position in Protestantism which it had not enjoyed elsewhere. But it must be frankly confessed that too often that position was an introverted one. The layman was used in the operation of the local church. Our new insight sees his place in the mission of the church in the world. Especially in Europe where the chasm between church and world is perhaps wider than in America, lay academies have been founded in which the committed Christian can be trained for effective witness in the world where he lives. What a leading Dutch theologian has called "the forgotten office in the Church" has now begun to come into its own. No one wishes to underestimate the necessity for the ministry of Word and Sacrament to the congregation gathered within the four walls of the church. But we have now begun to see how essential the ministry of the laity is in getting the gospel outside the four walls.

In this connection the reduced numbers of Christians may be a blessing in disguise. If they help us realize that being a Christian is more than spending an hour a week in the church building but involves nothing less than the offering of our total "secular" life in the service of Jesus Christ and his Kingdom, what we have lost in numbers will be more than compensated for by commitment. The fact that increasing numbers of laymen are asking seriously about their Christian vocation to be atomic scientists, teachers, lawyers, businessmen, barbers, or bus drivers is a hopeful sign.

And there we must bring our story to a close. But we must do so with the reminder that it is not our story but Christ's story. In a real sense the Acts of the Apostles is still being written. At this moment there are all kinds of threats and dangers. Many of them seem frightening indeed. But the pilgrim people of God is still on its journey through the wilderness. We may be on the verge of a new Dark Age for Christendom; we may be at the beginning of a new revival. However that may be, when the last chapter is written we may be certain that it will be *victory*. For it is not our church, but His church; and the gates of hell shall not prevail against it.

25

Conclusion: Good Friday and Easter

Now we have finished the story. What does it all mean? Is it only a confused jumble of names and dates, of places and people? Or did you see some kind of pattern emerging from the whole story? If so, what was its shape?

Let's begin by describing the pattern which for many years most American Protestants were sure they saw in the story of church history. It can best be defined by some words which used to appear on the bulletin board of a New England church. *We believe in the progress of mankind onward and upward forever.*

In fact, we could almost say that this was the favorite American interpretation of any kind of history. When we read the long story of human affairs this was the theme we were always sure we found there —progress. Things were getting better all the time. To be sure, the more intelligent student knew that there had been unhappy detours along the way. But not even these could obscure the fact that the world was getting better, its history one long march from darkness into light.

It is not difficult to understand why Americans came to think this way. Our theory was colored by our experiences of national expansion and scientific discovery. Since America was a growing land conquering not only the frontiers of geography but of knowledge as well, it was easy for us to suppose that the kind of progress which we were experiencing was the normal pattern of all history. *We believe in the progress of mankind onward and upward forever.*

CAN WE STILL BELIEVE IN PROGRESS?

For many Americans the progress theory is still the Christian theory. After all, if you read the Bible closely, does it not teach that history is moving toward some far-off glorious goal? Does it not speak about the coming of the Kingdom of God, the dawning of a new day in which nations shall beat their spears into plowshares? If words like these do not indicate some social ideal toward which the human story is steadily moving, what are we to make of them?

Similarly with the story of the church. Can it not be interpreted as the story of small beginnings, moving steadily into greatness, passing through the long period of the Dark Ages, gradually emerging into light with the Protestant Reformation, progressing into the enlightened and active Protestantism which we know in our own time? Would that not be a reasonable interpretation of all that we have read?

Of course, our twentieth century has given the progress theory some nasty shocks. Two world wars within twenty-five years hardly look like progress. Indeed, we begin to find ourselves looking back a little wistfully to those good old days when the world had not heard of atomic energy, international tension, and whole-scale oppression and brutality. This modern age has many people wondering about progress. Though it is true that we have the use of all kinds of mechanical gadgets that our fathers never dreamed of, is it true that human nature itself has made progress?

Let's think again about the story of the church. Think about the many times in the story when, humanly speaking at least, the church seemed ready to die, times when even though its external life seemed flourishing, it had already rotted out at the core. Take an honest look at the church in our own time, the millions that have been lost to Communism or to Islam, the other millions for whom the Christian gospel is simply no longer a relevant influence. Does this strike you as the progress of mankind onward and upward forever?

But what ever gave us the notion that the Bible endorsed our progress theory in the first place? If we really come to the Scriptures asking what they teach about history, do we find them saying that it is a straight line onward and upward forever? Or is this an idea which we have found in the Bible because we have wanted to find it there?

DEATH AND RESURRECTION

Let's have a look at the record. Because we have begun with the assumption that from Abraham to the present we are one people, let's recall the story of ancient Israel. It is, of course, impossible to compress Israel's entire history into a few pages. But we can take a sampling and see what it has to tell us.

There was, for instance, a crisis in the early history of that people when they were in revolt against their Egyptian masters. They had won a grudging permission to leave the land of their captivity and return to what had once been their homeland to reestablish their national life. It was a glorious moment. After four centuries of slavery they were at last free men and women.

Yet in the first flush of freedom they already stood on the brink of disaster. They found themselves trapped between an angry body of water which they had no way to cross and the approaching army of a slavemaster who had changed his mind. Their great adventure was over almost before it had begun. They knew it and surrendered to defeat in a helpless panic. Humanly speaking, that's where the story should have ended. But it didn't.

Or what about that dreadful moment in the life of the little kingdom of Judah? It was in the year 586 B.C. that Judah was overrun and destroyed by the great Babylonian Empire. Their defeat was a final one. Because the Babylonians did not feel they could trust the Jews, who had tried to sneak a pact with the Egyptians when they were conquered once before, they destroyed the city and deported almost the entire population. They left Jerusalem a smoking ruin with only a few old people poking around in its rubble.

That was the end of a great dream which had begun with men like David and Solomon. The holy empire with its capital city of God, his temple crowning its summit, was finished. In a few years it would disappear from history. The Jews and their religion would become extinct. They knew it, too, those exiles in Babylon who cried when they remembered what once had been and never would be again. Humanly speaking, that's how the story should have ended. But it didn't.

Now for an even more striking piece of evidence from the Bible—Jesus Christ. We all know his story very well. But have we ever thought of it in terms of a pattern? His public career began as a smashing success. People crowded around him so that more than once he had to escape them. At one point his popularity reached such a peak that there was a movement to make him king. There can be no question that had he wanted it, Jesus could have led a national uprising against Rome that might well have proved successful.

But the initial success began to change as the story unfolded. More and more people began to leave him. More and more the authorities who had disliked him from the first gained courage as they saw his popular support fade. When finally they realized that he could count on only a handful, they sprang their trap. He was arrested in Gethsemane. A kangaroo court condemned him to death; a weak-kneed Roman governor was frightened into compliance; and next morning there was a cross. What a tragic ending to such a hopeful beginning! Betrayed, denied by his own close associates, forsaken by most of his followers, supported only by a few women while the crowd spat out its hatred, Jesus died asking why God had forsaken him. Humanly speaking, that's how the story should have ended. But it didn't.

If the Christian claim is true, the story of Jesus Christ, foreshadowed in event after event in the Old Testament, is a capsule of

God's pattern for the history of his people. It is not the story of progress onward and upward forever. Israel at the Red Sea, Judah in Babylon, Jesus on the cross, it is the same story, the story of progress downward till matters seem hopeless. Then just when we think we can predict the result, God steps in to make the great reversal. And we bow our heads in wonder and say, "That's how the story should have ended. But it didn't."

GOOD FRIDAY AND EASTER

What is the Christian pattern of history? Good Friday and Easter, death and resurrection. The Christian pattern of history is neither pessimistic nor optimistic. Or rather, it is both. It is pessimistic about the human situation. The Bible knows that human beings, no matter what their skills and technologies, always work out their pride, their greed, their selfishness until they are brought to the end of a dead-end street—hopeless. "Age after age their tragic empires rise."[1] Though the theme may be played in a higher key, it is always the same theme.

Yet the Christian pattern of history is also optimistic. The Bible speaks of a God who is not an idle spectator of our human drama but an active participant in it; thus the biblical account affirms that it is always and exactly out of our human hopelessness that new life and new possibilities come from God. A new nation comes from the trap at the Red Sea; Easter comes from the cross. Human hopelessness and divine renewal, death and resurrection—this is how the Christian sees history.

If we have told the story of the church, of the people of God, correctly, this is the pattern which should be apparent. Naturally it is a much larger story than we have been able to tell within the compass of this book. The very universality of the Christian gospel would require a whole set of books if its story were to be told adequately.

Though we have not told the whole story, we have presented a number of samples. These samples have been from many different times and many different places. For, ever since Jesus Christ, the people of God have not been a single people living in one little country, but a new people gathered out of many lands and tongues and nations.

In one sense we have tried to tell the story for its own sake. There is something to be said for simply knowing the story of the Christian church about which all too many of us are ignorant. It is amazing how many blank pages the story has if told by many Christians. They know about a few of the highlights like the struggle of Martin Luther and the Protestant Reformation or perhaps they have a sprinkling of facts from the story of their own denomination. But usually that is about all. There can be no apology, therefore, for any attempt to acquaint us with at least some of the facts, some of the events, and some of the personalities in the story of the Christian church.

But we have had a much more important purpose in telling this story. We have tried to show how it illustrates the pattern of God's movement in history, the pattern of hopelessness and renewal, of death and resurrection. Of course we have not tried to point it out every time. That has been your task as a reader, to see beyond the facts to the pattern they demonstrate. Even as you read about Gregory and Aquinas, Luther and Calvin, Wesley and Edwards, did you see them not simply as men who led movements in history but as men whom God used for the accomplishment of his purposes?

There have been many Red Seas, many Calvaries in Christian history. Just when the church seemed about to disappear in the chaos of the barbarian invasions, there came a man named Benedict. Just when it seemed ready to die of its own carelessness and corruption, there came a man named Martin Luther. Just when the Church in England seemed to be drying up, there came a man named John Wesley.

And what about our own time? If the pattern is true, the story of the church should be one of the most hopeful and encouraging things we can read. Not because in the story of the church we read the progress of mankind onward and upward forever. Actually, as we have seen, the story of the church shows just as much selfishness, bitterness, hatred, and stupidity as we find in the story of the world. That's not so shocking as you may think when you remember that the story of the church is also the story of human beings.

Time and again, as we have seen, the people of God have teetered on the brink of destruction as the result of their own willful foolishness. It is in that unexpected divine renewal which has happened again and again that we find our anchor of hope. One renewal could have been mere coincidence. But a continuing series of them says that the story of God's people is also the story of God in history—our history. And if God is in our history, how can it be hopeless? He has some surprises in store for us too!

And why? *That the world may know.* The church has been preserved and will be preserved even from itself for no other reason—that through its very existence in this world, this world may know the power of God in Jesus Christ. That is why he called us into being as his people; that is why we are part of this holy fellowship; that is why the church still has a story to tell.

Notes

PART I

1. "The Didache" from *Holy Communion:* An Anthology of Christian Devotion, compiled by Massey H. Shepherd, Jr., © The Seabury Press, Inc., 1959.
2. *A Chain of Prayer Across the Ages* by Selina F. Fox, p. 69. Published by E. P. Dutton & Co., Inc., and reprinted with their permission. Also by permission of John Murray Ltd., London.
3. *Ibid.*, p. 70.

CHAPTER 2

1. From *Letters to Young Churches* © J. B. Phillips, 1947. Used by permission of The Macmillan Company.
2. Anne Fremantle (ed.), *A Treasury of Early Christianity* (New York: The Viking Press, Inc., 1953), pp. 42–43. By permission.

CHAPTER 3

1. J. Stevenson (ed.), *A New Eusebius* (New York: The Macmillan Company, 1957), p. 47. By permission of The Society for Promoting Christian Knowledge, London.
2. *Ibid.*, pp. 97–98.
3. From *Alexandrian Christianity*, ed. J. E. L. Oulton and Henry Chadwick. Published 1954, The Westminster Press.

CHAPTER 4

1. Philip Schaff and Henry Wace (eds.), "On the Incarnation of the Word of God," 20. 1, 2, 6. *A Select Library of Nicene and Post-Nicene Fathers of the Christian Church*, Second Series (New York: The Christian Literature Company; Oxford and London: Parker & Co., 1892), IV, 46–47.

PART II

1. Fox, *A Chain of Prayer Across the Ages, op. cit.*, p. 219.
2. *A Manual of Eastern Orthodox Prayers* (New York: The Macmillan Company, 1945), p. 32. By permission of The Society for Promoting Christian Knowledge, London.
3. Fox, *op. cit.*, p. 221.

CHAPTER 5

1. Whitney J. Oates (ed.), *Basic Writings of Saint Augustine* (New York: Random House, copyright 1948), II, 274. By permission.

CHAPTER 6

1. Leonard J. Doyle (trans.), *St. Benedict's Rule for Monasteries*, pp. 6, 17, 35, 49, 92 *passim*. Published by The Liturgical Press. Copyrighted by The Order of St. Benedict, Inc. Collegeville, Minnesota. By permission.

CHAPTER 7

1. Bede, *A History of the English Church and People*, trans. Leo Sherley-Price (Middlesex, England: Penguin Books Ltd., 1955), pp. 143–144. By permission.
2. Hugh Watt, *Representative Churchmen of Twenty Centuries* (London: James Clarke & Co. Ltd., n.d.), p. 104. By permission.
3. *Ibid.*, p. 106.
4. From *The Anglo-Saxon Missionaries in Germany*, translated and edited by C. H. Talbot, Copyright 1954 Sheed & Ward Inc., New York, pp. 6, 7. By permission.
5. *Ibid.*, pp. 37, 38, 39.

Chapter 8

1. Schaff and Wace, *Nicene and Post-Nicene Fathers, op. cit.,* XII, 9.
2. Oliver J. Thatcher and Edgar H. McNeal, *A Source Book for Mediaeval History* (New York: Charles Scribner's Sons, 1905), p. 107. By permission.
3. Herm. Adalbert. Daniel (compiler), *Thesaurus Hymnologicus* (Leipzig: Sumptibus J. T. Loeschke, 1855), II, 336.

Chapter 9

1. "The Liturgy of St. Chrysostom" from *Holy Communion:* An Anthology of Christian Devotion, compiled by Massey H. Shepherd, Jr., © The Seabury Press, Inc., 1959.
2. Mohammed Marmaduke Pickthall (trans.), *The Meaning of the Glorious Koran* (London: George Allen & Unwin Ltd.). By permission.

PART III

1. Bernard, Abbot of Clairvaux, *The Steps of Humility,* trans. George Bosworth Burch (Cambridge, Mass.: Harvard University Press, 1940), p. 67. By permission.
2. Fox, *A Chain of Prayer Across the Ages, op. cit.,* p. 30.
3. Thomas à Kempis, *The Imitation of Christ,* trans. Richard Whitford (New York: Pocket Books, Inc., 1953), p. 236.

Chapter 10

1. Williston Walker, *A History of the Christian Church* (revised ed.; New York: Charles Scribner's Sons, 1959), pp. 193–194. By permission.
2. Thatcher and McNeal, *A Source Book for Mediaeval History, op, cit.,* pp. 151–152.
3. *Ibid.,* pp. 155, 156.

Chapter 11

1. "Dominic," Encyclopædia Britannica (1910 ed.), VIII, 401. By permission.
2. Gerard K. Brady, *Saint Dominic, Pilgrim of Light* (New York: P. J. Kenedy & Sons; London: Burns & Oates Ltd., 1957), p. 106. By permission.
3. Watt, *Representative Churchmen of Twenty Centuries, op. cit.,* p. 162.
4. Father Cuthbert, O.S.F.C., *Life of St. Francis of Assisi* (London: Longmans, Green & Co. Ltd., 1956), p. 104. By permission.
5. Watt, *op. cit.,* pp. 169–170.
6. Williston Walker, *Great Men of the Christian Church* (New York: Harper & Row, Publishers, Incorporated, 1908), p. 173. By permission.

Chapter 12

1. Saxe Commins and Robert N. Linscott (eds.), *Man and Spirit: The Speculative Philosophers* (New York: Random House, Inc., copyright 1947; London: Burns & Oates Ltd.), pp. 29–67, *passim.* By permission.

Chapter 13

1. From *Advocates of Reform,* ed. Matthew Spinka. Published 1953 The Westminster Press. XIV, 49–51.
2. Used by permission, Moravian Church in America.

PART IV

1. Fox, *A Chain of Prayer Across the Ages, op. cit.,* p. 125.
2. Mary W. Tileston (compiler), *Prayers Ancient and Modern* (New York: Grosset & Dunlap, 1897, 1928). By permission.
3. Charles W. Baird, *The Presbyterian Liturgies* (Grand Rapids, Mich.: Baker Book House, 1960), p. 37. By permission.

Chapter 14

1. G. G. Findlay, *The Epistle to the Galatians* (The Expositor's Bible; New York: A. C. Armstrong & Son, 1893; London: Hodder & Stoughton, 1891), p. 3.

NOTES 223

2. Kenneth Scott Latourette, *A History of Christianity* (New York: Harper & Row, Publishers, Incorporated, 1953), p. 742. By permission.
3. Martin Luther, "Lectures on Galatians 1535," *Luther's Works*, eds. Jaroslav Pelikan and Walter A. Hansen (St. Louis, Mo.: Concordia Publishing House, 1963), XXVI, 3. By permission.

CHAPTER 15

1. John C. Wenger, *The Doctrines of the Mennonites* (Scottdale, Pa.: Mennonite Publishing House, 1950), p. 81. By permission.
2. From Henry S. Burrage's *Baptist Hymn Writers and Their Hymns*, 1888.

CHAPTER 16

1. From *Calvin: Institutes of the Christian Religion*, ed. John T. McNeill. Copyright © 1960, W. L. Jenkins. The Westminster Press. III. 7. 1.
2. *Ibid.*, IV. 3. 1, 2, 8, 9.
3. McNeill, *op. cit.*, IV. 1. 7, 9.
4. Jules Bonnet (ed.), *Letters of John Calvin* (Philadelphia: Presbyterian Board of Publication, 1858), II, 347–348.
5. Quoted in Andrew L. Drummond, *Story of American Protestantism* (Edinburgh and London: Oliver and Boyd, 1949; Boston: Beacon Press), p. 51.

CHAPTER 17

1. Walker, *Great Men of the Christian Church, op. cit.*, p. 268.
2. William Croft Dickinson (ed.), *Knox's History of the Reformation in Scotland* (Edinburgh and London: Thomas Nelson & Sons Ltd.; New York: the Philosophical Library, 1949), II, 557–558. By permission.
3. L. H. Lehmann (ed.), *The Drama of William of Orange* (Sea Cliff, N. Y.: Christ's Mission, 1937), pp. 114–116. By permission.

PART V

1. Tileston, *Prayers Ancient and Modern, op. cit.*, p. 184.
2. Eric Milner-White and G. W. Briggs (compilers), *Daily Prayer* (London: Oxford University Press, 1941), p. 178. By permission of Oxford University Press.
3. *Devotions and Prayers of John Wesley*, Compiled and Edited by Donald E. Demaray, Baker Book House, Grand Rapids, Michigan, 1957, p. 95.

CHAPTER 18

1. *The Church Teaches: Documents of the Church in English Translation* (Edited by Gerald Van Ackeren, S.J.) St. Louis, Mo.: B. Herder Book Co., 1955, pp. 8–9. By permission.
2. From *Creeds of the Churches* edited by John H. Leith. Copyright © 1963 by John H. Leith. Reprinted by permission of Doubleday & Company, Inc., pp. 309–310.

CHAPTER 19

1. John Geree, "The Character of an Old English Puritane," in Gordon S. Wakefield, *Puritan Devotion: Its Place in the Development of Christian Piety* (London: The Epworth Press, 1957), p. xxii. By permission.
2. Used by permission, Moravian Church in America.

CHAPTER 20

1. Quoted in Watt, *Representative Churchmen of Twenty Centuries, op. cit.*, p. 231.
2. *Ibid.*
3. Percy Livingstone Parker (ed.), *The Heart of John Wesley's Journal* (Westwood, N. J.: Fleming H. Revell Company, n.d.), p. 43. By permission.
4. Frank Baker (ed.), *Representative Verse of Charles Wesley* (Nashville: Abingdon Press, 1962), p. 3. By permission.
5. Parker, *op. cit.*, p. 47.
6. Baker, *op. cit.*, pp. 3–4.

7. Parker, *op. cit.*, pp. 45, 47, 55, 56, 459, 485.
8. John Calvin, *Institutes of the Christian Religion*, trans. Henry Beveridge (Edinburgh: T. & T. Clark, 1879), II, 281.

PART VI

1. Quoted in *Journal of the Presbyterian Historical Society*, Vol. II, No. 7 (1904), 366–367.
2. From *Prayers of the Social Awakening* by Walter Rauschenbusch. The Pilgrim Press, pp. 134–135. By permission.
3. "We Are One in Prayer" from *I Lie On My Mat And Pray* edited by Fritz Pawelzik. Copyrighted 1964 by Friendship Press, New York, N. Y. Used by permission.

Chapter 21

1. Quoted in Charles W. F. Smith, *Robert Hunt, Vicar of Jamestown* (Pamphlet in "Builders for Christ Series" [New York: The National Council of the Episcopal Church, 1957]), p. 12.
2. Drummond, *Story of American Protestantism, op. cit.*, pp. 50–51. Reprinted by permission of the Beacon Press.
3. *Ibid.*, p. 53.
4. William Warren Sweet, *The Story of Religion in America* (New York: Harper & Row, Publishers, Incorporated, 1939), p. 72. By permission.
5. James Kendall Hosmer (ed.), *John Winthrop's Journal: "History of New England,"* (New York: Barnes & Noble, Inc., 1908, 1959), I, 51–52. By permission.
6. *Ecclesiastical Records, State of New York* (Albany: James B. Lyon, State Printer, 1901), I, 52–53.
7. Drummond, *op. cit.*, pp. 43–44.
8. Charles Augustus Briggs in *American Presbyterianism: Its Origin and Early History* (New York: Charles Scribner's Sons, 1885), pp. xlix–l.
9. William C. Reichel (ed.), *Memorials of the Moravian Church* (Philadelphia: J. B. Lippincott & Co., 1870), I, 168, 174, 175.

Chapter 22

1. Sweet, *The Story of Religion in America, op. cit.*, p. 206.
2. Drummond, *Story of American Protestantism, op. cit.*, p. 118.
3. *Ibid.*, p. 120.
4. Leonard W. Labaree, "George Whitefield Comes to Middletown," *William and Mary Quarterly*, 3d Ser., VII (1950), 590–591. Williamsburg, Va.: Institute of Early American History and Culture. By permission.

Chapter 23

1. *The Panoplist, and Missionary Magazine*, No. 1, Vol. IX (1813), p. 39.
2. *Ibid.*, No. 2, pp. 234–237, *passim*.

Chapter 24

1. Hugh Ross Mackintosh, *Types of Modern Theology* (New York: Charles Scribner's Sons, 1937), p. 319. By permission.
2. Edmund Schlink, "The Witness of the German Church Struggle," *Man's Disorder and God's Design: The Amsterdam Assembly Series* (New York: Harper & Row, Publishers, Incorporated, n.d.), I, 100–101. By permission.
3. William Temple, *The Church Looks Forward* (New York: The Macmillan Company, 1944), pp. 2, 3. By permission of The Macmillan Company.
4. *Evanston Speaks:* Reports from the Second Assembly of the World Council of Churches (London: SCM Press for the WCC, 1954), pp. 104–105. By permission.

Chapter 25

1. From "Turn back, O man, forswear thy foolish ways" by Clifford Bax, 1916, in *The Hymnbook*. By permission of A. D. Peters & Co., London.